Polish Paradoxes

Polish Paradoxes

Edited by

Stanisław Gomułka and Antony Polonsky

ROUTLEDGE
London and New York

First published 1990
by Routledge
11 New Fetter Lane, London EC4P 4EE

Simultaneously published in the USA and Canada
by Routledge
a division of Routledge, Chapman and Hall, Inc.
29 West 35th Street, New York, NY 10001

Typeset in 10/12 Times by Columns of Reading

Printed in Great Britain by T J Press (Padstow) Ltd
Padstow, Cornwall

British Library Cataloguing in Publication Data

Gomułka, Stanisław
Polish paradoxes.
1. Poland, Social conditions, 1980 —
I. Title   II. Polonsky, Antony
943.8′056
ISBN 0–415–04375–1

Library of Congress Cataloging in Publication Data

Polish paradoxes/edited by Stanisław Gomułka and Antony Polonsky.
p.   cm.
Includes index.
ISBN 0–415–04375–1
1. Poland—Civilization—1945—   I. Gomułka, Stanisław.
II. Polonsky, Antony.
DK4442.P645   1989
943.805–dc20   89–6318

Contents

Contents

Acknowledgements

Ideas come by accident. The idea of this book was born during a conversation at Stanford University's Hoover Institution between Stanisław Gomułka and Melvyn Kraus in the summer of 1985. In response to an argument that post-war Poland is a country of exceptionally many and startling paradoxes, Dr Kraus responded: 'Polish Paradoxes is a splendid title for a book which should be written'. Back in London, a preliminary list of 'major paradoxes' was proposed. In this work Stanisław Gomułka was soon joined by Antony Polonsky. We decided to test the ground by inviting contributions from leading authors. Their positive, sometimes enthusiastic, responses removed our remaining doubts. As work on the project progressed, some topics were changed and new ones added, some authors withdrew and new ones joined, but the basic initial idea of the book has remained the same. In this formative stage of the project the advice and goodwill of several friends and colleagues was of great help to us. We wish to acknowledge in particular suggestions of Jerzy Jedlicki of the Institute of History of the Polish Academy of Sciences and George Schopflin of the LSE.

Eight of the authors represented in this volume decided to write their essays in Polish, their mother language. These essays were then translated into English in London. We wish to thank the translators, Vera Rich, Monika Bobinski, Jakub Basista and Irena Powell, for their painstaking work. The many re-typings of the essays were done at the London School of Economics and at Hampstead Secretarial Bureau. We would like to thank Prue Hutton, Sue Kirkbride, Pat Nutt and Colette Ritchie for their skilful work and attention to detail. The project was helped financially by an award from the Staff Research Fund of the LSE.

Our special thanks go above all to the authors of these twelve thought-provoking essays who contributed a great deal of effort in preparing their texts and were later gracious enough to respond in a most co-operative manner to suggested editorial revisions, whether of style or substance.

S.G. and A.P.

Introduction

Stanisław Gomułka and Antony Polonsky

London School of Economics and Political Science

There was something unhealthy, something perverted in our attitude to the world and I, as an artist, felt, in some measure, responsible for this fatal 'Polish legend'. I felt that one must somehow put an end to it. . . but how? The Poles, being a nation highly bound up in fantasies, illusions, phrases, legends, declamations, were also closed to that reality *in crudo, sans phrases*, which can break bones. . . . Only the sharpest realism could drag us out of the swamp of our 'legend'. . . [My goal was] to pry the Pole free of Poland, so that he would become simply a human being. (Witold Gombrowicz, 1969)

The essays in this volume were all written in the aftermath of the failure of what Tim Garton-Ash has called the 'Polish revolution'. The emergence of Solidarity as a trade union and social organization with a membership of nearly 10 million people shook the communist regime in Poland to its foundations and gave a severe shock to the rest of the Soviet bloc. Yet this great movement, the product of the aspirations of the overwhelming majority of the Polish people for greater control over their lives and for a freer and more representative political system, was, in 1981–2, crushed by an isolated and unpopular communist government with far less difficulty than might have been anticipated. It is this and the many similar paradoxes of the Polish scene which the authors of the essays in this book seek to explain. It is indeed tempting to regard the Solidarity experience until Spring 1989 as confirming the view that those very conditions which have formed the Polish political culture and which have equipped Poles to resist foreign domination and oppression also inhibit the adoption of those attitudes and policies which are necessary to resolve the country's persistent political and economic crises.

Paradox is no new feature of Polish political life. Even before the partitions of the eighteenth century, the constitution of the Polish-

Lithuanian Commonwealth with its peculiar and ultimately fatal characteristics, the *liberum veto* and the elective monarchy, was justified on the paradoxical grounds that *Polska nierządem stoi* (Poland survives by virtue of the absence of a central government). As is pointed out by Andrzej Walicki, the 'gentry democracy' which characterised pre-partition Poland bequeathed important and contradictory legacies to Polish political life. In spite of the existence of a large unfree and oppressed peasantry and a high level of social differentiation among the nobility, this 'gentry democracy' was undoubtedly a genuine phenomenon. All members of the *szlachta* (nobility), which made up over 10 per cent of the population, regarded themselves as entitled and indeed obliged to participate in political life, whether in the central parliament, the *Sejm*, in local parliaments (*Sejmiki* or dietines), or in the election of the monarch. *'Nic o nas bez nas'* ('Nothing concerning us without our consent') ran a widely repeated Polish principle of Polish gentry parliamentarism. This meant that when Poland was partitioned, there was a fairly large group of influential people who bitterly resented the autocratic rule of the partitioning powers, Russia, Prussia and Austria, states to which concepts such as consultation with their subjects or government by consent were largely alien. Linked with the belief in the importance of political participation was the concept of national sovereignty – the nation may have been embodied and represented by its nobility, but it had its own laws, its own traditions, its own rights, which should be respected. In the words of Hugo Kollątaj, one of the leading eighteenth-century political theorists and the advocate of a reformed gentry state:

> That every nation be free and independent, that every nation should be allowed to embrace that form of government which it prefers and that no foreign nation is entitled to interfere in its constitutional development – this is the first and most important maxim of the law of nations, so evident in the light of our century that no proofs are needed to justify it. A nation which has no right to rule its own country is not a nation.[1]

These gentry traditions were not specifically Polish. They were also strong in western Europe, particularly in the United Kingdom. But here, in conditions of national sovereignty, they led to the development of democratic institutions and the extension of civil rights to all persons of property, not just landowners. The consequence was the development of civil society and a shift of economic power to manufacturers and men of commerce. The traditions of political and economic liberation in the West thus lie at the root of a 'virtuous cycle': the rise and spread of economic wealth contributes to international political power and internal democratization, which in turn fosters further economic growth. In Poland, after the loss of political independence, much of the nation's energies was directed to its reacquisition and was lost to entrepreneurial activity. Polish gentry traditions activated these energies and, as a consequence, can be seen as lying at the root of the seemingly indomitable Polish desire for independence and self-government which frequently manifested itself throughout the nineteenth century, contributed in large measure to the re-establishment of an independent state in 1918, and was one of the factors which led to the emergence of Solidarity. In the words of Wojciech Karpiński, 'Solidarity was the product of the best features of the democratic tradition of the gentry.'[2] A similar view has been expressed by the British historian Norman Davies:

> Solidarity's organisational structure is strangely reminiscent of the *Sejm* (Diet) and *Sejmiki* (Dietines) of the Old Republic. Wałęsa, like the old Polish noblemen whom he so uncannily resembles, seems to have perceived instinctively that the main danger lay in the absolutist pretensions of state power. If this is so, the Polish working class can be seen reviving the political traditions of the Noble Democracy – traditions which appear to survive almost two centuries of suppression.[3]

But the political traditions created by the gentry inheritance were not all positive in their effects. In one respect, 'gentry democracy', with its egalitarianism, exemplified by the formula '*szlachcic na zagrodzie równy wojewodzie*' ('a nobleman on his small estate is equal to a palatine') stressed individualism. An extreme form of this individualism was the *liberum veto*, the principle of unanimity which paralysed the old Polish *Sejm*. It can be argued that the *liberum veto* was not only the reflection of a desire to respect minority opinions, but also the result of the belief that a collective unanimity embodied a higher form of consensus. In Marcin Król's words, 'The place of individual non-conformism was taken by social non-conformism of the group, which no longer required from the individual the courage of his convictions, but often did require personal courage' (p.72). This belief that one should not go against such a consensus was, as both Andrzej Walicki and Jerzy Holzer point out, a significant feature of the last months of the legal existence of Solidarity, when many who might otherwise have spoken out against a course of action they regarded as wrong-headed and potentially disastrous felt constrained to remain silent. Again, we may note that the power of the majority to silence internal opposition is not a specifically Polish phenomenon. In the case of Solidarity, there was also a very real concern that by challenging the majority decision in a democratic movement, one was indirectly aiding the oppressive government. Our point is, however, that in Poland, respect for simple majority decisions and for opposition views tends to lead either to unanimity and intolerance of dissent, or to anarchy. This is a tendency natural in societies with an under-developed political culture. Ruled as it was by autocratic and feudal powers, Poland did not have the opportunity to develop the early constitutional tradition of its nobility into a modern political culture.

The tradition of 'gentry democracy' was created in Poland before the development of capitalism and the liberal values bound up with it. This was to have serious consequences. In Andrzej Walicki's words:

> Poland had not passed through the school of liberal individualism, had not developed such 'bourgeois' values as economic capacity and industriousness, self-reliance in economic life, thrift and so forth. Its elite remained faithful to the values characteristic of the nobility, such as honour, courage in open fight (as distinct from civil courage), freedom conceived as participation in political power; it did not pay much attention to the prosaic, down-to-earth concerns of private law and could hardly understand Napoleon's famous dictum that the essence of freedom is a good Civil Code. (pp.27–8)

These attitudes contributed greatly to the anti-industrial and anti-bourgeois attitudes which were a feature of the Polish political culture in the eighteenth and nineteenth centuries, and which inhibited the emergence of a successful entrepreneurial class and the achievement of self-sustaining economic growth.

A final consequence of the habit of perceiving the nation in terms of the collective will was what Andrzej Walicki has called 'the widespread illusion that native rulers would have no other choice but to bow to the clearly expressed will of the nation'.[4] Because of this illusion, the crushing of Solidarity, although the attendant repression was relatively mild, was felt particularly painfully by many Poles, above all as a national humiliation and a national betrayal. The illusion also inhibited any clear-sighted analysis of the balance of power and of the behaviour of the Solidarity leadership in the run-up to the introduction of martial law. Criticism of their conduct of affairs was often seen as disloyal, and as collaboration with a deeply unpopular government, which by its actions had destroyed all vestiges of its political legitimacy. Similar taboos, as is pointed out by both Marcin Król and Jerzy Jedlicki, have characterized the discussions of Józef Poniatowski's politically suicidal loyalty to Napoleon in 1813, of the outbreak and conduct of the 1863 Insurrection, and of the political good sense of those who began the Warsaw uprising of 1944.

On the other hand, the restrained behaviour of the broad masses of the Polish people during the not infrequent uprisings of the last two centuries, including the 'Polish revolution' of 1980–1, may suggest that common sense and survival instinct, rather than the romantic ideas of the gentry and the intelligentsia, have guided their behaviour. The particular Polish predicament of a nation fighting desperately for the survival of its identity has meant, paradoxically, that the revolutionary spirit and readiness for sacrifice of its romantic insurrectionaries, and the denial to them by ordinary people of full support have both been needed. The challenges to the *status quo* have served the purpose of keeping the question of independence a burning issue at home and abroad. The denial of full support for these challenges has diminished their cost in circumstances in which success was not really possible. Indeed, as both Król and Jedlicki point out, through most of the nineteenth century the Poles were faced with the impossible choice of acquiescing in conditions which they found quite intolerable or revolution in a situation where an uprising was bound to fail. In the inter-war period, they were faced with an equally impossible choice between an alliance with Stalin's USSR or Hitler's Germany. In the post-war period, as Jerschina notes, the choice was between co-operation with an imposed regime, in the hope of gradual improvement, or terror and open occupation (see Chapter 4).

As a result of these adverse experiences, in Andrzej Walicki's words:

> The dominant form of the Polish national ideology became romantic nationalism, conceiving nations as moral entities and agents of universal progress: a nationalism passionately believing in the brotherhood of nations and in the ethicization of politics, whereby it was hoped to put an end to such political crimes as had culminated in the martyrdom of Poland. The most extreme and best articulated form of the romantic nationalism was religiously inspired romantic messianism, which saw the Poles as the chosen nation, the spiritual leaders of mankind and the sacred instrument of universal salvation. (pp.30–1)

This messianic romantic nationalism has been less dominant in Polish political culture in most recent times, but until 1918, its impact was both complex and potent. In the first place, the previous noble loyalty to the then no longer existing institutionalized forms of national life was superseded by loyalty to the national idea, which derived from national traditions and imposed on the nation its mission. In these circumstances, the nation ceased to be merely a group of citizens but became instead 'a community of spirits sharing a common destiny and realising a common task'. In the words of Adam Mickiewicz, the greatest of the Polish romantic poets, 'The Fatherland of the Poles is not a mere piece of land bound by frontiers which limit the national existence and activity of the Pole'.[5] The elevated character of the national dream also contrasted starkly with the bleak reality of everyday life, a feature of the Polish scene which, as Jerzy Jedlicki points out, has by no means disappeared. In one sense, romantic nationalism can be seen as an attempt to bridge this gap between 'Holy Ideals and Prosaic Life'. Słowacki, another of the great Polish romantic poets wrote, almost threateningly, that he would leave behind him a 'fatal force' of prophetic poetry, which 'itself invisible will crush you until you eaters-of-bread are made into angels'.[6]

An important component of Polish romantic nationalism was its internationalism, which saw the Polish revolution as an integral part of the European revolution, and which stressed that Poles would fight everywhere *za waszą i naszą wolność* ('for your freedom and ours'). This internationalism was undoubtedly a noble sentiment, but it had a number of deleterious consequences, which have persisted up to the present. It created among Poles an exaggerated belief in the willingness of the nations of the West to identify with the Polish struggle and to provide concrete aid in difficult situations. Conversely, when this aid was not forthcoming, it led to a feeling that the West in the pursuit of short-term interests had betrayed its own long-term values, was corrupted, and that the Poles alone were holding up the banner of these values. It was Mickiewicz who told the Polish refugees to France after the failure of the 1831 uprising to regard themselves while in the materialistic, mercantile West as 'apostles among the idolaters', pilgrims of freedom, precursors of a new era of Christian politics in Europe.[7]

Romantic patriotic ideals were widely accepted by the educated classes in Poland. But they could not be put into practice or their espousal could have serious and unpleasant consequences. Most people faced with this dilemma created a division, acknowledging the authority of the partitioning powers in everyday life, for which no responsibility was felt and preserving what Jedlicki calls a patriotic 'sanctuary . . . in the privacy of the home and heart' (p.55). It was this national schizophrenia which the poet Norwid was alluding to when on the eve of the 1863 uprising he distinguished between 'Poland as a society' and 'Poland as a nation' (see Chapter 1, pp.32–3).

This division between a sacred patriotic sphere and the greyness of everyday life, with its corollary of the absence of many of the characteristics of a developed civil society has also been a feature of communist Poland. Its consequences on everyday life are tellingly documented by Janine Wedel (Chapter 12) and have been investigated by sociologists like Mira Marody (Chapter 11), Stefan Nowak and Adam Podgórecki. Nowak has shown that the overwhelming majority of Poles do not identify with the institutions in which they work and do not think in terms of public good on the institutional level. Andrzej Walicki summarises his findings as follows:

> [The Poles'] loyalties and feelings of belonging are two-sided. First they belong and are loyal to different primary face-to-face groups – from the family and groups of friends to informal cliques, mafias and other personalised groups pursuing their interests in a half-legal or illegal way. From this lowest level of integration we have a sudden leap to the most abstract and most sublimated level: the level of national solidarity. Thus an average Pole does not belong to a large-scale

institutionalised civil society, he belongs to different primary groups and secondly he belongs to his nation; not a nation as a system of political and economic institutions, but a nation as national tradition, national culture, the sphere of uniting symbols, of sublimated lofty patriotic feelings.[8]

Nowak's 'social vacuum' is the legacy of Polish history of the last two centuries, when institutions were, for the most part, the instruments of oppression by foreign powers rather than the means of organizing individual effort for the people's common good. What this has meant in present-day Poland is the coexistence of the absence of any real work-ethic with strongly patriotic feelings. The general demoralization of the work force is widely to be found in socialist societies, including the USSR where the policy of *perestroika* is partly intended to change long-established working habits. What may seem to be paradoxical in Poland is that it has been impossible to translate patriotic feelings into policies which could create a properly functioning economic system. This issue lies at the heart of the economic crisis which is addressed in Chapters 6–10, particularly by Wiktor Herer and Władysław Sadowski (Chapter 6).

The insurrections of the nineteenth century all failed. This has created a cult of heroic failure, the belief that political actions should not be judged by whether they succeed, but by their moral impact, a phenomenon discussed by Król, Jedlicki and Walicki. As Andrzej Bryk has written:

Modern Polish history has been a story of nearly consistent defeat and internal failure. A defeated people lives by myths, clings to myths. Apologetic and martyrological visions of national history only mirror an incurable romantic despair. Poles thus look at their history in terms of 'honour' versus 'shame' because categories of victory or national success are largely beyond the modern Polish consciousness and any of the institutions which shape it. Honour seems to Poles the only reliable justification of the national existence.[9]

This has had important consequences in the adoption of specific political strategies. In the words of the writer Witold Zalewski, 'I think that our awareness of the inevitability of defeat forces us to embark on actions bringing about this defeat. We have been used to treat defeat as a kind of value'.[10] Partly, this was a result of the nineteenth-century experience when, as Marcin Król points out, 'Political thought was condemned to reckoning with the national situation rather than developing its own logic and internal cohesion' (p.65).

This is not to say that these values have gone unchallenged. Even before the 1863 uprising, as Jerzy Jedlicki explains, a movement developed in Russian Poland, modelled on Western positivism, which stressed the need to abandon romantic dreams and concentrate on realizable goals. Independence could not be obtained, and Polish society should concentrate rather on building up its economic strength by participating in the capitalist revolution which was now beginning to penetrate to the Tsarist Empire. This would enable other unresolved problems, such as the status of the peasantry, of women and of the Jews to be dealt with in a civilized and liberal manner which would help establish the foundations of a civil society. Warsaw positivism gained greatly in influence as a result of the catastrophic failure of the 1863 Uprising and acquired many impressive advocates, including the writer Bolesław Prus and the political theorist Alexander Swiętochowski, editor of the main positivist newspaper *Prawda*. But although a degree of industrialization was achieved, material gains seemed to many among the educated of little significance in the face of the increasingly repressive character of Tsarism in Poland. With the revival of nationalism in the 1890s, positivism came to seem little more than a servile and time-serving justification of alien rule.

Similarly, with this revival of nationalism, there emerged in Poland, under the ideological guidance of Roman Dmowski, a movement which was the Polish variant of the general European reaction against the dominant ideologies of liberalism and capitalism and which elsewhere produced thinkers like Corradini, Pareto, Gustave le Bon and Charles Maurras. Like its West European radical right wing counterparts, this movement was strongly social-darwinist, seeing the nation as an organism fated to struggle against other national organisms to ensure its survival and development. In Dmowski's words:

The surface of the globe is not a museum to preserve ethnographic displays in order, unities each in its place. Humanity is going forward swiftly, and in the contest of the nations, each is bound to do as much as it can for progress, for civilisation, to raise the value of man. . . [Yet] the fact is that continual improvement and progress are not natural characteristics of man – the majority of today's population of the earth is standing still and not advancing at all. And the greatest factor in progress is competition, the need continually to improve the weapons which enable one to defend one's own existence. . . . Is this a philosophy of struggle and oppression? . . . Perhaps. But what if this struggle and this oppression are a reality, and universal peace and universal freedom a fiction. . .? One must have the courage to look the facts in the face.[11]

Dmowski also set out a cogent critique of gentry romanticism which is clearly expounded by Andrzej Walicki. To quote him:

1 Against an idealistic belief in justice he set the view that international

relations are subject to severe laws of the struggle for survival and that it is stupid to believe in the final victory of the 'right cause', since the fate of any cause depends first of all on material forces.

2   Against 'political romanticism', that is, 'building political activity on purely illusory grounds' and 'embarking on political activity with no prior estimation of the means at disposal', he set a programme of 'political realism', with special stress on the difficult geopolitical situation of Poland.

3   Against such concepts as the 'national idea', national honour, or national glory, he set the concept of the *national interest*, emphasizing that each nation has a natural right to national egoism and that the brotherhood of nations is a naïve illusion.

4   Finally, he offered a new, simple definition of nation which rejected both the old Polish tradition of defining nation in purely political terms, irrespective of ethnic criteria, and the romantic tradition of defining 'Polishness' in terms of certain spiritual values inherent in the national tradition and in the national mission. He thought of nations as the natural product of ethnic differentiation, defining them in terms of language and ethnic origin. (p.34)

It was this definition of the nation which lay at the root of Dmowski's hostility to non-Polish groups within the borders of the former Polish-Lithuanian Commonwealth. In particular, he regarded the large Jewish community in Poland as unassimilable and a barrier to the creation of an organic national community. The National Democratic movement (*Endecja* – its followers were called *Endecy*), of which he was the main ideologist, became increasingly powerful in Poland, both before the First World War and in the inter-war period. The politicians who adhered to its views, whether in the National Party or in the various smaller fascist groups which seceded from it, never succeeded in establishing themselves in power, although an increasing section of Polish society had accepted their view of the world by 1939. Their influence diminished somewhat in the post-1945 era, both because of communist repression and because of the general compromising of radical right wing views as a result of the fascist experience in Europe. There have been a number of attempts to revive this tradition of Polish political realism both with, and more generally without, its anti-semitic component. Indeed, the Polish People's Republic – mono ethnic and mono-religious, anti-German and allied with Russia – bears a striking resemblance to Dmowski's blueprint for the future of Poland as set out in *Myśli nowoczesnego Polaka* (*Thoughts of a Modern Pole*, Lwów, 1903). His idea of 'political realism' was embraced wholeheartedly by Polish communists during and after World War II. This was especially evident in the policies and attitudes of their more national-oriented wing, led by Władysław Gomułka. The new western

9

borders and the satisfactory outcome of the Polish-Soviet confrontation in October 1956 have been its greatest successes and major influences on the modern political culture in Poland. Dmowski's political ideas have also been popularized in the form of the neo-Endek views of the Catholic publicist Andrzej Micewski and by the explicitly National Democratic group of Alexander Hall.

The imperatives of running a state in the inter-war period caused a diminution in the appeal of romantic and insurrectionary political views. But they gained a new strength in the conditions of brutal Nazi and Soviet occupation after 1939. The Polish underground state, one of the largest and best organized anti-Nazi resistance movements in Europe, drew much of its inspiration from these traditions. They were given a further lease of life by the imposition after 1944 of an unpopular and unrepresentative communist regime, ultimately controlled by Poland's historical foe. Indeed in the post-war years, political romanticism gained significant new adherents. But it has lost many more as a result of such brutal lessons in political realism as the Yalta agreements, the disastrous outcome of the Warsaw Uprising in 1944, the domestic impact of continuous communist rule for two generations and the international implications of the Soviet-American parity in nuclear arms. Yet the influence of 'dreams', 'myths' and other similar syndromes of the romantic tradition remains powerful in post-war Poland.

In the nineteenth century, the values of romantic nationalism were widely adopted by the intelligentsia in Poland, a separate culturally homogeneous stratum, characteristic of central and eastern Europe and made up of those possessing academic secondary education. As Maria Hirszowicz points out (Chapter 7, p. 139), the intelligentsia did not exist as a separate stratum in western Europe 'where the educated strata were from the start fragmented by serving different classes and institutions. In conditions of a rapidly developing economy . . . [the] emergence of political parties and the expansion of public and private services, educated people were to be found everywhere, wherever general knowledge and specialised training were necessary: their status was determined primarily by the prestige of the professions they pursued and the positions which they occupied in the political and social structures.' As she notes:

In Russia and in Poland the situation was completely different: the practical applications of education were limited by the backwardness of social and economic life, while at the same time the advance of progress and the desire for social change manifested themselves primarily in the realms of culture, ideology, and social and political thought. The cultural heritage of the Enlightenment, the belief in progress, the budding movements of the working masses, and national aspirations reflected themselves in the East in the new mood of the educated elites, who resented their marginal position and aspired to the function of spiritual leadership. In partitioned Poland the importance of the national problem enhanced the leadership functions of the educated stratum: the Polish intelligentsia became the major force in preserving national traditions, developing national identity and cultivating the idea of national independence. (pp.139–40)

In inter-war Poland, the intelligentsia became more stratified and fragmented and began to lose this special role which it had claimed for itself, which was in fact a reflection of similar noble claims. One might have expected this process to have continued at an accelerated pace under the communists, who introduced a programme of rapid industrialization and mass education which not only greatly increased the size of the intelligentsia, but opened up for it a much wider range of employment possibilities. To quote Maria Hirszowicz again:

the development of communist Poland between 1945 and 1980 brought about the rise of a 'new intelligentsia', which was closely linked to the establishment, serving the authorities as administrators, managers, professionals, teachers and doctors. There were reasons to believe that the new intelligentsia was on the way to merging with the Party state bureaucracy in a process which could be described as the bureaucratization of the intelligentsia and the professionalization of the bureaucracy. (p.140)

Yet as the economic and political crisis deepened in the last years of Gierek's rule, a process graphically described by Jerzy Holzer (Chapter 5), the ethos of the old Polish intelligentsia, which had seemed moribund, revived and assumed a new and vigorous life. This took communist theorists by surprise. One of them, Stefan Żiółkiewski, had written in 1962:

The traditional normative model of an intelligentsia as envisaged by Żeromski and Nałkowska was possible only in a society in which the masses were deprived. The liquidation of those deprivations transforms the normative and statistical patterns of the intelligentsia and limits the specific and distinctive nature of the traditional extra-occupational, totality-oriented role of this intelligentsia.[12]

The intensified political and cultural activity of the intelligentsia, which affected wide groups of people and extended over the whole country, was one of the main factors which led to the emergence and success of Solidarity. It was characteristic that the demands of the intelligentsia did not focus in these years on their sectional or material interests but expressed, in a quite traditional fashion, the demands and aspirations of society, or, perhaps more accurately, of the nation as a whole. This was also a feature of the political aspirations of the increasingly sophisticated working class, chronicled by Jerzy Holzer, himself the author of the standard history of Solidarity, which came to see the establishment of free trade unions as the only way of checking the authoritarian nature of the government (see Chapter 5).

The survival of the traditional role of the intelligentsia and the growing political awareness of the politicized sections of the working class brought about increased contact of both a personal and institutional character between these two groups. This development was linked with another characteristic Polish development, the revival of the influence of the Catholic Church within both the intelligentsia and the working class. Although the Church had been a bulwark of 'Polishness' during the period of the partitions, in the inter-war period its political influence had been on the decline (Jerschina, Chapter 4). This process had been to some extent arrested by the brutality of the occupiers during the Second World War; yet the Church's initial reaction to the establishment of communist rule was hesitant and even confused. Given the exhaustion of Polish society after 1945, it had sought to avoid outright conflict with the new rulers of the country, aware that certain communist reforms, including the land reform, nationalization of industry, banks and commerce, and the annexation of the formerly German western and northern territories, were popular in the country. Indeed, the period of accelerated social and economic changes were difficult ones for the Church, with society becoming increasingly secularized and many socially upwardly mobile peasants and workers leaving the fold. Yet at the same time, the Church succeeded in retaining much of its influence, which it was able to employ in helping the new national communist regime of Władysław Gomułka to stabilise itself after 1956. It performed a similar role for Gierek after 1970 and for Jaruzelski after the 'state of war' of 13 December 1981. The results of this strategy, above all the product of the extremely astute Primate of Poland, Cardinal Stefan Wyszyński, are well summarised by Jan Jerschina (Chapter 4):

> The Church . . . was transformed from a *victim* into a *mediator*, and so into an actor in the politico-historical processes, a co-creator of change in society, its consciousness and its bonds with pre-war Poland. As circumstances developed, by continuing this role of mediator it became ever more and more the *partner* of the authorities. (pp.89–90).

In the 1970s, the Church reaped the benefit of its social and educational policies. As Gierek's promises of economic well-being proved vain and the government's popularity fell sharply, the tide of secularization began to recede. Religious observance and loyalty to the Church became increasingly widespread not only in the traditionally Catholic countryside but also in the bulk of the new working class. This was not only the result of a disillusionment with the materialism fostered by the Gierek regime but also reflected a more deep-seated rejection of the communist regime among those very people who were expected to be its strongest supporters, an irony clearly highlighted by Jerzy Holzer. Jerschina stresses the role of the Church's own actions, under the guidance of Cardinal Wyszyński:

The Church proposed an ideology which was broader, philosophically and morally richer, and also more profound, being rooted both in the national traditions of Poland and in the culture of the West. The 1970s, instead of being the years of victorious secularism, appealing to the consumerism of the urban population, became instead years of religious renewal. (p.92)

The religious revival also affected the intelligentsia. Cardinal Glemp, Cardinal Wyszyński's successor as primate, has described this process in a characteristic way:

Before the Second World War, the intelligentsia adopted mostly an unfavourable, indifferent, or opportunistic stance. There were also in that group some who sympathised with communism.
    After the war the new generation of intelligentsia surrendered relatively easily to Marxist ideology. They joined the Party without playing a leading part. The disappointment came only later. Many then protested against the methods of the system. Later the adherents of the Marxist ideology joined Solidarity. Others preferred to stay apart and simply turned in their Party cards. Embittered, they regarded their life, or at least a considerable part of it, as wasted. This applied, above all, to the creative intelligentsia who did not know the Church or knew it simply from folk traditions. Against that background, there appeared a new attitude on the part of the intelligentsia towards the Church. This was expressed in the respect for its deeper spiritual life and its role in maintaining patriotic attitudes.[13]

Cardinal Glemp's claims are confirmed by independent observers. According to Maria Hirszowicz:

the intelligentsia see in the Church the institution which helps them to protect their basic rights and creates the outlet for activities which are otherwise not tolerated by the establishment. The majority of the intelligentsia in Poland is therefore fully committed to the Church, both in spiritual and political terms. (p.147)

The same point is articulated by Janine Wedel: 'The Church's rhetoric affirmed Solidarity's challenge. Pope John Paul II's homilies during his

1983 visit to Poland under martial law stressed the fundamental dignity of humanity. With its slogan, "to regain dignity", Solidarity [and the Church] brought humiliation into public consciousness and generated open discussion' (p.252).

These were the intellectual traditions and social forces which provide the seedbed for the Solidarity movement. Its emergence, flourishing and suppression by the government is succinctly described by Jerzy Holzer. Whilst not sparing in his criticism of the mistakes and miscalculations of the Solidarity leadership, he does not believe that any other course of action they could have pursued would have proved more successful. Ultimately the communist authorities were bound to attempt to crush Solidarity, in the early 1980s since they could not accept so drastic a limitation on their monopoly of power as that constituted by the emergence of this movement. The suppression of Solidarity was, from the government's point of view, reasonably successful. Yet as Holzer has pointed out 'the true paradox of the Polish situation lies in the fact that the defeat of Solidarity is also a defeat for the communist authorities' (p.114). This is because the government has been able to contain the challenge of the political opposition only at great expense in terms of its ideological claims and political legitimacy. Moreover, it is still faced by a deep-rooted, persistent and fundamental economic crisis, which renders the stabilization it has achieved shallow-based and shaky. The re-emergence of Solidarity as a legal opposition since autumn 1988 is an admission on the part of the government that Poland has entered a stage when some power-sharing is inevitable. By this latest turn of events, Solidarity is proving to be the agency which has begun the end of Soviet-style communism in Poland. The marriage of old gentry traditions and post-war industrialization and urbanization is at last bringing Poland into twentieth-century Europe.

The reasons for the present economic crisis are analysed in Chapters 7–10. Wiktor Herer and Władysław Sadowski see its roots as lying in those specific features of the Polish past which we have already analysed. Severe economic difficulties, they argue, are common to many socialist countries and should be traced, in part at least, to their common Soviet-type economic system. Yet the Polish economic collapse of the 1980s was unusually severe – in 1982, national income was 25 per cent lower than in 1979, and by 1988, it was still, in per capita terms, 10 per cent lower than it had been in 1978. This collapse, in their view, was no accident, and can only be explained by reference to those Polish national characteristics which made a centrally planned economy work particularly badly in Poland. Paradoxically, it is precisely that same Polish individualism which has undermined the functioning of the old-style Soviet-inspired economic system in Poland which will make it possible for them to operate a freer, market-based system successfully.

According to them: 'The command system and the policy of central allocation handed the economy over to the bureaucrats. . . . Its main thrust was *discipline, hierarchical submission and blind obedience* – in other words, *everything that was alien to the Poles*' (p.122). As a result, they argue, the Polish economy was not only inefficient but also more inefficient than the economies of its neighbours, where the cultural traditions are judged to be less incompatible with the requirements of the collectivist system. Another cause of the crisis was the strong demonstration effect of pre-war Poland's islands of prosperity and of the capitalist West, fuelling aspirations to achieve quickly a high standard of living. The existence of a defiant working class, unwilling to accept what was on offer, gave the situation a specifically Polish character. As the authors write: 'Such a combination could only end in a bloodbath or madness in economic policy. In the early 1970s it led to the latter, with well-known consequences, and in the early 1980s it led to the imposition of the "state of war"' (p.135).

Jadwiga Staniszkis looks at the prospect of reforms in Poland, given the vested interests of the communist authorities, the USSR and the Polish people. She expatiates on the fundamental paradox that while there seems to be universal support for a far-reaching economic reform involving the use of the market as the main regulator of economic life, there is also widespread opposition, both within the party bureaucracy and in society, to the implications of such a reform. She takes the view that only a radical reform can succeed, one as a result of which the political authorities would divest themselves of the ownership of most of the means of production. She regards this as a necessary condition for economic reforms to be effective, as only in this way can detailed bureaucratic intervention in the day-to-day functioning of the economy be brought to an end. Yet such a reform will not, in her view, be acceptable to the communist authorities in Poland or elsewhere for the foreseeable future, since it will involve them losing too much power. It will also prove unacceptable to society at large because of its consequences – greater work discipline, unemployment and greater inequality. It will also come up against the now deep-rooted egalitarianism of Polish society, one of the few areas where communist ideology has taken root, a point which is also made by Holzer. A more feasible, if less drastic, solution would be a reform which would allow various private and other non-state sections of the economy to develop at the expense of the state sector. These would produce the wealth which will maintain the still large and mostly inefficient state sector which would in her phrase be 'de-articulated'. Such a reform might be a prelude to the more radical solution later on.

Lena Kolarska-Bobińska investigates more deeply the attitudes to a market-oriented economic reform held by various social groups. This study, based on sociological research unique in Eastern Europe, takes a less gloomy view than that held by Staniszkis. While opposition to reform was fairly strong in the early 1980s, the persistence of the economic crisis has made Poles more willing to accept radical measures. In this respect, the economic crisis has, paradoxically, proved a valuable learning experience both for the authorities and for the nation.

Staniszkis' views on the importance of the private sector are fleshed out by Jacek Rostowski. In his view, the traditional communist-socialist economy in Poland is in a state of terminal decay and is being replaced by what he refers to as a 'mixed economy kleptocracy'. He shows both the great variety of forms of private economic activity in Poland and their increasing scale. Whether they can provide the motor to drive forward the whole Polish economy remains open to question.

The economic and political crises described in this book have made Poland a country of paradoxes. It is probably the most pro-American country in Europe and yet the Soviet Union's most important ally; one of the most religious countries in the world and yet communist-ruled; instinctively pro-western yet frequently ignored or even abandoned by the West; a nation in which individualism is particularly strong, yet which has an economy based on collectivist principles; a nation marked by its fervent patriotism which has been under foreign domination for most of the past two centuries; a land of extreme shortages and poor standards and yet a nation reluctant to embrace the principles of competition and efficiency. These antinomies have only been sharpened by the defeat of Solidarity in 1981. As Jerzy Holzer points out, 'Besides the kind of compromise with Solidarity rejected in December 1981, only two others now seem possible: either a further crisis and Poland's humiliation in the world, as well as in the communist bloc, or a spontaneous rebellion, the catalyst of which may well be the young workers from the big towns, but which will probably result in a further crisis' (p.114).

Faced with these two extremely unattractive alternatives, the rulers of Poland today have, in fact, no viable alternative to a policy of political democratization and economic reform. Democratization – the concession of a guaranteed legal status to the opposition and a degree of power-sharing – seems necessary to give the government greater authority to introduce reforms that are, in the short term, costly but represent the only way of avoiding further major economic decline. The authors of this volume display an impressive degree of intellectual sophistication and political understanding. It is our hope that these qualities are shared by both the ruling elite and a sufficient part of their compatriots. Much wisdom, understanding and tolerance will be needed to resolve the Polish crisis. If these characteristics are not allowed their full play, the paradoxes described in this volume will soon be supplanted by new and far less agreeable ones. The recent changes in the USSR and East-West relations also give Poland the chance to play a fuller part in the unification of Europe. The country's historical role of a bridge between the civilizations of Europe's two distinct and competing parts was at the root of its misfortunes during the last two centuries. Now we may be entering a new era of co-operation, of building a 'common European home', in the construction of which the bridge role may prove, this time, to be Poland's asset, offering its people the chance, at last, to be free and to come to terms with reality, assigning many of the paradoxes our authors have outlined to the pages of history.

Notes

1 Kołłątaj, H. *et al.* (1868) *O ustanowieniu i upadku konstytucji 3 maja* (On the creation and fall of the constitution of 3 May), 2nd edn, Paris, vol.1, 5–6.
2 Karpiński, W. (1983) *Amerykańskie cienie* (American shadows), Paris, 52.
3 Davies, N. (1981) *God's Playground: A History of Poland*, Oxford, vol.2, 723–4.
4 Quoted in Walicki, A. (1988) *The Three Traditions in Polish Patriotism. Some Peculiarities and Vicissitudes of the Polish National Consciousness, Past and Present* (Indiana University pamphlet), Indiana, 22. This is an extended version of Chapter 1.
5 Chapter 1, p.31, below.
6 Chapter 2, pp.46–7 below.
7 Chapter 2, p.46, below.
8 Walicki, A. *op. cit.,* 28.
9 Bryk, A. (1989) 'Polish-Jewish Relations during the Holocaust. The Hidden Complex of the Polish Mind', in A. Polonsky (ed.) *'My Brother's Keeper'. Recent Polish Debates on the Holocaust*, London, 161.
10 *'Jakby życie było zdradą'* ('As if life was a betrayal'). A discussion between M. Janion, W. Zalewski, W. Terlecki, A. Wajda and M. Bajer. *Tygodnik Powszechny*, 27 January 1985.
11 *Myśli nowoczesnego Polaka* (*Thoughts of a Modern Pole*), first published Lwów, 1903. This quotation is on p.87 of the edition published in London in 1953.
12 Żiółkiewski, S. (1962) *'O polityce kulturalnej PRL w lalach 1945–1948'*, *Kultura i Społeczeństwo*, vol.6, no.4, 12–13.
13 Glemp, A. (1987), *'Droga Kościoła w Polsce Ludowej'* ('The Church's Road in People's Poland') *Przegląd Katolicki*, 24 May.

Part I

History and politics

1

The three traditions in Polish patriotism

Andrzej Walicki

University of Notre Dame, Indiana

Poland is a country where everything has a historical dimension. We are living, as it were, with the entire burden of our history on our shoulders, without being able to forget about the past, or to liberate ourselves from its omnipresent influence. This explains why history as a discipline is so popular in Poland: we have more than a hundred historical periodicals and the number of historical publications per year is close on 6,000. Books on historical topics – not only historical novels but also memoirs and scholarly works – disappear immediately from the bookshops.

That is why the problem of Polish patriotism, or nationalism, must be approached historically. It is a very complex problem, because the Polish national consciousness contains elements of different historical origin and of equally different present implications. In more or less 'normal' times we are often unaware of the potential conflict between different ingredients in our love for our fatherland, but in a time of trouble the essential heterogeneity and incompatibility between the different streams in Polish patriotism and the different constituent parts of the Polish national consciousness become evident.

I have no space to dwell on all aspects of this complex topic. In the present essay I shall concentrate on three historical traditions of Polish 'nationalism': first, the tradition which conceives of the nation as subject to the collective *will* and the national will as the only legitimation of political power; second, that which conceives of the nation in terms of the ethical *ideal* inherent in its historical heritage; and, third, the tradition which thinks of the nation in terms of the national *interest*. In short, I am going to deal with three different conceptions of nationalism: the nationalism of the national will, of the national ideal, and of the national interest. The first of these provided the legitimation for the democracy of the gentry – the peculiarly Polish political structure which took final shape in the sixteenth century; the second characterized the romantic view of the nation and of patriotic duty – a view which has taken deep roots in Poland and is still very much alive today; the third dominates the anti-romantic forms of Polish nationalism, especially modern integral nationalism, as represented by the influential ideology of National Democracy.

It seems proper to begin with a semantic digression on the two crucial words: 'nation' and 'nationalism'. In the English language the term 'nation' is closely associated, sometimes even synonymous, with the term 'state'. In Poland, as in other east European countries whose national consciousness was growing in the period when they did not yet achieve or (as in the case of Poland) were deprived of their own statehood, the semantic difference between the two terms is felt very strongly. In France the term 'nationalité', especially when used in passports and other official documents, means simply 'citizenship of the state'; an attempt to classify French citizens according to their native language and ethnic background would be felt as incompatible with democratic principles. In Poland state citizenship and nationality are seen as two different things and an attempt to identify the two would be regarded as a brutal violation of the most elementary human right. If 'nationality' and 'state citizenship' were equivalent, the nineteenth-century Poles should have been considered to be Russians or Germans; needless to say, the whole of nineteenth-century Polish history was a struggle to preserve and develop Polish national identity and, therefore, nothing was more alien and more horrifying to Polish patriots than the idea of identifying nation with state, nationality with citizenship and patriotism with loyalty to the existing state. The same was true for Ukrainians living in the inter-war Polish state: they were Polish citizens but not Poles, and attempts to classify them as Poles would have been felt by them, quite rightly, as a policy of enforced polonization and not a step towards ensuring democratic equality among the citizens of Poland.

We must be aware that it was not always so in the Polish case. In the Polish-Lithuanian state before partition the word 'nation' (*natio*), already widely used in the sixteenth century, had a distinctively political, rather than linguistic or ethnic connotation. The 'nation' was conceived as a body politic, embracing all active citizens (i.e. all members of the gentry) irrespective of their native language or ethnic background. This tradition of multi-ethnic and multi-lingual nationalism survived in Poland until the middle of the nineteenth century, but finally gave way to a new conception of nation, based upon linguistic and ethnic criteria.

The word 'nationalism', derived from 'nation', is also used in Poland in a different sense from in the West. To put it simply, in the Polish language the term 'nationalism' is used in its most narrow sense, defining the ideology and practice of a chauvinistic and narrow-minded national egoism, while in western languages, especially in English, the same word comprises, as a rule, *every* concern with winning national independence, awakening national consciousness, or preserving the national identity. According to Carlton Hayes, an eminent American student of nationalist movements, 'nationalism may be defined as a fusion of patriotism with a consciousness of nationality'.[1] Considered in this way, Polish romantic patriotism *is*, of course, an example of the most ardent and highly developed nationalism. The average educated Pole would, of course, protest against such a classification, pointing out that Polish romantic patriotism was inseparably bound up with the idea of the brotherhood of nations, as expressed in the famous slogan of the Polish uprising of 1830–1, 'For your freedom and ours'. He would be surprised and indignant to be told that Adam Mickiewicz was not only the greatest Polish poet but also one of the greatest Polish nationalists. He would be right, moreover, in insisting on the essential difference between the noble, idealistic patriotism of the romantic epoch and the brutal nationalism of the later period. But it does not follow from this that the word 'nationalism' should be used only in its narrow and pejorative meaning.

I think that contemporary English usage of the term 'nationalism' has many obvious advantages and, therefore, I shall not try to change it. At the same time, however, I should like to stress that although I use the word 'nationalism' in its *broadest* sense, one of my main aims is to contribute to a clearer understanding of important *differences* between the various types of nationalist thinking. We must always remember, I think, that nationalism, like socialism, is not singular, but plural.

Let us pass now to the first of the three problems mentioned above, to the legacy of the Polish 'democracy of the gentry'.

The peculiarly Polish political structure called the 'democracy of the gentry' took final shape in the sixteenth century, i.e. in Poland's 'Golden Age'. Its genesis, however, can be traced back to the first half of the fifteenth century. In the beginning the Polish gentry obtained from the king a firm assurance of their negative rights – the inviolability of private property (1422), of private households and, most importantly, the assurance of personal immunity (*'Neminem captivabimus nisi iure victum'*, 1430). This increase in their 'negative freedoms' was paralleled by an increase in their strictly *political* rights and their share in ruling the state. The year 1493 was the date of the formal establishment of the parliamentary system in Poland, with the Great Diet as a legislative power. The members of the Chamber of Deputies were dependent on specific 'instructions', received from their local gentry councils, called 'dietines'. Besides proclaiming the laws, the Great Diet fixed taxation, controlled the administration and the finances of the state, received the reports of foreign ambassadors and envoys, and, above all, decided on all important questions of foreign politics, especially on peace and war. The king was forbidden to declare war for personal or dynastic reasons. In 1505 the Great Diet in Radom strengthened this constitutional development by promulgating the famous law of '*Nihil Novi*' – the law which obliged the king to refrain from introducing any changes in the established system, except with the agreement of the Diet.

Further constitutional development took place after the extinction of the Jagiellonian dynasty. In theory Poland had been an elective monarchy since 1382, that is, since the extinction of the Piast dynasty; in practice, however, until the death of the last of the Jagiellons (1572) – mainly because of the fact that the Jagiellons had hereditary rights to the Lithuanian throne – the dynastic principle was observed. Afterwards, from the time of the election of Henry de Valois in 1573, every newly elected King of Poland had to swear to protect the existing laws and liberties of the country and never to violate them. Each Polish noble felt proud not only of being an 'elector' of the king but also of the right to become king himself. This was by no means a purely theoretical right: in fact four kings were elected in Poland not from among royal families but from the ranks of the Polish nobility. One of these was Jan Sobieski, who in 1683 defended the Hapsburg Empire against the Turkish invasion.

It is obvious that the 'democracy of the gentry' was restricted, by definition, to one estate only; some historians, especially German and Russian, have concluded from this that it was in fact a form of absolute (although collective) political power. On the other hand it is undeniable that sixteenth-century Poland was, as the American historian R.H. Lord put it, 'the freest state in Europe, the state in which the greatest degree of constitutional, civic and intellectual liberty prevailed'.[2] It was a democracy, because it was based upon the principle of the sovereignty of the people. It was a democracy *of the gentry* because the sovereign people were composed of, and limited to, the members of the gentry. But the Polish gentry was an extremely numerous group; in the sixteenth century 11 to 13 per cent of the total population of the Polish-Lithuanian Commonwealth consisted of noblemen who were represented in parliament, whereas in sixteenth-century England the corresponding figure was only 5 per cent. From this point of view the old Polish democracy was impressive even if measured by nineteenth-century standards: the Polish romantic poet, Zygmunt Krasiński, was right to remind Lamartine, who had called Poland 'an aristocracy without a people', that in the bourgeois France of Louis Philippe only 1.5 per cent of the population had the right to vote.[3]

From the socio-economic point of view the Polish (or polonized) nobility was an extremely differentiated group. At the top of it were great magnates, at the bottom the noble proletariat, the *nobiles pauperes* who had to work for their living and who were often as poor as the peasantry. In spite of these differences all the members of the nobility embraced the doctrine of the juridical and political equality of all the nobles. The ideal to which they aspired was expressed in their favourite saying: 'the nobleman on his little plot of land is the equal of the Palatine' (*Szlachcic na zagrodzie równy wojewodzie*). Of course, in reality it was not so. It is a rather general rule that societies cannot live up to their values. Nevertheless, it was true that many efforts were made to equalize the nobility, or at least, to uphold the image of their theoretical equality. The Polish king had no right to bestow aristocratic titles on the nobility of his country; only some ancient Lithuanian and Ruthenian families were allowed to use their inherited ducal titles. The difference between the most powerful magnate and the poorest nobleman was accepted as a difference in wealth, but not as a difference in political or social status. The accepted form of addressing every member of the noble estate by another noble was 'Sir brother'.

Let us turn now to the problem of the nation-building processes and the national consciousness in Poland. In the vast literature on nationalism two theses are widely accepted: first, that modern nations are the products of capitalist development; second, that modern national consciousness is a correlate of the process of democratization. The first thesis claims that the growing socialisation of production and large-scale economic integration destroys the barriers dividing provinces and estates, increases horizontal and vertical social mobility, intensifies contacts between different people (discovering, by the same token, the importance of a commonly understood national language), unifies laws and, finally, creates national markets and nation-states. The second thesis maintains that the idea of national sovereignty is closely bound up, logically and historically, with the democratic idea of the sovereignty of the people, that the development of a national consciousness depends on the numbers of politically active or, at least, politically conscious people, i.e. on the degree of political and social democratization.

It is evident that the strong, deeply rooted traditions of the democracy of the gentry greatly influenced the processes of nation-building in Poland, especially in the sphere of national consciousness. Their effects, I think, were at once positive and negative. Basically we may say that they were positive as regards the development of national consciousness, and negative as regards economic modernization.

Hans Kohn, a leading American historian and theorist of modern nationalism, maintains that the 'Western' type of nationalism was bound up with the idea of the sovereignty of the people, with government by consent and a constitutional conception of the state, and that it was incompatible with an absolutist monarchy and inconceivable without the idea of political democracy.[4] We may add that conditions for this type of national consciousness were much better in the Polish-Lithuanian Commonwealth than in western Europe. If 'nationalism' means that loyalty to the nation comes before loyalty to the king or multiple loyalties to supra-national feudal authorities, the Polish gentry was 'nationalistic' from the beginnings of 'gentry democracy', and Frycz Modrzewski – the greatest thinker of the Polish Renaissance, who advocated, among other things, treating burghers and peasants as equal before the law and establishing a Polish national Church – should be recognized as one of the first great theorists of 'political' nationalism.

The idea of the 'sovereignty of the nation of the gentry' in its relation to the king paved the way for modern ideas of national sovereignty and the right to national self-determination – ideas which appeared in Poland earlier than in any other European country, and, as has been shown by Jean Fabre, had some influence on the republican current in the French Enlightenment.[5] This is quite understandable: as soon as Polish political freedom became endangered from outside rather than from inside, the entire libertarian tradition of the 'gentry democracy' produced powerful arguments for national independence.

The fragility of Polish independence in the eighteenth century gave birth to a rich theoretical literature dealing with the problems of the law of nations. A physiocrat, Hieronim Stroynowski, put forward a theory that every nation had four natural rights: (1) the right to free and independent existence; (2) the right to defend itself by force; (3) the right to the certainty that international agreements would not be violated; and finally, (4) the right to demand help from other nations.[6] Similar ideas were developed by many other Polish jurists of the Age of Enlightenment. It should be stressed that the right to self-determination was never restricted, explicitly or implicitly, to European peoples: Polish public opinion did not sympathize with the ideology of colonialism and took the part of the distant colonized peoples.

After the second partition of Poland Hugo Kołłątaj, a leading political thinker of the Polish Enlightenment, formulated the common conviction of his generation thus:

> That every nation be free and independent, that every nation should be allowed to embrace that form of government which it prefers and that no foreign nation is entitled to interfere in its constitutional development – that is the first and most important maxim of the law of nations, so evident in the light of our century that no proofs are needed to justify it. A nation which has no right to rule in its own country is not a nation.[7]

It is a commonplace that in the eighteenth century the Polish 'democracy of the gentry' degenerated into anarchy, actively supported by the neighbouring absolute monarchies whose hirelings used the right of veto to block all attempts at progressive legislation. The necessary reforms came too late to save the existence of the Polish-Lithuanian state.

Nevertheless, as Rousseau had rightly predicted, it was easier to swallow Poland than to digest it. Maurycy Mochnacki, the romantic literary critic who in the uprising of 1830–31 emerged as an outstanding intellectual leader of the Left, asserted with good reason that after the downfall of the state the republic traditions of the gentry democracy, quite irrespective of their functioning in the recent past, did much to support the inner vitality of the nation and the spirit of resistance against the partitioning powers. If Poland had been an absolute monarchy, he argued, its society would have become passive, devoid of civic spirit and unable to defend itself. In other words, the downfall of the Polish state would then have meant the dissolution of the Polish nation. If Poland had 'not yet been lost' (to quote from the Polish national anthem), it was because a large percentage of its population felt itself to be a nation, endowed with an inalienable right to sovereignty.

Many contemporary historians fully agree with this view. A Polish historian, Janusz Tazbir, has recently pointed out that in the changed conditions even the ancient vices of the gentry showed their positive side: stubborn conservatism changed into a stubborn determination to preserve national tradition and identity, the long-established habit of opposing royal power became resistance to the foreign yoke, and so forth.[8]

Thus we may conclude that the 'democracy of the gentry', whose 'golden age' coincided with the 'golden age' of Poland, has greatly contributed to the formation of the modern Polish nation. Its main legacy – the twin ideas of the 'sovereignty of the people' and 'sovereignty of the nation' – were easily modernized, that is, related to the entire population of the country, and not to one estate only. In the last decades of the 'gentry republic' an impressive re-emergence of active patriotism took place and the partitioning powers proved unable to break it. The tradition of independence and active citizenship, the long-established habit of distinguishing between 'a nation' and 'a mere state', enabled nineteenth-century Poles to feel themselves to be a 'historical nation', although one temporarily (and illegitimately) deprived of its own statehood.

However, there was also the other side of the coin. For a long time – much too long – the democratic tradition existed in Poland without capitalism and without the liberal values bound up with it. The under-development of modern social structures was paralleled by a psychological unpreparedness for the requirements of modernity. Poland had not passed through the school of liberal individualism, had not developed such 'bourgeois' values as economic capacity and industriousness, self-reliance in economic life, thrift, and so forth. Its elite remained faithful to the values characteristic of the nobility, such as honour, courage in open fight (as distinct from civil courage), freedom conceived as participation in political power; it did not pay much attention to the prosaic, down-to-earth concerns of private law and could hardly understand Napoleon's famous dictum that the essence of freedom is a good Civil Code. The democratic ideologies of the Polish intelligentsia remained significantly related to the 'democracy of the gentry' in their emphasis on disinterestedness and sacrifice; even peaceful 'organic work', in order to be accepted, had to take the form of, or at least be presented as, a *disinterested public service*, a patriotic duty. Thus, the Polish democratic tradition could contribute very little to the release of the economic energy of the nation. Even more: its inherent hostility towards 'bourgeois-liberal' values created psychological obstacles for genuine economic modernization.

We face, therefore, a seeming paradox which explains, I think, a great deal in Polish history. The same national tradition functioned in two different ways in the process of forming the modern Polish nation. With respect to such preconditions of modern nationhood as active citizenship and political nationalism, centred on the question of national independence, its role was both considerable and positive. At the same time, with respect to capitalist development, so essential for modern national formations, its role was much slighter, ambiguous, sometimes simply negative.

The astonishing vitality of the positive aspect of the Polish national heritage has been revealed in recent years by the Solidarity movement in Poland. Norman Davies, the author of *God's Playground: A History of Poland* (1981), comments that Solidarity's organizational structure 'is strangely reminiscent of the *Sejm* (Diet) and the *Sejmiki* (Dietines) of the Old Republic. Wałęsa, like the old Polish noblemen whom he so uncannily resembles, seems to have perceived instinctively that the main danger lay in the absolutist pretensions of state power. If this is so, the Polish working class may be seen reviving the political traditions of the Noble Democracy – traditions which appear to survive almost two centuries of suppression'.[9]

A similar assessment was made by the American historian, Martin Malia, who wrote: 'it is not too much to say that this young working class, in its mentality at least, resembles nothing more than a gigantic plebeian *szlachta* (gentry), insisting on the principle "nothing about us without us" and aspiring to the "golden freedom" of its ancestral lords'.[10]

On closer examination, however, even the valuable aspect of the legacy of the democracy of the gentry turns out to have its other side, which makes it somewhat archaic and not particularly suitable for the requirements of modern nationhood. In spite of its long parliamentary tradition Poland has experienced very little truly *modern* parliamentary government or truly modern democratic decision-making. The explanation of this sad fact can be found in two characteristic features of the Polish 'democracy of the gentry', the only form of democracy to have taken strong root in Poland.

The first may be defined as a penchant for direct democracy, as distinct from the modern principle of representation. 'The kernel of the Polish nation', wrote Adam Mickiewicz, 'was an assembly, a meeting of free people, a *dietine* (*sejmik*). The history of Poland is the history of various assemblies, sometimes debating together and sometimes not, often quarrelling with or even hostile to one another, acting, as it were, with no set purpose. But it had also a moral focus which rested with the so-called general assembly – the *Diet* (*Sejm*).'[11] The members of the Diet, however, were bound by specific instructions from their local dietines, and the authority of the Diet was moral rather than legal. It decided on moral issues, as for instance on the righteousness of declaring war, but its decisions were not legally binding. The same was true of the national leadership of Solidarity and turned out to be its greatest weakness.

The second archaic feature of the Polish parliamentary system was the principle of unanimity and its converse – the notorious *liberum veto*. It was taken for granted that the minority would accept the views of the majority not only legally but morally, giving up their separate position and thus saving the unity of the corporate will of the nation; at the same time each member of the Diet had an inalienable right of veto and, if this right was used, the Diet was automatically dissolved and *all* laws voted during the session were annulled. This was based on the belief that, if an individual member of the Diet had the courage to use his right of 'free protest', his reasons must be very strong and it would therefore be better to make no decision at all; in other words, the exercise of the right of veto was interpreted as an indication that there was something fundamentally wrong with the proposed decision, that the will of the majority was deprived of divine blessing. The ideological justification of this view may be defined as anti-authoritarian collectivism; *anti-authoritarian*, because it recognized that a mechanical majority was not enough, that there could be cases in which the entire collective had to respect the will of one of its members; *collectivism*, because it was assumed that *as a rule* an individual, or minority, had to bow to majority opinion and accept it as *morally binding*. I think that this collectivist aspect of the Polish mind is very much alive today. Patriotism is often used in Poland as a means of applying ruthless moral pressure, majority opinion tends to be seen as *morally binding*, and great civic courage is needed to defend one's right to truly independent judgement.

Let us pass now to a brief discussion of my second and third points: the legacy of romanticism and the anti-romantic forms of nationalism. As we know, Poland in the nineteenth century was a stateless nation, divided between the three conservative states, Russia, Austria and Prussia, pillars of the reactionary Holy Alliance. Nevertheless for a long time – at least until the insurrection of 1863–4 – Poles saw themselves as a 'political nation', owing its existence to the political will of its members, irrespective of language or ethnic origin. True, the influence of romanticism with its stress on a distinctively national culture and, also, the example of Germany – a nation deprived of political unity but held together by a common culture – greatly increased the importance of language as a criterion of nationality. But it can safely be said that, for a Polish patriot in the first half of the nineteenth century, to be a Pole meant being loyal to the former Polish Commonwealth. One could speak Ukrainian or any other non-Polish language and still consider oneself, and be considered by others, as Polish, because 'Polishness' was not yet defined in terms of language and ethnic background. (In other words, the notion of being '*gente Ruthenus, natione Polonus*' was still in use, although it conflicted with the newly awakened Ukrainian national consciousness.)

It may be difficult to understand how it was possible to conceive the inhabitants of the former Poland as members of a 'political nation' when the Polish state had ceased to exist. At the beginning it was also difficult for the Poles. The last partition of Poland was seen by many Polish patriots (including the greatest political thinker of the Polish Enlightenment, Hugo Kołłątaj) as the end of the Polish nation. Soon, however, a different feeling prevailed and a distinction was made between a 'mere state' and a genuine 'political nation' whose spirit can live even if its earthly body (the state) has been destroyed. 'Mere state' is an artefact, a soulless machine, while a nation is a community held together by ties of common history and by the common political will to preserve, or to regain, its independent statehood. Membership in a state is compulsory, based on a purely territorial principle, while a political nation owes its existence to the will of its members. It was assumed, of course, that the overwhelming majority of politically conscious inhabitants of the former Commonwealth desired the restoration of the Polish state, quite irrespective of their language.

After the defeat of the 1830–1 uprising all vestiges of independent Polish statehood completely disappeared and the intellectual elite of the nation, including our greatest romantic poets, found itself in political exile, mainly in France. The influence of romantic ideas, the tragedy of emigration, the strange combination of national humiliation with an increased feeling of national importance, stemming from an awareness of the all-European significance of the Polish cause, all these factors exerted a powerful influence on the Polish national consciousness. The dominant form of the Polish national ideology became romantic nationalism, conceiving nations as moral entities and agents of universal progress; a nationalism passionately believing in the brotherhood of nations and in the ethicisation of politics, whereby it was hoped to put an end to such political crimes as had culminated in the martyrdom of Poland. The most extreme and best-articulated form of this romantic nationalism was religiously inspired romantic messianism, which saw Poland as the chosen nation, the spiritual leader of mankind and the sacred instrument of universal salvation.

We have no time to analyse the rich texture of Polish messianism and other forms of Polish nationalist thought in the romantic epoch. Let us indicate instead some practical consequences of this peculiar form of national consciousness. First, loyalty to defunct institutionalized forms of national life was replaced by loyalty to the 'national idea', as manifested in the national tradition and revealed in the national mission; the nation ceased to be conceived of as a certain empirical reality, becoming instead 'a community of spirits sharing a common destiny and realizing a common task'. Responsibility for current national affairs, especially for such prosaic aspects as, for instance, economic growth, was replaced by a concern for maintaining the memory of an idealized past and by dreams of an ideal future. In other words, 'Polishness' was transformed into a lofty idea, and national existence was accordingly conceived of as keeping this idea alive by the power of the spirit, manifesting itself in heroic deeds, without reference to their practical results. 'The Fatherland of the Poles', proclaimed Mickiewicz, 'is not a mere piece of land bound by frontiers which limit the national existence and activity of the Pole.'[12] The Fatherland of the Poles is an idea which has never really existed, since the actual Poland never fulfilled all the conditions necessary for its materialization.

This romantic conception of patriotism, conceiving of the love of Fatherland as a love for Poland's spiritual heritage and for the 'Polish idea', is still very much alive among the Poles. The Archbishop of Cracow, Karol Wojtyla, now Pope John Paul II, expressed this view as follows: 'Each of us possesses a heritage within us – a heritage to which generations and centuries of achievement and calamity, of triumph and failure, have contributed: a heritage which somehow takes deeper root and grows new tissues from every one of us. We cannot live without it. It is our own soul. It is this heritage, variously labelled the Fatherland, or the Nation, by which we live.'

We should recognize the unique nobility of this conception. Patriotism conceived of as passionate loyalty to a certain tradition and a certain ideal is immune to the usual pitfalls and dangers of a more prosaic, down-to-earth nationalism, as expressed in the saying 'my country, right or wrong'. On the other hand, it involves the danger of indifference to the prosaic needs of the really existing fatherland, generates an excessive love for symbolic gestures, and too often encourages heroic action without responsible calculation of the chances of victory.

It has been aptly observed that the Poles are peculiarly fond of celebrating their defeats while other nations celebrate only their victories. It should be added that to romantic patriotism the difference between defeat and victory is not essential: a heroic defeat is in fact a spiritual victory, since defeat in the struggle for a just cause helps to keep alive the national idea. This attitude easily degenerates into a cult of national martyrdom, through the romantic belief that great sufferings, and especially the shedding of blood, serve as a purifying force for the general redemption and regeneration of mankind.

Equally ambiguous is the fate of another ingredient in the Polish romantic heritage: the belief in the brotherhood of nations and in the particular Polish mission within universal history. This ardent conviction explains why so many Poles have fought for the national or social freedom of other nations, providing leadership for the revolutions in Germany, Italy, Hungary, and even military leaders for the Paris Commune. This was indeed a unique and greatly admired phenomenon in European history: even Karl Marx, generally so critical of sentimental outbursts, called Poland 'an immortal knight of Europe', a 'necessary nation', a nation of 'twenty million heroes', defending the West against the Asiatic despotism of Russia.[13] But the converse of this was, and still is, the notoriously naïve belief that the nations of the West are always willing to help Poland, to come to its rescue in time of trouble, and that their help is something which the Poles have 'deserved' for their services in the cause of European civilization and freedom.

We should also remember that the Poles of the romantic epoch were still a nation of the gentry, lacking the 'bourgeois' capacity for well-organized hard work, and suffering instead from acute feelings of national humiliation, which found expression in outbursts of emotional patriotism. In the stateless conditions of existence in Poland, it was difficult for Polish patriots, deeply imbued as they were with the knightly traditions of the gentry, to find a legal outlet for patriotic public activity. The ethos of public service in the political sphere, characteristic of the ancient democracy of the gentry, became transformed, very one-sidedly, into the ethos of an open struggle on the battlefield, in accordance with the gospel of heroism preached by the great romantic poets. Under the influence of messianic romanticism the very idea of a nation became unduly spiritualized, divorced from empirical reality; patriotism was identified as service of the glorious 'national idea', which was found in the past and would be triumphant again in the future, and not as the prosaic daily task of making life more bearable in the present. The view that it is possible to serve one's nation by furthering worthy individual interests in the sphere of civil society appeared only with the so-called 'Warsaw Positivists' of the 1870s, and even then proved to be short-lived.

In this way the legacy of the gentry democracy, combined with the legacy of romantic nationalism, created important psychological obstacles to the emergence and respectability of 'bourgeois virtues' in Poland. Cyprian Norwid, on the eve of the desperate uprising of 1863, summarized this situation by contrasting 'Poland as a society' and 'Poland as a nation'. According to his famous diagnosis the Poles were supreme as a nation because their patriotism in crucial moments was superb; they were least admirable as a society because they were deficient in the virtues of will and character indispensable to normal, everyday life. Let me quote:

> This is Polish society! – this is the nation which is undeniably great so far as *patriotism* is concerned but which *as a society* represents nothing. . . .
> We are no *society* at all.
> We are a great *national* banner.[14]

It is fascinating to see how little the Poles have changed since the time these words were written. Norwid's diagnosis has found spectacular confirmation in the works of contemporary Polish sociologists, who – using the methods of modern American sociology – have examined the attitudes and state of mind of the citizens of the People's Republic of Poland. The main result of their works was well summarized by Professor Stefan Nowak.[15] He has found that an overwhelming majority of Poles do not identify with the institutions in which they work, do not think in terms of public good on the institutional level. Their loyalties and their feelings of belonging are two-sided. First, they belong and are loyal to different primary face-to-face groups – from the family and groups of friends to informal cliques, mafias, and other personalized groups pursuing their interests in a half-legal, or illegal way. From this lowest level of integration we have a sudden leap to the highest, most abstract and most sublimated, symbolic level: the level of national solidarity. Thus, an average Pole does not belong to a large-scale institutionalized civil society; he belongs to different primary groups and, secondly, he belongs to his nation; not a nation as a system of political and economic institutions, but a nation as national tradition, national culture, the sphere of uniting symbols, of sublimated, lofty, patriotic feelings.

From its very beginning romantic patriotism, or nationalism, coexisted in Poland with different attempts to create a distinctively Polish tradition of political realism, which conceived of patriotism as serving national interests and defined these interests on the basis of the existing balance of power. Before the 1890s they took the forms of 'organic labour' which concentrated on the tasks of the economic and cultural progress of civilization, and of a programme of political conciliation with the partitioning powers. In principle there was no necessary connection between the two: the supporters of political conciliation might neglect economic modernization while people engaged in 'organic labour' might be apolitical or combine their concern for modernization with active commitment to the struggle for independence.

In practice, however, the defeats of the successive insurrections paved the way for the view that 'organic labour' must involve acceptance of existing political realities. Aleksander Świętochowski, the ideological leader of the so-called Warsaw positivists, proclaimed in 1882 that Poles must abandon their political aspirations. Thus, he was politically less ambitious than Aleksander Wielopolski, a statesman of 'loyalist' persuasion who did much to restore the autonomy of the Congress Kingdom but whose efforts were brought to nothing by the romantic uprising of 1863.

Roman Dmowski, the founder of modern, integral nationalism in Poland, had the merit of rejecting 'political romanticism' without abandoning his far-reaching political aspirations. For this reason his conception of political realism, embraced and promoted by the party of National Democracy (the so-called *endecy*), was more influential than earlier forms of anti-romantic political thinking and deserves special consideration in the present context.

Dmowski's criticism of romantic nationalism may be summed up in four points.

1　Against an idealistic belief in justice he set the view that international relations are subject to severe laws of the struggle for survival and that it is stupid to believe in the final victory of the 'right cause', since the fate of any cause depends first of all on material forces.

2　Against 'political romanticism', that is, 'building political activity on purely illusory grounds' and 'embarking on political activity with no prior estimation of the means at disposal',[16] he set a programme of 'political realism', with special stress on the difficult geopolitical situation of Poland.

3　Against such concepts as the 'national idea', national honour, or national glory, he set the concept of the *national interest*, emphasizing that each nation has a natural right to national egoism and that the brotherhood of nations is a naïve illusion.

4　Finally, he offered a new, simple definition of nation which rejected both the old Polish tradition of defining nation in purely political terms, irrespective of ethnic criteria, and the romantic tradition of defining 'Polishness' in terms of certain spiritual values inherent in the national tradition and in the national mission. He thought of nations as the natural product of ethnic differentiation, defining them in terms of language and ethnic origin. His nationalism was meant as consistent, unreflective loyalty to one's nation, so conceived, and not as loyalty to the state, let alone a romantic 'national idea'.

The romantic appeals to a supra-national 'justice' and the other illusions of Polish patriots of the romantic epoch were seen by Dmowski as a result of Poland's abnormal historical evolution. From his point of view, strongly influenced, as we can see, by social Darwinism, the best traditions of the Old Polish Commonwealth, such as religious toleration, attachment to civil liberties, and political freedom, even the equality of the Lithuanian and Ukrainian gentry, were merely expressions of political immaturity and the laziness of a comfortable elite lacking experience of everyday struggle. Even worse, in his eyes, was the romantic idealization of ancient Poland. He saw it as an idealization of weakness, an effort to comfort the Poles with the thought that their alleged moral superiority was more important than victory in the struggle and lording over others. He found especially repellent such messianic ideas as the 'crucifixion' of Poland and the Poles' sacred mission to fight for the salvation of all other nations. Each nation, he maintained, should think only of its own interests; no nation can claim to be innocent. The partitions of Poland were not a 'crime', but the natural result of Poland's weakness. The Poles should not appeal to a non-existent conscience of mankind but should instead learn from their enemies how to win in a brutal struggle. Their struggle should not only be defensive but aggressive as well. It should be directed not only against the partitioning powers but also against national minorities, especially the Ukrainians in Galicia and the Jews.

In this way political realism became consciously opposed to noble idealism in the choice of both the ends and the means of political struggle. This has created an extremely uncomfortable situation for those Poles who want to combine political realism with political morality.

Nevertheless, whether we like it or not, it is clear that Dmowski still remains the main theorist both of political realism in Poland, and also of the 'nationalism of the national interest' (as opposed to the nationalism of the consciously expressed national will). There are, however, different kinds of political realist in Poland: some active within the ranks of the broadly conceived opposition, especially the Catholic intellectual establishment, others supporting Jaruzelski's government as a 'lesser evil', still others, and the most numerous perhaps, supporting the regime whole-heartedly, seeing the existing form of the Polish state as the only realistic solution to the Polish question. Jaruzelski himself seems to have been motivated by a sort of political realism and by a nationalism of the national interest: in proclaiming martial law he openly stated that it was a tragic necessity because the national will had become suicidal, incompatible with the realistically conceived conditions of national existence.

Especially interesting is the resurgence of interest in Dmowski's ideas among the democratic opposition in Poland, including the members of KOR (Workers' Defence Committee). The ideas of the early National Democratic Party (as expressed in its programme of 1903) appealed to them as an impressive attempt to go beyond a political organic labour while, at the same time, stopping short of national insurrection.[17] The

35

National Democrats tried to put pressure on the Russian authorities to force them to make further and further concessions; at the same time they put concerted moral pressure on their compatriots by boycotting collaborators, urging people to sign various collective petitions to the government and, above all, creating a sense of national solidarity which, they hoped, would ensure for their party the position of moral arbiter in national affairs, forcing hesitant individuals to be obedient to its will. They also engaged in underground educative and publishing activity aimed at awakening the masses and forming political elites among them. The activization of the masses thus achieved was to serve as the most powerful means of extracting concessions. Thus, the 'realism' of this programme, consisting in emphatic rejection of romantic revolutionism, was very different from the 'cabinet' realism of Wielopolski.[18] It was a programme of mass participation in an active struggle for national ends; a programme organizing Polish society, making it self-conscious and in control of its own affairs.

The intellectual leaders of KOR saw this aspect of Dmowski's programme as anticipating their own political strategy.[19]

After the crushing of the Solidarity movement, the discussions about political realism in Poland naturally became even more topical. The very fact of the quick and successful execution of the difficult operation of subjecting the country to military rule proved, in Dmowski's words, that Solidarity was basing its political prospects 'on illusory grounds' and embarking on political activity 'with no prior estimation of the means at disposal'.[20] Thus, in *this* sense, the outcome of events strongly supported the views of the political realists. We must also remember that this was a very broad category of people, ranging from outright supporters of government to the great Primate of Poland, Cardinal Stefan Wyszyński, who from the very beginning warned the new trade unions, while emphatically stressing their right to independence, against engaging in emotion-laden political conflict. The official establishment was clever enough to avoid arguments drawn from communist ideology, appealing instead to political common sense and reminding people of the hard facts of life, in particular Poland's dependence on its powerful eastern ally. The logic of this argument was unshakeable although the price of using it was great: the legitimacy of communist rule in Poland was reduced thereby to a question of external necessity and to the proverbial 'lesser evil'.

On the other hand it became immediately clear to all sensitive people that Dmowski's formula of political realism was too narrow. It was clearly unrealistic to expect that politicians, or even generals, could afford to ignore the moral attitudes and feelings of the nation. Although Solidarity was physically defeated public opinion did not turn against the Solidarity radicals, did not urge Lech Wałęsa, who was known as a moderate, to cut himself off from them, as the price of a better bargaining position with the military rulers; on the contrary, it was curiously, irrationally obvious that any move in this direction would be severely condemned, that moral solidarity with the defeated was stronger than the political will to survive and save as much as possible through a workable compromise. Dmowski's warnings against naïve beliefs 'in justice ruling the relations between nations, in the success of impartial European opinion in claiming one's due rights' were conveniently forgotten while the attitude he had ridiculed – a stubborn 'trust in the final victory of the right cause' – came to be dominant and strong enough to *demand* obedience. The leaders of the opposition were not ashamed of having been taken by surprise and badly mistaken in their prognoses; rather they felt proud to have served the right cause irrespective of the outcome. '*Gloria Victis*!' sounded everywhere; this formula, coined by a nineteenth-century Polish writer,[21] seemed universally acceptable while its opposite – the severe '*Vae Victis*!' of the ancient Romans – was felt as inapposite and emotionally repugnant. The language of sober realism became suspicious, as a possible rationalization of moral surrender, while romantic paradoxes had sometimes brilliant careers.[22]

To sum up. I have already indicated in what sense the legacy of the 'democracy of the gentry' can be seen as still alive and relevant for a better understanding of recent events in Poland. There is no need to stress the relevance of the Polish romantic tradition – the impact of romantic ideas upon contemporary Poles, especially upon the best members of the Polish intelligentsia, seems to be obvious. Much more difficult is to define the role of Dmowski's ideas in contemporary Polish patriotism. Let me try to say a few words about it.

A Polish nineteenth-century philosopher, Bronislaw Trentowski, postulated a synthesis of realism and idealism in politics, in which cold realism in the choice of means would be combined with noble idealism in the choice of ends.[23] It was easier, however, to theorize about such a synthesis than to make it a real force which could change the tragic course of Polish history.

One of the reasons for this failure is the fact that political realism in Poland has become too strongly associated with Dmowski's gospel of national immoralism, which has made it repellent to noble-minded people, while the romantic tradition has become enshrined in Polish history, the highest tribunal for the Polish national conscience. That is why in times of national emergency romantic attitudes always prevail. In such times the best representatives of political realism become afraid of being associated with those who use the slogans of realism for the defence of their own dirty interests; this leads them to join the camp of political idealists, thus indeed saving their moral reputation, but at the cost of their political life, allowing the cause of realism to be monopolized, as it were, by people with dirty hands. In order to change this pattern a new kind of Polish patriotism must be developed: a patriotism free from the archaic features of the democratic legacy of Old Poland, critical of romantic illusions, but no less critical of Dmowski's version of political realism.

The aim of this essay has been to show that it may be useful to analyse some problems of contemporary Poland against the background of Polish historical tradition. Each of the three traditions presented above has its merits as well as its pitfalls. Political realism should not be associated exclusively with Dmowski's, that is, with politics seen in terms of material forces and geopolitical considerations alone. More importantly, communists should not be able to present themselves as possessing a virtually unchallenged monopoly of political realism in contemporary Poland. The elaboration of a truly modern Polish school of political realism, suitable for coping with present problems and taking into account the peculiarities of the historically shaped national character of the Poles, is, in my view, an urgent task for independent political thinkers in Poland.

Notes

1 Hayes, C.J.H. (1960) *Nationalism: a Religion*, New York, 2.
2 Haskins, C.H. and Lord, R.H. (1920) *Some Problems of Peace Conference*, Cambridge, Mass., 22–3.
3 See Lednicki, W. (1944) *Life and Culture of Poland as Reflected in Polish Literature*, New York, 3–4.
4 Kohn, H. (1968), 'Nationalism', in *International Encyclopedia of the Social Sciences*, ed. D.L. Sills, vol. XI. See also Kohn, H. (1957) *The Idea of Nationalism. A Study of Its Origin and Background*, 6th edn, New York, 3 and 103.
5 See Fabre, J. (1963) *Lumières et romantisme: énergie et nostalgie de Rousseau à Mickiewicz*, Paris, 131–49.
6 Stroynowski, H. (1791) *Nauka prawa przyrodzonego, politycznego, ekonomiki i prawa narodów*, Wilno, IV, 5.
7 Kołłątaj, H. *et al.* (1868) *O ustanowieniu i upadku konstytucji 3 maja*, 2nd edn, Paris, vol. 1, 5–6.
8 Tazbir, J. (1978) *Kultura, Szlachecka w Polsce*, Warsaw, 71–2.
9 Davies, N. (1981) *God's Playground: A History of Poland*, Oxford, vol. 2, 723–4.
10 Malia, M. (1983) 'Poland's Eternal Return', *New York Review of Books*, 29 September, 26. See also Ash, T.G. (1985) *The Polish Revolution: Solidarity*, London. One of the chapters in Ash's book bears the title 'Noble Democracy'.
11 Mickiewicz, A. (1955) *Dzieła*, Warsaw, vol. 10, 42–3.
12 Ibid., vol. 8, 36.
13 Cf. Marx, K. and Engels, F. (1952) *The Russian Menace to Europe*. Glencoe, Ill., 105–8.
14 Norwid, C.K. (1971–6) *Dzieła wszystkie*, Warsaw, vol. 9, 63–4.

15 Nowak, S. (1981) 'Values and Attitudes of Polish People', *Scientific American*, vol. 245, No. 1 (July). The Polish original was published in *Polaków portret własny*, Cracow, 1979.

16 Dmowski, R. (1908) *Rosja, Niemcy i kwestia polska*, Lwów, 212.

17 See Cywiński, B. (1974) *Rodowody niepokornych*, Warsaw, pp. 325–52; Toruńczyk, B. (ed.) (1983) *Narodowa Demokracja. Antologia myśli politycznej 'Przeglądu Wszechpolskiego'*, London; Michnik, A., (1984) *Szanse polskiej demokracji*, London, 214–41.

18 See Hall, A. (1985) 'Dwa realizmy', *Tygodnik Powszechny*, no. 28 (14 July).

19 See Michnik, *Szanse*, p.231, and Kuroń, J. (1984) *Polityka i odpowiedzialność'*, London, 215.

20 See above, note 16.

21 Eliza Orzeszkowa. *Gloria victis* is the title of her short story about the defeated uprising of 1863–4.

22 See Walicki, A. (1985) 'The Paradoxes of Jaruzelski's Poland', *Archives Européennes de Sociologie*, vol. 16, no. 2, 167–92.

23 See Trentowski, B. (1970) *Chowanna, czyli system pedagogiki narodowej*, edited and introduced by A. Walicki, Wroclaw.

2

Holy ideals and prosaic life, or the Devil's alternatives

Jerzy Jedlicki

Institute of History, Polish Academy of Sciences, Warsaw

Instead of an introduction

In February 1987, I received a letter from the editor of an important Catholic monthly in Kraków. The editor informed me that he wanted to put out a number dedicated to the question of 'Polishness', so as to try to 'grasp the sense and content of this elastic and often misapplied concept and to define the contours of the reality which it conceals'. The editorial board therefore approached more than twenty intellectuals, asking them to reply to the question: 'What are the images, stereotypes, and historical, cultural and religious associations which you connect with the concept of Polishness?'

For a long time I put off replying. At last, I wrote, with unconcealed reluctance, several pages, the gist of which was that such a question should rather be put to foreigners, since the Poles are too egocentric and even narcissistic a nation. In very truth, public discussions of the virtues and failings of the Polish national character have been a favourite theme of our journalism for close on two centuries: this collective obsession for self-analysis has thus become the very hallmark of our character and culture.

Having thus freed myself from one obligation, I then had to come to grips with another, which had been hanging fire from the previous year. For back in March 1986, the editors of this volume had commissioned from me a contribution to the projected collection *Polish Paradoxes*. 'We should very much like you to do an article on "The role of the irrational and the mystical in Polish history",' Antony Polonsky wrote. I did not agree to the title in this form, since it implied a foregone conclusion or, if you prefer, a stereotype. I did not know, I replied, any rational criterion which would allow one to distinguish rational actions from irrational (unless – I should add – we understand 'rational' to mean everything which turns out to be effective, and then triumphant; it then appears that the world has been run by people more rational than others).

I promised, however, that I would write something about 'paradoxes', or rather about the contradictions and tensions which have arisen in the confrontation of holy ideals with prosaic life. But I still did not know how I should tackle this. And then, once again, I thought of that concept of *polskość*.

How should one properly translate it into English? 'Polishness'? This seems to have a somewhat artificial sound. The Polish-English dictionary does not give an exact equivalent, but instead defines it by some possible meanings. '*Polskość* = Polish character, or: traits, nationality, origin, descent, provenance.'[1] It is interesting that the corresponding word *angielskość* (Englishness), constructed analogously to *polskość*, has a false ring to the Polish ear. There is the legitimate form *angielszczyzna*, which can mean firstly, 'English language', and secondly, 'things English', 'the English way of life', although in this second and now archaic meaning, it has derogatory overtones, similar to *francuszczyzna* (French manners and customs, things French) and in general, any sort of *cudzoziemszczyzna* (foreign influence). But *polskość* is a word that is fully natural and living, that sounds equally well in a historical dissertation and in current speech. It can signify everything that the dictionary says, but it also signifies, as it were, something more, something elusive. *Polskość* signifies the very essence of being a Pole.

If a word comes into existence and endures, that means that this word is necessary for something. For what was, and is, *polskość* necessary for the Poles? The *Concise Dictionary of the Polish Language* cites only two typical expressions, 'To show one's Polishness', and 'To give evidence of Polishness'.[2] One might also add the formerly common 'defence of Polishness' or 'stand on guard for Polishness'. From such uses of the word there rise up together both pride and misgivings. Polishness is emphasised in those situations where it is either not entirely self-evident or not entirely secure. We speak only rarely therefore of the Polishness of the gentry (except for polonised noble families in Lithuania or the Ukraine), but often of the Polishness of the peasants, especially in the ethnic borderland. No one spoke of the Polishness of Kraków or Warsaw, even after the partitions, but about the Polishness of Lwów or Silesia. Not about the Polishness of Słowacki (which no one questioned), but about the Polishness of Chopin (where there was some doubt). Uncertainty, and a feeling of being under threat, were impressed into the language.

History and legends

Unless one takes into account this constant feeling of being under threat it is impossible to understand either Polish culture or the Polish type of national consciousness. This is not simply a matter of a threat to the political existence of the nation, but also of a threat to Polish assets in various fields (territory, administration, economy, education, language), and of a threat to a collective feeling of one's own worth. All nations of central and south-eastern Europe have an underlying inferiority complex, but against this background Poland (like Hungary) constitutes a special case. The others, from Finland to Greece, had during the nineteenth century first of all to develop their name, their literary language, history, and national consciousness, and finally to strive for independence. Poland had had all these things, but nevertheless had lost control of her vast territory, a historical catastrophe without precedent in Europe.

At first, the consequences of this were not clear. To the people of the Age of Enlightenment, the existence of a nation without a state seemed impossible. In defiance of this, the soldiers' song sung in Italy by the Polish legion in Bonaparte's army expressed the hope that 'Poland has not yet died, so long as we are alive'.[3] The Warsaw Society of the Friends of Learning, founded in 1800 under Prussian rule, set itself the task of rescuing what still could be saved: the native language and national relics. This passive programme gave place to an active policy again, when the defeat of Prussia and the entry of the French armies into Warsaw evoked hopes that Napoleon would re-establish Poland. This hope vanished after the defeat of 1812. The Kingdom of Poland, under the sceptre of Tsar Alexander I, which was set up after the Congress of Vienna, permitted the preservation in one part of the former territory of the Commonwealth of autonomy and national institutions, but this could in no way satisfy Polish aspirations for sovereignty and unification.

Two social classes were the subjects of these aspirations, and in general of Polish political life. One was the landed nobility. As the only power-holding estate in the Commonwealth before the partitions, the nobility lost the most from the political point of view, but also still had the most to lose: ownership of land together with the right to the service of the peasants; a privileged position in the social hierarchy; civil rights. It is obvious that every attempt to overturn the established, post-Vienna order portended for the nobility hope in the case of success and catastrophe in the case of defeat. The landed gentry was for the most part of a conservative disposition: however, the preservation of fidelity to the Polish republican tradition set it at odds with the existing political order of Europe. Restoration was not possible without revolution, and this constituted the irresoluble paradox of Polish conservatism in the nineteenth century. The alternative was to acquiesce with the partitions, so as to preserve a social or maybe even political position in one or the other of the partitioning states, at the price of abandoning the idea of independence. The posture of the landed gentry, which was, moreover, burdened with the historical guilt for the loss of the country, oscillated between these two extremes, of revolt and resignation.

The other politically active social milieu still did not have a name. It consisted of young officers, minor officials, journalists, literary figures, artists; in other words people with secondary or university education, but without an established social status, and often, too, without a profession. They were drawn partly from the impoverished or landless gentry, partly from the bourgeoisie or from polonised foreign families. They most willingly put on the name of patriots. This was a restless element, which gathered principally in Warsaw, inclining towards political (and after 1831 also social) radicalism, providing numerous members for secret independence organisations, initiating all the Polish uprisings, and drawing into them the less eager gentry. Their principal weapon was the Word: the word of poetry, the word of the press, the word of patriotic and democratic manifestos.

Bearers of the Word were, as is well known, the leaven of all national renaissance movements in nineteenth-century Europe. Among the Germans and the Italians, in Greece and in Serbia, in Hungary and the Czech lands, the 'awakeners' of national consciousness and harbingers of national unification were the historians, ethnographers, philologists, philosophers, and poets. In Poland their role was easier inasmuch as here it did not cause a break in the continuity of historical tradition. Only the partitions – in the recent past – had created such a threat. In the face of this threat it had become necessary to establish safeguards, and to create from words a strong fortress of nationhood. Hence it was precisely the preservation of tradition, the enrichment of the content of the symbols uniting the nation, and the imbuing of them with an almost religious significance which became the principal imperative of literature and art. It was not simply that history had to legitimize in the eyes of the world Poland's right to an independent existence; the hallowed tradition had also to nourish, organize and to extend to all, even to the still indifferent social classes, the feeling of nationhood and the desire for independence. The idealism of literature had thus to replace, over a long period, the material and unifying force of the state.

In this respect memories of the last years of the Commonwealth became especially significant. Even during his lifetime, the most popular Polish hero was Tadeusz Kościuszko, the leader of the 1794 uprising, the defeat of which hastened the downfall of the Polish state. His cult was seemingly paradoxical. Kościuszko was undoubtedly a noble and illustrious man, a sincere patriot and democrat, but he displayed no great talents either as a military leader or as a politician. It is not a praiseworthy victory, but a most bitter defeat which is associated with his name. But what of that? Poland in defeat needed not so much the memory of military triumphs as the legend of a knight without blemish, whose name and deeds could become holy for all classes of the nation.

In 1794, in the small and far from decisive battle of Racławice, Kościuszko gained victory due to the gallant attack of untrained peasant scythemen on a Russian battery. From this time, the scythe mounted on end became for ever a part of the treasury of national symbols. On several occasions, indeed, the radical democrats threatened the gentry with this peasant's scythe, but they did not prevail; in literature and in the national imagination the myth of the scytheman remained constantly as a living personification of commoners' patriotism and of the brotherhood of all estates in the fight for freedom.

Likewise the Constitution of 3 May 1791 became a holy treasure of the nation and is so honoured until this day. At first glance, this is in no way remarkable: the American constitution, which dates from four years earlier, is likewise honoured. But while the American constitution formed the nation, and, albeit with amendments, is still in force two centuries later, the Polish constitution endured barely a year, and, by the reaction of Russia which it improvidently provoked, it was a cause rather of the destruction than of the salvation of Poland. What of that? In the canon of tradition, the Constitution of 3 May finds a place not as an act of political deliberation, but as a beautiful ideological document of the Enlightenment, a model of peaceful reform of government, while with the passage of time, it was remembered not even as a document (since it was only rarely published, and its detailed content was never and still is not generally known), but as a date symbolizing rebirth in defeat. It is not the results of it which count, but the intention, the word, the sign.

These and many similar historical legends, symbols, songs and images have created an ever richer treasury of national mythology, which – like all such treasures – has had an enormous integrating effect. The commonplace 'antithesis' of emotion and reason is of no use in the analysis of myths. A national bond without a state is an organization of feelings directed towards common symbols. Therefore he who acknowledges the preservation of national identity as an intrinsic good must proceed by building a national *sacrum* and binding the people ever more strongly to it. It is still necessary, however, to consider the price which is paid for such a cultural configuration.

Romantic education

The 'holiness' of the native land had its origins in a convention of late classicism, which was characterized by the pathos of solemn oratory, the poetic grandiloquence, the pictorial allegory. The philosophy and aestheticism of romanticism, which reached Wilno and Warsaw around 1820, accorded better with the outlook and desires of the younger generation. Romanticism revealed to them the means of expressing an enormous range of feelings: love and vengeance, pride and humility, rapture and despair; it unleashed the imagination and allowed them to seek completely new principles for the natural order and history. Young poets like Mickiewicz and young critics with Mochnacki at their head eagerly and rapidly learned how to make use of the opportunities opened up to them by the new poetics, fostering a new kind of sensitivity and spiritual outlook on the world. First and foremost, however, romanticism became for them and through them a school of nonconformity: the patriotic conspiracies and the national revolution of 1830–1 became, as it were, a continuation of the literary revolution.

The uprising was defeated, yet poetry triumphed. The romantic generation had to strain their forces to the uttermost in somewhat special conditions – emigration, especially to France, where after 1831 was to be found the majority of the Polish political, military and literary elite, in a community of several thousand refugees who were compromised in the eyes of the Tsarist regime. In Paris and in several provincial towns they created a fairly isolated society of lone men, without families and without property, living from day to day on handouts from the French government, convinced that soon a general European war for liberation of the subjugated peoples would break out and would enable them to return to their homeland in soldiers' glory. While awaiting this moment they quarrelled bitterly about why the rising had failed; they divided into mutually warring factions, issued newspapers and manifestos, gave offence one to the other, and were all sick with longing for home and country, which most of them were fated never to see again. But nevertheless, in this somewhat pathological atmosphere, there were born political programmes and ideas of social reform which would guide and inspire the country for many years, and poetry and drama which still remains unsurpassed.

The situation in which these works were written put a special seal on them. The native land was far away, preserved in memory, in history and in imagination. The emigration could live only by its sense of mission, which had to rely on the preservation of the Word and on preparations – spiritual, ideological, and finally military – for the day of liberation.

Their ideas and aims underwent sublimation. The typical hero of the dramas of Mickiewicz and Słowacki became the youth who from being a romantic individualist (a spurned lover, oversensitive poet, sick with the spleen of a dandy) was transformed into a man who contends with God over the 'governance of souls' and the might of the Word; or into a conspirator, an avenger, a martyr, who by his individual deed and sacrifice tries to save the homeland. The Polish martyrdom and sacrifice thus had to redeem and save humanity. For, of course, the suffering of nations, the loss of freedom, the struggle of the patriots must have some higher meaning; history cannot be a chaos of random events nor the triumph of brute force over liberty. In seeking this meaning, the romantic poets and thinkers experienced mystical revelations, or built up complicated messianic, historiosophic, and palingenetic systems. What mattered was that the whole of the cosmos, nature itself, and first and foremost history, became books of lore, filled with signs which could be read only by the initiated. In the book of history, or in the plans of God, Poland, humiliated, crucified, yet destined to rise again from the dead in the future, had acquired a special mission, to lead the whole of humanity on the road to the millennium of liberty, justice and peace. Mickiewicz told the Polish refugees to regard themselves while in the materialistic, mercantile West as 'apostles among the idolaters', pilgrims of freedom, precursors of a new era of Christian politics in Europe.[4]

A national megalomania? Without doubt. And yet this was not the arrogance of conquerors, but the faith of the homeless and degraded that they would be lifted up, if they kept the spirit of self-sacrifice and the might of the Word alive in themselves. The individual was elevated to the heights of the nation, the nation to that of humanity, humanity to that of God. Romantic poetry, history, philosophy, religion and politics were braided into a single prophetic whole, a kind of theology of liberation, the aim of which was not to set pragmatic directives, but to puzzle out the spiritual goal of history and to establish an ethical measure for judging politics.

The Polish romantics were conscious of the abyss which gaped between their visionary outlook and the far from poetic everyday life in Poland and in emigration. They had not the least inclination to idealize Polish society: they spoke to their compatriots truths which were bitter, derisive, even disdainful, especially when it was a matter of those 'who stand at the head of the people', that is, aristocrats, the Tsarist courtiers, and armchair cosmopolitans. But most of them also felt a repulsion for the pettiness of everyday affairs, the intellectual sloth of the gentry, and the squabbles of the *émigré* politicians. The abyss between ideal and life, between *sacrum* and *profanum*, was yet another reason for them not to lower their aspirations. They believed that God was testing the nation, that He was chastising it 'with the whips of the Mongols' so as to temper it for great deeds. The Poles – Mickiewicz proclaimed – still lacked that 'holy fire', the power to realize their vision which France possessed.[5] Thus Polish romanticism was an unattainable striving for greatness, a search for spiritual change. It was not the ideal which had to conform to life; everyday life had to raise itself up to the ideal. In the poem which he entitled *My Testament* Słowacki wrote that he would leave behind him a 'fatal force' of prophetic poetry, which 'itself invisible will crush you until you eaters-of-bread are made into angels'.[6] And this formula remained the most concise and popular message of the romanticists.

The vicious circle

This calling of the nation to great historic destinies, what resonance did it arouse in a country intimidated after recent repressions, impoverished, and split up by frontiers into small portions isolated from the world? Each portion, moreover, was under strict police observation, deprived of universities, associations, and libraries, virtually without industry, and with a peasant question that was growing ever more threatening. Everything here seemed to be small and miserably provincial. Young people were lucky if, on leaving school, they were able to get a civil service post as a clerk, or as an unpaid legal trainee 'with prospects'. Europe, which only a short while ago had been close and attainable, with its economic, political, and intellectual movements, had now become somewhere over the hills and far away.

In the Russian sector which, ironically, was still officially called the Kingdom of Poland, the very possession and reading of forbidden books, the more so lending them to someone else, became a crime against the state. So here, all the conspiracies began with books, and a large number of them never managed to get past this stage. These small-format books, smuggled past the border patrols, appeared in strange sets: there were first and foremost the manifestos and brochures of the Polish Democratic Society in Exile, together with the poetry of Mickiewicz; then, depending on circumstances, there were Lamennais, Mochnacki, Tocqueville.

Recently there appeared several volumes of legal depositions from the 1830s and 1840s. These contain repeated descriptions of first encounters with a forbidden book or first conversations with an underground activist. These were moments of almost religious revelation: moreover a great number of the democratic brochures had titles such as 'Catechism', 'Prophetic words', 'Truths of life', and so on. Everything suddenly became simple and clear: the enfranchisement of the common people, the social revolution as a condition of the liberation of Poland and, afterwards, the creation of a single great homeland of free and equal people. What did this have in common with poetry? Romantic poetry was not, indeed, a political programme, nor did it resemble the language of ideology. True, but poetry aroused in young souls an enormous yearning for an ideal, for impulsive action; it created an emotional aura of the search for revelation. The experience of these young men in their twenties, sensitive but under-educated, was spiritual emptiness, boredom and barrenness of existence. From this emptiness in a single moment they entered into a world of fullness. Conspirator I testified:

We were in a strange position: we were young, we had the desire to work, we needed an occupation, but poetry repelled us and tormented us, portraying in so deceptive a manner the emptiness around us and the emptiness before us. Such was the state of our intellect, when the idea of democracy appeared. . . . This frenzied idea from the beginning obsessed us so forcefully that it drove out every other feeling from our hearts.[7]

Conspirator II:

My temperament contains a kind of germ of romanticism. From my earliest years, everything poetic fired my imagination and held an irresistible attraction for me . . . The new democratic theory, which demanded so much reasoning, has for me an enchanting allure. It seemed to me that I had found the philosophers' stone, which would heal all the ills of mankind.[8]

Conspirator III:

At that time I had no fixed way of thinking or viewing affairs. My powers of reasoning were completely dormant, but my imagination was fired by reading poetry and was ready to accept any system of thought whatsoever, provided it was presented in a poetic manner. I did not deliberate about political systems at all; I had only a vague idea about them.[9]

Together with the books there appeared a charismatic emissary: the messenger from the Paris Society or a Galician plot. He brought the principles of the 'political creed', the statutes of organization, the rules of conspiracy.

At this point, I started to go crazy. I thought: 'I am only nineteen years [old] but I am a political person, I can be of service to my country, to humanity', and this appealed to my pride and I decided to dedicate myself to this.[10]

Another said:

From the beginning I was stupefied by this new, imaginary dignity of mine. I was so young, yet I thought, I am already to the world a moral and political person. I regarded myself as more superior a being than I knew myself to be.[11]

Henceforward the unbearable ordinariness of a life stripped of values was only a pale background, an illusion. The true life was conspiracy – the order of friends who possessed the truth and who had decided to be its apostles. They divided among themselves the provinces which they had to convert to the democratic faith. In the beginning, each of them activated of them activated several colleagues. Then they had to enlighten the common people. Once the people were enlightened, it would know its rights, dignity and power, and there would be no holding it. Then all this loathsome reality, privileges, injustice and servitude would collapse, maybe even without bloodshed, and there would come into being the sovereignty of the people – in Poland and in the world. As one of them wrote:

> We know that all people are by nature equal and free, but we know too that this freedom and equality exists in full nowhere in the world . . . Further, we know that it is our duty to implant that equality and freedom among our neighbours, and once we know all this, what should we do? Overturn the present, existing order of the world and make it such that the inhabitants of this world may all proclaim, with a single voice: 'We are happy!' This is the enigma and the aim of our life.[12]

They were earnest and serious, they renounced the frivolous pleasures of youth. But it was no longer poetry or fiery imagination which guided their steps but the patently self-evident truth, which admitted not the least doubt. They felt the approach of the life-giving storm, and they were afraid they would miss their opportunity. Perhaps next spring . . .

The police normally rounded them up in a single night. No, they were not beaten up. The military commission of enquiry was patient, it scolded, it threatened, it waited. Block Ten of the Warsaw Citadel had thick, solid walls, like the whole enormous dominion of Nicholas I. Beyond these walls, outside, life flowed on as before, and hardly anyone noticed that these young men had disappeared. They were alone, and there was only a handful of them. Each of them was alone in his cell, faced the commission alone. Alone in the face of the immutable order of the world. What in hell had they taken on? With what means? In whose name, anyway? Days, weeks, months passed in these solitary meditations. Doubt, terror, hopelessness ate into their souls. Suddenly there came a blinding flash: everything that they had believed in was some kind of insanity, madness, delusion, childish naïvety.

The detainee was coming to his senses; the reality of life was regaining its rights. The detainee had grown up: he was ready to trample underfoot his ideals of the recent past and to pass judgement on himself.

> Five years have gone by since I went to confession. Finally the divine finger of Providence has prompted me to make a general confession, before the Supreme Commission, of almost my whole life, of all my thoughts, words, deeds and feelings. And this confession comes at the most fitting moment, since I had endured a great deal, and professing the sincere truth brings peace of mind, and I was now properly

prepared, because my confession is accompanied by sincere and bitter repentance. I only beg the Supreme Commission to deign to be patient, for I must pour it all out, I must lay bare my whole soul.[13]

And he laid it bare, he made a deposition of all that he had thought, all that he had done, and all that he knew in secret.

I have nothing further to add to my deposition, nothing to strike out or change. I am convinced that I not only erred in my behaviour but that I became truly a criminal, for no one has any right neither in deed nor in word to rise up against the institutions, whose order proceeds from laws of God which surpass our understanding. It remains only for me to beg the indulgence of a benevolent government to condescend to mitigate the punishment which I have deserved in consideration of my youth and my sincere undertaking to atone for the rest of my life for the wicked wrongdoings I have previously committed.[14]

The vicious circle closed. The attempt to break free from captivity, from a living death, ended, for a great number, in a still harsher captivity, and the denial of self, friends, and ideas. And there remained still a long epilogue. The process of Tsarist military law knew no public court hearing. The sentence was handed down in the absence of the accused, on the basis of the investigation dossier. For reading forbidden books and membership of secret societies, the benevolent government sentenced the repentant criminals to years of forced labour followed by Siberian exile. Some of them, when their sentences expired, returned to Poland, sometimes we see them later in some kind of legal work or – yet again – secret work. But in the end we do not know which of the changes of heart of the years of their youth they regarded as self-deception.

Negation of a negation, or ironic tragedy. The political history of Poland under the partitions might be told from the viewpoint of a devil whose aim is to ensure that every attempt at freedom leads with inexorable logic to a still more repressive servitude, and trusting in ideals ends in compromising them. But it can also be told as a ceaseless struggle against the Satan of despair, cynicism and inertia. Both these viewpoints are present in Polish romanticism, especially in Słowacki, and later – years later – in Żeromski and Wyspiański. They still persist to the present day, carrying on an unsuppressible dialogue on the sense and senselessness of rebellion against superior force, or against reality.

The myth of the common people

It was the century of progress, and this concept applied not only to science, industry and civilization, but also, and in Poland first and foremost, to the history of the spirit. Coming down to earth from the heights of philosophy and poetry, it was understood that every effort and sacrifice, even if vain today, were seeds which would bear fruit in the future. In the economics of the romantics, nothing went to waste, since history was the constant progress of the peoples towards freedom and brotherhood, the unfolding of thought and the maturing of deeds.

In Poland, it was democratic thought that unfolded, revolutionary deeds that matured. Each generation of insurgents drew conclusions from the experiences and failures of its older brothers. The November uprising (1830–1) collapsed since the nobility failed and the common people did not rise. The common people did not join in, because Poland was not as yet their country. Poland would become their country when she abolished privileges and proclaimed the principle of government by the people. The Polish Democracy camp made this proclamation but knowledge of this fact had not filtered down to the common people. And anyway the people were not interested in principles.

The democrats of the 1840s, who were more mature than their predecessors, knew that if they wanted to achieve something, they must produce facts, because ideals and promises of themselves achieve nothing. They would have to make a fact of the abolition of serfdom and feudal dues, and of the restoration to the people of the unconditional possession of the land they worked. If on the first day of the rising a revolutionary decree of this type was proclaimed to the people, then the cause of Poland would have become the people's cause too.

In 1846, in the Russian and Prussian sectors, the planned outbreak of an uprising was forestalled by the police who caught the conspirators. In the Austrian sector the rising did break out. The insurgents – who in this sector were for the most part from the nobility – proclaimed freedom and the granting of freehold tenure to the people. The peasants, however, trusted the Imperial officials and their promptings: they killed the 'Poles', or bound them and handed them over to the police. Where they had the chance, they robbed manor houses and murdered the squires, including those who had not favoured the rising. This was the greatest moral failure of Polish democracy. The common people – despite the great myth of the romanticists and the revolutionary intelligentsia – did not reciprocate the love extended to them. The insurgents were denied even the honour of a soldier's death. The devil's laughter rolled long over the Polish land.

The golden mean

In 1859 in Warsaw, Narcyza Żmichowska, a writer who had already served a sentence for taking part in underground activities during the 1840s, wrote a letter to one of the activists of the political emigration, who was thinking about reviving clandestine work in the Kingdom of Poland:

It would appear that the victims thrown into the abyss of twenty and more years, those banishments to Siberia, those incarcerations behind prison walls, and those scaffolds, instead of at least fertilising the soil of the homeland, actually made it more barren. For this is what really happened, nothing else. The most precious blood of the nation drained away from two veins: emigration and underground activity. . . . Yet underground activity represented every noble feeling in the whole national intelligentsia. The fact that those engaged in underground activity, workers and thinkers, the links between the past and the time to come, those who in our dismembered Commonwealth were the only dignitaries and officials of national causes, guarantors of the continuity of our political history, these consecrated and elect people left *virtually not a trace* behind them, while their endeavours petered out in complete bankruptcy – ah, that became ultra-difficult for us to explain to ourselves. Who was at fault? The country or them?[15]

What was usually called 'organic work', or the development of the internal autonomy of the country, was an effort to break free from these accursed alternatives. The starting-point of this approach was a diagnosis of the state of society that was even more gloomy than that from which the underground activists began. Servitude tempers a few individuals, but for the most part it corrupts and degrades. The lack of one's own administration, of even local self-rule, national institutions, or education, the impossibility of implementing agrarian reform or of carrying through any economic or social policy whatsoever – all this the protagonists of 'organic work' believed was exacerbating class distinctions, destroying every tissue of the social organism, and reducing people's aspirations to the most trivial, mundane materialism. But they were also convinced that the expenditure of its entire moral energy in the hopeless struggle could only drag the country out of its torpor for a moment. Poland needed ideals that were more prosaic, closer to the notions and primary needs of society as a whole. She needed an intelligentsia which would not waste their moral and intellectual forces on the threshold of life, but which would train themselves, work in the professions and make their way up to prestigious positions from which they would be able to exert an influence on the state of the country's affairs and public opinion.

Żmichowska, who was typical of a small circle of the Warsaw intelligentsia, favoured a programme of non-clandestine work but not one, however, limited to a framework of legality that was too narrow to get anything done.

The Muscovite government forbids everything, and it is impossible even to predict what today or tomorrow will raise its fears . . . It forbids people to study Polish history, it forbids them to write, read or speak about Poland, it forbids them to fraternize with the peasants, to enlighten the artisans, to organize mutual assistance for paying school fees and university tuition or for buying scholarly works. And so anyone who wants to train himself must day in day out do what the government forbids, must at every step put himself at own risk and must do so *today*, without the mould of underground work, among everyday life, within the limits of his day-to-day relations. That is how we began to work.[16]

One has to remark that this infant design of the building of a citizens' society in the face of the Imperial Power, the ethos of civil courage and civil resistance without bravura, with a calculated degree of risk, this design was born only when the repressiveness of the Tsarist regime diminished, in the first years of the reign of Alexander II. For to put this theory into practice, one had to have at least a certain minimum of legal elbow-room for the Word and for social work. But the easing of pressure and the ferment for reform in the Russian state evoked in the Kingdom of Poland also the desire to renew secret work for independence. Thus, a classical auction began, in which the more radical and lofty ideal always beats the moderate card. Żmichowska observed with anxiety a new generation of youth which, dependent only on itself in a society without recognized authorities, 'whatever it does, knows that until it makes an uprising it will not have achieved anything'.[17]

Germs of organic work did, indeed, awaken hope, but however . . . 'But however all this work and hope could easily be destroyed; it only needs an artificial warmth to bring it too far on, or if this national work which is to lead the nation first and foremost to self-awareness, if this work dissipates itself too early on external concerns or an attempt at a rising, tomorrow a Sahara-like drought will return.'[18] And so, indeed, it came to pass.

Two cultures or double-thinking?

I have confined myself to the period between the November rising of 1830 to 1831 and the January rising of 1863 to 1864, since it is precisely here that the dilemma which concerns us is most sharply evident. This is the time of maximisation of the ideals and hopes of the moral elite of the nation – both in emigration and at home – and at the same time the minimalization of the aspirations of the 'eaters of bread', that is, the social classes which were nationally conscious and had at least elementary education: the landed nobility, the professional intelligentsia, and the Polish petty bourgeoisie. But this gulf between holy ideals and the prose of everyday life is by no means something especially Polish. Ideologies and programmes that are sober, pragmatic and Fabian are normally predominant only in those peoples and social classes which have in their hands the instruments to realize them, such as government, parliament, a free press, legal parties and social organizations. Peoples and classes who are without these instruments are doomed to Utopian programmes. Their ideological and political vanguards are as a rule romantic and revolutionary, and dream of a total remaking of the world. When there is an arbitrary authority, when the system of government knows no civil rights nor mediation bodies, then ideas of moderation, compromise and organic work cannot take root and show their worth in obvious successes. Their action is principally one of education, and hence slow, their emotional appeal is by nature weak, and so they lose out – on the one hand to the romantic maximalism of the vanguard and on the other to the conservative inertia of the life of society and the egoism of private interests.

A similar cleavage may be observed in culture, and this, in the conditions of mid-nineteenth-century Poland, was especially drastic. The peaks of Polish literature, especially poetry, soared high, but seemed sometimes to be lost in mystical clouds. The sciences and arts, without universities, laboratories or state patronage, and dependent mainly on the philanthropy of a handful of the more enlightened aristocrats, lingered virtually at an amateur level. The sparse professional intelligentsia, which in part had been educated abroad, had the greatest difficulty in defending its material and moral independence, but in spite of all barriers (censorship, passports, financial) it tried to maintain its contacts with the European intellectual movement, including the Polish emigration. Secondary schooling, which in all three partitions was under the vigilant eye of the bureaucracy, became ossified and conservative. The intellectual level of the landed nobility covered a wide range, but parochial narrow-mindedness, traditionalism, and a lack of demand for higher culture predominated. The peasants were still completely cut off from education and from taking part in the changes of civilization; the Church satisfied their spiritual needs and their life obeyed the standards of archaic local peasant culture.

All in all, the culture of 'society' (taken here in the sense of those strata of the nation which had at least an elementary education), over a period of prolonged political stabilization, was characterized by triviality, eclectism, formlessness, a lack of a definite hierarchy of values. The nobleman's honour could perfectly well come coupled with a speculator's greed, cosmopolitanism with xenophobia, superficial democratism with contempt for the 'boor' and the Jew. A similar lack of guidelines characterized everyday relationships with the authorities of the partitioning powers. They were perceived as foreign, yet familiar, harsh, yet maintainers of law and order. The owners of estates in general considered it no crime to call in the civil and military authorities to deal with restive peasants, and taking up a civil service or military career was not considered incompatible with patriotism. Voluntarily acting as an informer was rather despised, but making statements demanded by the police passed as permissible. The everyday ethos was governed first and foremost by the principle of adapting oneself to current conditions, and in that sense, it legitimized those conditions.

It is easy to see that the romantic ethos of uncompromised fidelity to one's ideals was the antithesis of this pragmatic and spineless morality. Moreover, it was a passionate protest against the opportunism and idle swinishness of life. It would appear that between two such spiritual stances there could exist nothing in common but mutual contempt, for 'fantasies' on the one hand, for 'baseness' on the other. And yet, there was a web which linked them.

The paradox of the romantic culture lay in the fact that the Word, which aimed at becoming the Deed, which aimed at acquiring the power to create history, was an elite and esoteric matter. The texts of the romantic poets and philosophers are predominantly difficult and obscure, and demand either a commentary or a special gift in the reader enabling him to attune himself to the tone, the language, the ideas and the imagery of the author. There are very few who can rise to such an effort. To get into a wider circulation in society, romantic literature had to overcome not only the barriers of state frontiers or censorship but also an intellectual barrier. Somehow it managed this, but with enormous losses in transmission. For the wider public in Poland received and adopted only individual stanzas, dramatic scenes, quotations, sentences, slogans, like Mickiewicz's 'Gauge your strength by your purpose' or 'Heed thy heart and look to the hearts of others'.[19] And so great poetry, deprived of its internal tensions, its metaphysics and irony, its wrestling with God, was transformed all too easily into high-flown phraseology, and then into sentimentalism or a patriotic reveille. In this way, there arose a stereotyped canon of simplified romanticism, which itself created the core of a Polish sanctuary, in which there were laid up relics of the past, historical legends, Kościuszko's oath and the scythes of Racławice, the Union with Lithuania and the Constitution of the Third of May, the song of the Legions and the hymn 'God Who Saved Poland', the White Eagle, the national colours, and Our Lady of Częstochowa 'Who has the Polish nation under Her special protection'. Every nation has similar symbols, but when they become the object of public worship or even obligatory ceremonial, then they surely lose something of their hallowed nature. In Poland, this very rich sanctuary had to be long preserved in the privacy of the home and heart as a common mystery of the Poles, the deposit of truth of the nation and a condition of its existence.

This sanctuary was of no great use in everyday life. It was even unseemly to profane its sanctity in the turmoil of petty interests. These two spheres were thus conveniently separated. One was governed by the rule of adaptation, and the other by holy duty. The despot's order gained a not too eager acceptance in the sphere of everyday life, and at the same time was ceremonially repudiated in the symbolic sphere. Such double-thinking may, it is well known, persist for a long time, fairly painlessly, without evoking a particularly strong dissonance of conviction: in the end even children know that prayer is one thing and life is another, and that one thinks (and not merely speaks) one way at home and another in school. Dissonances could arise rather in the world of sacral values: for example, between the axiology of patriotism and the commandments of universal religion. These dissonances were obviously present in the ideas of the romantic movement, which in a number of ways fell outside the orthodox teaching of the Catholic Church. But this was no concern of simplified romanticism, which was joined in harmony with religion, in a single syndrome of patriotic devotion.

The homeland was concealed in a chapel, in poetry, in an attic where relics from the last uprising were hidden; it was thus a kind of conspiracy but one which was, as it were, so far no threat to the stabilized order. It was only the plots of the revolutionaries which strove to disturb this order, but without results, and usually without even the sympathy of their compatriots.

The avalanche

Matters remained in this condition until such time as one of the partitioning powers was itself in a state of crisis, due to military defeat, the death of the ruler, the swelling discontent of various classes of the population, or the restless expectation of reforms long-overdue. Then a current ran through the conquered and subjugated country; suddenly everyone felt that it was impossible to go on living in the same old way, that something must change. The demeanour of adaptation ceased to satisfy. Apathy and passivity vanished; he who was alive began to act. The advocates of 'conciliation' quickly seized the moment: they wrote 'Memorials to the Emperor'; they made up delegations to dignitaries of the state; they offered their services to get some concessions as a trade-off, for example, the restoration of Polish schools, local self-government, maybe even a certain autonomy for the country. The government, although it was weak – or else because it was weak – tried to take evasive action, to make vague promises, to play for time.

The opponents of conformism, too, made use of the expectations which had been aroused. New secret circles sprang up, and now suddenly expanded with unparalleled ease, for it was now time to awaken society from its slumbers. The most effective means of communication and emotional mobilization lay in demonstrations. In the beginning, these took the form of requiems for the repose of the souls of national poets and heroes, the commemoration of major anniversaries. The crowd of participants grew, born on a tide of emotion. Forbidden songs were called to mind, which had not been sung for decades. Singing these songs together gave a hitherto unknown feeling of unity. Emblems hitherto adored in secret now appeared in public. The *sacrum* began to govern the behaviour of the people. And one day, the singing throng poured out from the churches into the streets.

The authorities were horrified, disorientated. One day they withdrew and tried persuasion, the next they gave the order to shoot. The blood of innocent victims flowed. Słowacki's 'eaters of bread' had become 'angels'. The revolutionaries were no longer alone. The mass movement gathered momentum. The secret circles which were its mainspring got into touch with each other, joined forces, and began to make plans for a national rising.

Then the conciliators said to the government, if you agree to concessions and reforms, we will calm the people; if not, you will have a revolution. Then the revolutionaries pointed at the conciliators, saying: 'Behold those who renounced independence for a droplet of the Emperor's favour!' The 'organic workers' tried mediation: they called on the conciliators to make bolder efforts, and at the same time, tried in vain to calm down the fervent youth.

In the end, the authorities decided in favour of concessions in the spirit of liberalism, on social reforms and restoration of the old national institutions. But this was always too little, too late: the aspirations of the movement for change grew at a violent rate, and they were not satisfied today with what yesterday would have been a triumph. The conciliators went to the government not in the glory of statesmen but with the brand of traitors.

The preparations for the rising always went badly. There was always a lack of means. The arms transport got stuck somewhere on the frontier. There were squabbles with the *émigrés* over the military leadership. Some of the most gifted leaders of the organization fell into the hands of the police. The outbreak must be deferred. No, the outbreak cannot be deferred, because the police already have a list of suspects. Any day there might be a raid and compulsory enlistment in the army. Do we have to let them pick us off, like chicks from a nest? We haven't got a chance. We have got a chance if we take them by surprise. Everything depends on striking first: if we survive a couple of days and issue our decrees, then the common people will follow us. It won't be any use, we have no weapons. We'll liberate some from the arsenals and strongholds. We can't take on such a responsibility. We must take responsibility. We must wait for a better moment. We can't wait, the time for action is here. The people are already tired. Nothing of the sort, the lads want to fight. Hold them back. We can't hold them back, they'll start on their own. We shall

all perish, and Poland will perish with us. Victory or death! This is mere rhetoric. There is no turning back any more.

There was no turning back now. Those who had created the events and considered that they were leading them found themselves caught in the trap of their inexorable logic. When, in January 1863, the secret national government decided that the uprising should break out, they were in a situation in which they had practically no choice. And at that point the moderates who were against a rising had no choice either. For once the rising had broken out in spite of their warnings, thus burying every chance of a bloodless solution of the crisis, the dictates of honour or patriotic duty and political foresight left them no other road but to join in with the intention, if possible, of influencing the future course of events. The results are well known; the nightmare of disaster, devastation and Tsarist reprisals always exceeded all previous expectations.

After each such experience, the liberation movement, learning from the mistakes of its predecessors, went a further stage along the road, marked out a wider circle of society and together with it drew into the whirlpool more victims, and in the end resulted in a more profound failure and a more permanent state of prostration after the next disaster. This form of progress made the Polish situation a devil's alternative. One might say that the curse of the country was its men of ideas, who were not reconciled to the oppression of the nation and the wrongs of society, and who by their determination constantly brewed new disasters for themselves and their homeland.

So it has been said, and more than once. After the failure of the rising once again there always began the bitter mutual recriminations of fellow-countrymen as to who was guilty and who had the right to judge. Those chiefly responsible, however, were no longer there to answer accusations.

Over the years, a legend grew up about them. In a country still subjugated, in a society which in day-to-day matters managed as best it could, homage was secretly paid to the heroic partisans of 1863, and their relics were received reverently into the national sanctuary. The painful reckonings of faults and errors were put aside more and more often with the words that 'their blood was not shed in vain', that 'without risings we should not be a nation', or with other bracing expressions which attenuated the tragic nature of Polish destiny.

The aftermath or the Polish 'Forma'

People who have lived through the same cycle of events – for example, a national revolution – together, afterwards invest it with the most diverse meanings and draw from it the most contradictory conclusions: from glorification to condemnation, and see their own participation in it as glory or insanity. In this matter nothing is defined unequivocally by the experience alone.

The Polish experience of the nineteenth century was, and to this day is, interpreted in a variety of ways. Depending on the values adopted, we have had conservative, positivist, nationalist and socialist constructions put on history, and within the framework of each there is yet another great range of variants. There is no doubt, however, that the interpretation which had the most powerful effect on the Polish consciousness and subconsciousness was the post-romantic interpretation. More precisely: that made in the spirit of the simplified romanticism we have described above. For this endowed the recent history of the nation with a meaning that was most understandable, flattering and comforting, and which therefore proved most resistant to the action of time.

All other ideological expositions of Polish history started life as polemics against this romantic canonisation of history. What is more important, almost all major Polish literature from the mid-nineteenth century, and also serious political writing and philosophical criticism of culture, was turned against this spiritual outlook and contended with it. Simplified romanticism, as the most popular form of patriotism, was attacked for its intellectual shallowness, for its cult of optimistic martyrology, for its aestheticisation of wars and uprisings, for the moral intolerance of the heroic stereotype it fostered, for its disregard of productive work and the ethos of civil society, for a lack of respect for human individuality. And also for the national insularity favoured by the myth of Poland as a chosen and exceptional nation, the bulwark of Europe. In indefatigable debate with this – as Stanisław Brzozowski called it – 'Polish Oberammergau',[20] every possible strategy was used. Up to the recovery of independence it was principally a serious critique, armed with philosophical earnestness, didactic and moral passion, bitter irony and gloomy derision. It fought the pathos of the apologia with the pathos of the critique, and, on occasion, with the language of the romantics. The quietism of simplified romanticism was unmasked by appeal to Mickiewicz, to the ideals of the original romanticism, urging action and passion. They took satisfaction (Żeromski, in particular) in setting the moral pathos of the idea of the homeland, freedom, and the obligations of the intelligentsia towards the common people, against the hopelessness and repulsive destitution of the everyday existence of the Polish peasantry and proletariat. The counterpoise as much exposed reality as ideas, and first and foremost represented an ironic image of their mutual mismatch.

Independence changed the situation inasmuch as simplified romanticism now laid aside its mourning, worked its way into school textbooks and dictated the rituals of state celebrations. The patterns of virtues and postures it created had no application to everyday life; they were patterns of the sentimental 'experiences' of history and poetry. And it was in this form that they became the subject of parody. From Stanisław Ignacy Witkiewicz, and more especially from Gombrowicz onwards, there exists in Polish literature a type of critique of the romantic canon, in *buffo* style but significantly more venomous, poking merciless fun at the very style of that 'experience', the patriotic phraseology, the quixotic theatricality of its gestures and poses. It is a significant thing that this current of mockery survived the war, the occupation and the Warsaw uprising and reappeared in the grotesques of Galczyński, the films of Munk, and the theatre of Różewicz and Mrożek.

And who opposed all these anti-romantic campaigns, waged by the most illustrious minds and pens in Poland? Mainly minor poets and political writers, secondary-school teachers, preachers, former combatants grown bitter in emigration, civil servants responsible for moral and spiritual upbringing. Not really much of a troop. But what of that? Simplified romanticism did not need even them. It could defend itself by its own persistence and regeneration in spite of all exorcism, since the situation which had created it continued to persist and regenerate itself. That situation was the expropriation of the people's sovereign rights and the sense of powerlessness which arose from it. Romantic patriotism made up for this powerlessness by a feeling of being in the right, of faith in the meaning of sacrifice and in the divine justice in history. It did not so much create history as make it easier to endure. No other intellectual outlook so far could replace it in the task of integrating the national community in the hour of trial. And inasmuch as it did not replace it, it could not triumph over it.

Hence the more abject and degraded reality became and the less the chance of changing it, the greater the inclination to lofty, milleniary, transcendental ideals. The worse the position as regards those examples with which a person or a nation draws comparisons, the greater the need to raise one's ideal self-estimation. But these comforts are paid for by mystification of one's consciousness and the pulling of stupid, pretentious faces. These Polish faces and complexes appear most often when a Pole is confronted by the West. For then he feels towards that West, with its wonders, its prosperity and contented calm, admiration and rejection, humility and pride, when he considers that he has endured more and has achieved less than is due to him. He is extremely touchy and the lower his condition, the more he is aware of his individual and national honour. He will not allow a foreigner to mock at his sanctities, but he applauds his own sarcastic writers, especially if first they win world renown. In and out of season he recalls that we gave the world Chopin and Pułaski and that we are a heroic nation.

So in the end, this holy battle of reason and literature against the pathetically banal turns out simply to be the grappling of the Poles with

Polishness, which means something elusive which pinches, chafes and shackles them, but without which they cannot go on. Gombrowicz, of course, called this something the 'Forma' and missed no opportunity to free first himself and then his compatriots from this tight and ludicrous Forma.

> There was something unhealthy, something perverted in our attitude to the world, and I, as an artist, felt, in some measure, responsible for this fatal 'Polish legend', and I felt that one must somehow put an end to it, but how? . . . The Poles, being a nation highly bound up in fantasies, illusions, phrases, legends, declamations were also close to that reality *in crudo*, *sans phrases*, which can break bones. This was a trump to be played to advantage. Only the sharpest realism could drag us out of the swamp of our 'legend' . . . To pry the Pole free of Poland, so that he would become simply a human being. Or to make the Pole into an anti-Pole. . . Hence my whole 'programme' was contained first and foremost in a tone, in a style, in my brazenly thumbing my nose at tragedy, in my unceremonious approach to the sanctities of a thousand years. Literature is not a dame school, it is the creation in words of an accomplished fact.[21]

Unfortunately, to change attitudes on the scale of a whole community, it is not sufficient to create facts in words. So long as there are no suitable facts in history, refined literary strategies would likewise go for nothing. After 13 December 1981, at patriotic services in a Warsaw church they sang this heartrending song: 'My native land, How oft did blood bathe thee, What great wounds now scathe thee, How long didst thou withstand, My native land'. And in a theatre a few streets away they were putting on, to a full house, a play by Gombrowicz or Mrożek.

And so the world goes on.

Notes

1 Stanisławski, Jan (1975) *Wielki słownik polsko-angielski* (The Great Polish-English Dictionary), Warsaw: Wiedza Powszechna, vol. 2, 94.
2 Skorupka, S. *et al.* (eds) (1974) *Mały słownik języka polskiego*, Warsaw: PWN, 596.
3 After 1918, this song, with slightly different words, became the Polish national anthem.
4 Mickiewicz, Adam (1950) *Księgi narodu polskiego i pielgrzymstwa polskiego* (The Books of the Polish Nation and Polish Pilgrimage), *Dzieła* (Works), national edition, vol. 6, Warsaw Czytelnik, 7–55.
5 Mickiewicz, Adam (1955) *Literatura słowiańska* (Slavonic Literature), *Dzieła* (Works), vol. 10, Warsaw, 422–3.
6 Słowacki, Juliusz (1949) *Dzieła* (Works), vol. 1 Wrocław: Ossolineum, 113.

7 Djakov, V. A. *et al.* (1978) *Stowarzyszenie Ludu Polskiego w Królestwie Polskim*, Wrocław: Ossolineum, 278–9. This volume has been edited and published in a joint Soviet–Polish series 'Polskie ruchy społeczno-polityczne i życie literackie 1832–1855: studia i dokumenty' (Polish social and political movements and literary life, 1832–1855: studies and documents).

8 Ibid., 332.

9 Ibid., 249.

10 Djakov, V.A. *et al.* (1981) *Rewolucyjna konspiracja w Królestwie Polskim w latach 1840–1845*, Wrocław: Ossolineum, p. 347 (in the same series).

11 *Stowarzyszenie Ludu Polskiego*, 302.

12 Ibid., 197.

13 *Rewolucyjna konspiracja*, 235.

14 *Stowarzyszenie Ludu Polskiego*, 263.

15 Żmichowska, Narcyza (1960) *Listy* (Letters), ed. M. Romankówna, vol. 2, Wrocław: Ossolineum, 381–2.

16 Ibid., 388.

17 Ibid., 389.

18 Ibid., 389–90.

19 Mickiewicz, Adam (1949) 'Pieśń Filaretów' and 'Romantyczność', in *Dzieła*, vol. 1, Warsaw: Czytelnik, 11, 106.

20 Brzozowski, Stanisław (1910) *Legenda Młodej Polski* (The Legend of Young Poland), Lwów, 189 ff.

21 De Roux, Dominique (1969) *Rozmowy z Gombrowiczem* (Talks with Gombrowicz), Paris: Instytut Literacki, 89–91.

Translated by Vera Rich.

3

The Polish syndrome of incompleteness

Marcin Król

Respublica, *Warsaw*

The history of Poland since the partitions up to the present day is either extremely boring or extremely interesting depending on by whom and how it is looked at. It depends most of all on the temperament of the observer. The epic temperament, the temperament of the crusader, conquistador, conqueror of new territories, or finally of someone who revels in the variety and quality of his material acquisitions, will not find here much nourishment. Whereas the lyrical temperament, the temperament of a romantic, of a man of imagination, man of the theatre, one who revels in surreality and derives more pleasure from the word than the fact, from the emotion rather than the deed, from the beauty of a gesture rather than from its result, from purity of heart rather than from a radically consistent way of thinking, will find no difficulty in feeling at home in modern Polish history.

Among the Poles themselves therefore those who are by nature of an active temperament do not fare so well, and even worse is the case of those whose emotional impulses are restrained by scepticism and irony. One has to assume that nature bestows her gifts on all nations equally and that the Poles therefore have had their share of a variety of temperaments in proportions similar to other nations. To get a better understanding of the logic of Polish alternatives of choice and of the logic of Polish thinking let us first have a look at some earlier and then at some modern cases.

The efforts of those historians who in the 1950s attempted to find in modern Polish history examples of class struggle in accordance with Marxist doctrine had truly meagre results. This is not by any means because the relationships between particular social classes or groups in Poland were idyllic, nor was it because there was no brutal exploitation (particularly in villages). The reason is that throughout the nineteenth century in Poland there arose no revolutionary ideology which would have appealed to the oppressed and exploited communities.

Here is the first, characteristic case of the Polish discord between situation and thought – a discord which prevented the growth of radicalism and equally made action difficult if not often impossible. Yet nineteenth-century Poland witnessed the emergence, both inside the country as well as within the emigrant communities, of revolutionary and radical ideologies. Among the *émigrés*, the radical pre-socialists, although not numerous, demanded that *szlachta* be put to the sword; inside the country the ideologues of the proletariat proclaimed radical social reforms which in the end led to their death in martyrdom. Neither the former nor the latter, nor their few predecessors or followers ever achieved any social support or any intellectual influence. While in Russia in the 1870s and 1880s a few young men moved in the space of two or three years from a fascination with the peasantry to active terrorism, in Poland political terror never appeared in practice and was rare even in theory.

The Polish author Zygmunt Krasiński wrote a drama in which the defeat of both revolution and counter-revolution is portrayed in a masterly way. Nevertheless, his 'Un-divine comedy' (*Nie-boska komedia*) is not about Poland as neither revolution nor counter-revolution ever took place there. If the radical revolutionaries, socialists and later Marxists had any opportunities, these only occurred abroad, so it is not surprising that at first they attempted to export revolution beyond the European continent (Gurowski, Królikowski, Polish People's Communes – Gminy Ludu Polskiego). Later the logic of Polish alternatives pushed them towards positions which effectively denied the desire of the enormous majority of the population for national independence. Such was the tragic case of Rosa Luxemburg, a personage not liked in Poland even today and therefore underestimated. But the fact is that Rosa Luxemburg was very closely connected with Poland, its language and customs. She was also undoubtedly one of the most interesting and distinguished minds among the European Marxists of her generation. It was the consistency of her revolutionary thinking which, as she was very much aware, had no chance in a Polish national state and which pushed her towards an internationalism which rejected the goal of independence.

The weight and the absolute intellectual dominance of the national question created in Poland a situation in which there was no room for a consistent non-Utopian socialist-Marxist thinker. For a radical socialist there were two choices: that of Rosa Luxemburg or that of Stanisław Brzozowski. One led to socialism but away from Polishness, the other from socialism to Polishness in its religious and romantic (and therefore only acceptable) version. For ordinary socialists, that is for minds of a rather practical bent, not so much prone towards consistency and speculation, half-way solutions were usually feasible. There was one man who rose above these restricting circumstances, who stated (with the demagogic skill common to all great politicians and also with their common instinct and courage to be inconsistent) there will be no socialism without independence and no independence without socialism. Piłsudski repeated this thought or rather non-thought (as its logic is not very clear) in many versions. Its pertinence could only be proved and has been proved in modern Polish history by successful armed struggle.

The situation within the radical right was identical with that within the radical left. There were only two possible solutions: everyone who by virtue of his temperament consistently followed the lines indicated by the doctrine had to face a choice between conservative doctrine or Polishness. In this case, too, radical conservatives were few and far between (like Henryk Rzewuski). The majority of the conservatives spent their time seeking for more tortured solutions which would somehow enable them to appease some dictates of doctrine with the rejection of the status quo and at least allow for the idea of a national insurrection.

Consistency in political thinking is a virtue but only up to a point. Reality – and not only in Poland – always forces one to opt for specific solutions which are never fully compatible with the doctrine. One does not know whether the doctrine of socialism (or conservatism for that matter) really exists, and if one were to accept that it does, who was its creator and who the judge of its orthodoxy. Doctrines so understood exist only within totalitarian ideologies. On the other hand, political thought, like all thought, is bound by the rules of logic and an imperative to think things through to the end and consistently draw all the conclusions which can be deduced from the premises. The freedom with which political thought could be applied to specific situations in the free countries of nineteenth-century Europe was one thing; but the situation in Poland, where there was a brake put on even at the threshold of political reflection, was quite different. Political thought was condemned to reckoning with the national situation rather than developing its own logic and internal cohesion.

Inevitably, compared with the European background, and there was none other, this gave Polish thought its intellectually second-rate character. Its task lay not in a rational exploration of new eventualities, but in examining the ways of adapting European thinking to the specifically Polish alternatives. From time to time an illusion was created that this specific situation would give birth to 'Polish' political thought, which would be recognized as an equal among the main European currents of socialism, conservatism or liberalism. This of course was not a possibility, and only bastardised forms could appear which were not acceptable to anybody.

It is easy to see that a serious thinker would have had to seek salvation in flight. The flight might take the form of complete abandonment of political theory. One could devote one's talent and interest to the field of historical research or art – both are marked by relatively high Polish achievement. Conversely, the flight might take one in the opposite direction, into pure activism, not supported by any ideological argument – this accounts for the innumerable circles, plots and small conspiracies.

In a very few individual cases, the bastard would be transformed into a hybrid. Thought would be unexpectedly generated by a situation which was intellectually unacceptable and then, by some mysterious coincidence, it would find its own direction and have intellectually outstanding results. The results would mainly be in the form of notes, observations, first ideas rather than completed and comprehensive studies. This can be seen in the works of Maurycy Mochnacki and Stanisław Brzozowski. Almost all the rest of Polish political thought became a vehicle for expressing the national sentiment rather than speculating about solutions, which were anyway non-existent. It represented a way of thinking which was never thought through to the end as the end was not there to be seen; a way of thinking which was always incomplete, for freedom is essential for completion; not fully aware of itself, as full awareness can only be achieved by independent reasoning. And the political reasoning in Poland was always dependent; before it ever had time to follow its own cause it was forced to go on applying half-baked formulas to situations which had no solutions.

The logic of Polish political thought was undoubtedly influenced not only by restrictions forced on political reasoning itself, but also by the conclusions drawn from historical experience. Not much can be said by the historian on the topic of the conclusion-drawing process, except that intuition and instinct played a greater role here than critical reasoning, that collective emotions were of more significance than a political reflection reclusive by nature. The following example may perhaps illustrate it better than any analysis.

In 1813 Prince Józef Poniatowski, following his withdrawal from Moscow, found himself with his large and well-trained army in Kraków. Tsar Alexander I put forward, through his intermediaries, a suggestion that the Polish army should change its allegiance to the Russian side. Napoleon, although not yet defeated, was undoubtedly losing the war. Both Alexander and Napoleon at various times made promises to the effect that, circumstances permitting, they would endeavour in recognition of Polish co-operation to reactivate the Polish state. The promises were as vague as they were uncertain. Prince Józef's Polish army was stationed on Polish soil, and had it stayed in Poland instead of following Napoleon to France, it would have undoubtedly had a role to play in the diplomatic calculations of the Vienna Congress. It would have meant the betrayal of Napoleon, but in history such acts of betrayal are not few in number. Furthermore, loyalty should have been truly binding only to the homeland, and not to the Emperor who had done practically nothing for

Poland. Whatever (good or bad) one can say about Prince Poniatowski, one thing is certain: he was never a political thinker. He, therefore, against or rather ignoring all political arguments, led his army to Napoleon and at an opportune moment himself perished.

This was the first example in the post-partition history of Poland of a pattern of political behaviour, which would repeat itself under changing circumstance with unchanged logic – from the November Uprising through the Warsaw Uprising up to Solidarity and the events of 1982–6. People who were in charge of decision-taking obviously searched for rational arguments, but we know what a minimal role cool political thinking played in these events, notwithstanding political affiliation and notwithstanding whether it was action-oriented or whether it aimed at withdrawal from action. Inadvertently, events were taking place *alongside* political thinking. Poles did not rise at the time of the Crimean War, precisely when, as a result of the advantageous political configuration in Europe, cool thinking should have indicated the existence of a chance for success. The reason was that past experiences, examined intuitively and instinctively, taught the Poles that they had no chance, that is no political chance, in the Europe of the day with its predispositions. Prince Józef Poniatowski's attitude, oriented rather towards values, gestures and the meaning of symbols, respecting emotions rather than the rights or wrongs of the political reasoning, became the model of the citizens' attitude. This might be the reason why there never was any real collaboration with the enemy and no Quislings in Poland; why in the period of Solidarity more room and attention were devoted to the problem of Katyn, than for instance to the problem of the necessary structural reforms of the economy. Poles have treated all great national undertakings – not consciously but again intuitively and instinctively – as causes lost from the start. The only exception to this was provided by the amazing history of the political activities of Józef Piłsudski. Without doubting for a moment his political talent, one has to admit nevertheless that his was the only case when the political configuration in Europe was for once favourable to the Polish cause.

In such a situation what course of action was supposed to be taken by people who by virtue of their temperament were unable to abandon the habits of thinking in political categories and approaching emotions with scepticism; who wanted to look not at the symbols but beyond them? They were faced with several choices, none of them very good but some worse than others. The worst was to see the logic of the national issue as fundamentally mistaken, to see the reality of gesture and symbol as a non-reality. It was still not too bad when they ended up, as was not unusual in spite of the commonly held beliefs in Poland, in a flight from Polishness, Poland and from the whole set of those incomplete, inconsistent and impossible situations. They would normally become absorbed into the countries (including Russia) in which they happened to settle and they would, without much trouble, forget about Poland.

It was much worse, when a cool political temperament was combined with civil courage and the will to act, as in the case of Alexander Wielkopolski or – *toutes proportions gardées* – of Bolesław Piasecki. The political activity of the first was perfectly justified on grounds of reason and the actions of the second, particularly in the immediate post-war period, although there is a certain unwillingness to admit it today, were also dictated by valid reasons. Yet their failures were both cruel and unavoidable. There are periods in history – and in Poland such a period has lasted with short intervals for 200 years – when all political game-playing is impossible. And not because it is morally reprehensible or badly executed, but because it is doomed to failure from the start; and besides, it is embarrassing to sit down to the game having always too little money.

We are fortunate to have at our disposal an example of a related temperament, the example provided by the writings and political activity of Stefan Kisielewski. Where does this basic difference come from? The mystery of talent, like any other mystery, cannot be explained. But one might be able perhaps to point to a difference which was decisive. Kisielewski often stated himself that he found the logic of national thinking irritating, its symbols ridiculous, its emotions something he could not share, its moralizing, whose boundaries he constantly overstepped, narrow. Yet it had represented for him a part of reality which had to be reckoned with, whereas for Wielopolski and Piasecki it was that part of reality which had to be rejected. Reality, however, is not something that can just be rejected. But what is of more interest to us here is the question of how Kisielewski coped with the Polish alternatives. He often said of himself that his position was 'for a hunchback not too bad'. The hump on the hunchback's back in this case was the ever-growing dissonance between the logic of the national situation and his desire for freedom in thinking. And it is not too bad as long as one has got sufficient spiritual energy at least to consider such a state of affairs as interesting and find in it an inspiration for one's thoughts. Nevertheless, the work of Kisielewski, undoubtedly the most outstanding and the most independent thinker of the post-war epoch, is incomplete, defective and affected by signs of his hitting his head against a brick wall.

Adam Michnik, a man who is also willing to think politically – that is, soberly and critically – seemed to have hit upon a different solution when he declared his 'loyalty to lost causes'. This solution is based on a retreat before the power and strength of the national logic; on abandonment of independence in the face of the canons of public morality, on a recognition of the secondary role of political thinking after loyalty and the duty to bear witness. In every conflicting or potentially conflicting situation between ethics and politics, this solution dictates the ethical stand that is on the side of the historically determined ethics of the Polish communal life. To declare oneself for these absolute values is a patently obvious matter, and not a matter of choice.

The problem of the historically determined ethics of Polish communal life leads us to one further element of the alternatives with which we have concerned ourselves here. It reveals one further limitation whose existence defines the shape of the specifically Polish incompleteness of thought, speech and action.

These ethics are not without their code, though such a code has never been written down. Its two basic commandments are: 'be faithful' and 'be loyal to your comrades in arms'. The first may obviously be treated as an absolute norm, the second on the other hand is always relative by nature. The absolute precepts of the first commandment may refer to the religious sphere, which was often the case in the post-partition history of Poland. But it has never been sufficient just on its own, and on occasions it has found itself in conflict with the patriotic stance. It may also refer to one's sense of honour, or for that matter to faithfully following one's own conscience. It is a well-known fact that honour is, and, at the same time, is not a Christian concept, whereas faithful following of one's own conscience is a privilege of the few; a privilege gained with difficulty and completely unsuitable as a general attitudinal model. In difficult times the hardest thing to do is to follow the verdict of conscience. Few, and only a few, have ever succeeded. And hence this sort of loyalty requires personal models, not of the 'Gilgamesh, Hector or Roland' type but those like Prince Józcf, Walerian Łukasiński, Szymon Konarski or Romuald Traugutt.

'Be faithful' means also: 'do not change your mind about to which absolute values you are being faithful'. This command was often difficult to observe undividedly. While the values to be observed by the individual did not belong to this world, there was a constant possibility of the verification of faithfulness. When, however, they became identified with communal aims or national aims, then faithfulness and political tactics often found themselves in conflict. The conduct of the Polish government in London in 1944 provides a good example here. Historians and intellectuals discuss to this day (this is after all their profession) the subject of what that government could and should have done. Looking at it from our perspective, we can see that the Polish government found itself in an impossible situation, that is, a situation in which tactical considerations were in obvious conflict with the command of loyalty. Under the circumstances they took a stand in accordance with national logic, that is, an apolitical stand. What clinched that choice was not the distrust of the Soviet Union or the Allies, or the question of Katyn and the borders in the East, but the abandonment of political in favour of ethical categories. The results, from a political point of view, were exactly what were to be expected, as they have to be when one withdraws from the political game. Personally, I have little faith in the argument that that political game should have been entered into. Intuition and instinct suggested to those people the only possible solution when faced with defeat – to withdraw and to rise to the only level at which the defeat might prove fruitful one day.

It is quite understandable that people with truly political and active temperaments had the greatest difficulty in accepting this solution. They had to try, as it still seemed possible in the first period after the war to act while remaining at the same time faithful to basic values. Soon, however, it proved impossible and the Polish alternatives proved to be no alternatives at all. Later generations held it against them that they never prepared themselves for the eventual possibility of yet another crisis; so their contribution to political thinking which should have covered every contingency was minimal. But one of the causes of the specifically Polish incompleteness is the fact that in situations without choice, it is very difficult to achieve a rational, boldly formulated and forward-looking political ideology.

There also appeared another strongly restricting factor. There is only superficially a strong and safe link between the command 'be faithful' and 'be loyal to your comrades in arms'. Faithfulness may be tantamount to loyalty, but it may also not be tantamount at all, or even be contrary to it. All combatants are familiar with situations in which some, having experienced persecution and accusations of unorthodoxy, find the road to future activities barred, and others who, sometimes by chance, avoided such persecution and are willing to continue their activity. Such was the case of the 'Stańczyk' group in Galicia in the late 1860s. The subsequent confrontation which took place within the conservative grouping as well as between them and their opponents, interesting as it was, was only marginally concerned with the ideological and political content of conservative opinion in Kraków. Much more significant, at least in the initial phase, was the indignation aroused by their criticism of the January Uprising, in which after all the majority of them took part. Similar in character was the controversy over the Warsaw Uprising in the immediate post-war period (mainly in the pages of *Tygodnik Powszechny*) which was abandoned soon after it started, not necessarily due to the political situation and censorship. It was not continued abroad in the *émigré* community either, where the freedom to express opinions was not restricted. The anti-uprising irony of the Stańczyk group, or for that matter the questioning by Stefan Kisielewski of the meaning of the sacrifice of 1944, was seen as socially reprehensible. It transgressed the command of loyalty; yet no one denied either the Stańczyk group or Kisielewski their faithfulness to fundamental ideals.

Faithfulness can be observed by reckoning just with oneself, but loyalty can be observed only by conforming to the currently binding group precepts. One might add that the precepts change, and that the public life of all groups subjected to overwhelming pressures relies to a large extent on the continuous upholding, verification and renewal of those precepts, those formulas of loyalty. In the case of the public life of a community, in contrast to the case of the inner life of the individual, one cannot create commandments which would be binding once and for all. As the situation keeps changing there is no such thing as an objective fact; everything becomes a subject for interpretation. This may be the reason why until quite recently one talked about Mochnacki and Brzozowski – perhaps the two most eminent Polish thinkers of the nineteenth and twentieth centuries – mainly in terms of their ambiguous political biographies rather than in terms of their intellectual achievements. One can even detect in many publications some kind of satisfaction, as though these biographies proved the thesis that the nation does not need any of this excessive sophistry which often leads to the path of collaboration with the enemy.

Naturally it was always those who were defeated who spoke most about loyalty. The disputes within the *émigré* community after the November Uprising of 1830 or after 1945 concentrated mainly on the question of loyalty. Even seemingly meritorious disputes, i.e. those concerning foreign or social policy, were nothing but the loyalty debate in another form. The 'loyals' kept together notwithstanding their quarrels. The 'faithful', however, remained lonely. Particularly so when, faithful to their aims and values, they perceived the need for a change of tactics. This was the case of Mochnacki after the November Uprising and also, for some time after 1945, the case of *Kultura* and its editor Jerzy Giedroyć. Naturally there was not always a conflict between faithfulness and loyalty: but it was almost always generated when attempts were made to subjugate the command of faithfulness to the command of loyalty. One can be faithful to certain values and ideals, and consequently loyal towards one's own group, to the extent to which the group adheres to those values; one cannot, however, be loyal first and then from the sense of loyalty derive the sense of primary values. That is to say one can, but such a sequence either gives rise to the utilitarian treatment of values or – even worse – to its complete subordination to the *esprit de corps*.

Nevertheless conflicting situations occurred in moral and intellectual life less often than one would have thought. Judging by Polish diaries from the nineteenth and twentieth centuries, every effort was made to avoid a situation of conflict, to live and act within the area where the values of faithfulness and loyalty overlapped, no matter how small that area was. The oceans of patriotic banality which flow through those diaries do not necessarily prove that the authors were blessed with brains no bigger than a pea. This patriotic banality is often accompanied by an accurate and critical description of customs, international relations or *émigré* life. Resorting to patriotic banality or, to avoid pejorative terms, to the patriotic minimum was a natural result of the desire to avoid conflicts, which no one likes. There was no shortage of people who opposed the November, the January or the Warsaw Uprisings. However, Józef Kalasanty Szaniawski left his extremely penetrating observations in manuscript form and removed himself in time to Vienna; the Rev. Hieronim Kajsiewicz found his famous 'Letter to my brothers. . .' shamelessly exploited by the Russian authorities; Paweł Popiel spoke out late and hardly anyone listened to him; Kazimierz Sosnkowski, who seemed to be opposed to the Warsaw Uprising, left London at the critical moment for Italy.

The history of Poland interpreted in terms of the command of loyalty indicates very clearly that protest was as a rule fruitless, and often ended in disaster for the protesters. How much safer it was, therefore, and how much more sensible from the point of view of the effectiveness of one's action, to satisfy the patriotic minimum. These repeated victories of loyalty over faithfulness in conflict situations, or the more commonly occurring pattern of satisfying the patriotic minimum, had their consequences. The patriotic minimum was indispensable in difficult times as the best form of defence. It proved, however, banal and depressingly ineffective at a time of crisis. Yet nonconformist attitudes have become practically excluded from national life. The place of individual non-conformism was taken by social nonconformism of the group, which no longer required from the individual the courage of his convictions, but often did require personal courage. The main consequence, however, was the disappearance or virtual disappearance from Polish culture of the problem of conscience, that is the problem of the individual versus God, or in wider terms, of the individual versus the absolute. As a result a serious philosophy never developed in Poland and the few, not fully successful, attempts – like those of Stanisław Ignacy Witkiewicz – are treated to this day as original, strange, ridiculous or at best prophetic.

A surprising phenomenon, which is in complete contrast with what has been said above, emerged in the form of great Polish romantic poetry and its excellent modern successor. Why was it that only the poets (music and painting are more difficult to assess) escaped that limited pressure?

One can never fully answer this type of question. But if Polish culture (and indirectly also political thought) found anywhere a measure of fulfilment, acquired a dimension and a free and unrestricted life, it was precisely in poetry. How did it come about then that poetry slipped through the net of the constraints to which the collective life was subjugated?

First, it was due to the double nature of poetry itself. Good poetry, because of its rhythm, melody and melancholy, always makes easy and satisfying reading, and in Poland it also constituted patriotic reading, either directly or indirectly, as a way of keeping the language alive. Good poetry, however, has another level which is hidden to a lesser or greater extent. There the poet is completely independent of social reception. He faces first of all only himself and then a few readers. This duality does not exist in prose.

Second, romantic Polish poetry fell on the propitious ground of national feelings and the bard became in his own right an indispensable element of the patriotic minimum. Acknowledged as a bard, his special rights had to be recognized: the right to solitude, to an unconventional stand, to abstaining from social or political involvement, and even the right to a morally suspect style of life. The bard was automatically loyal by virtue of being a bard. And the elements in his poetry which were out of character with his prophetic role were either simply ignored or sometimes subjected to an alternative, more nationalistic, interpretation.

And third, for the reasons mentioned above, talented people, or if one prefers, the culture itself, perceived this outlet for independent and therefore creative activity, and it attracted a large number of good candidates who perhaps under a different set of circumstances would have never found their poetic vocation. In poetry one could best succeed in expressing the thoughts and impressions which were little in agreement with the order of the spirit and sensitivity. Poetry in Poland was therefore for social and spiritual reasons the most feasible of forms, and yet even the greatest poetry was permanently and firmly incorporated into the patriotic minimum.

This is a suitable moment to mention one more intriguing element of Polish political culture which, although not fully realized, constituted one more curb on temperaments unable to accept Polish restless clumsiness.

Polish nationalism was never threatening and yet it was a nuisance. The 200-year-long existence outside reality, and the commandment of loyalty, led in Poland to the formation of patriotic attitudes of a particular type. They had enormous power before which literally everything had to give way, and they lacked any doubts. This is clear and understandable. What is not so clear is the phenomenon of nationalism. What was it for? The last hundred years in Poland never gave a single opportunity for a justifiable fear that the national identity or consciousness might be lost. Situations kept continuously emerging, as in a film, which favoured defensive and patriotic attitudes. There were many threats of a social, economic and political nature, but none that would endanger the national consciousness. Yet it is nationalism that is the most dynamic and forever recurring trend in Polish political thinking. One can to a certain extent understand (though not justify) the phenomenon of German nationalism at the time of the Weimar Republic or at the beginning of the 1930s in

Berlin. Yet in Poland the corresponding attitudes were in a minority or non-existent.

Polish nationalism as an allegedly defensive tactic was not needed either for interior purposes, as no threat was forthcoming, nor for exterior purposes, as the universal patriotism constituted a sufficient response. Polish nationalism is and always has been the simplest and the most reliable surrogate for political thinking. Not because of its easy social appeal as an ideology, although that is also true, but because it is not and has virtually never been an authentic ideology of authentic political thought. It is a formula designating what is there already; it is a way of avoiding the contradictions mentioned earlier. Nationalism solves in one go all the Polish paradoxes. A nationalist lives comfortably without having to trouble himself constantly and irritatingly with problems like how to reconcile the loneliness of the individual with the solidarity of the crowd, how to reconcile the national with the universal, how to reconcile cool thinking with the force of patriotic emotion, how to reconcile the left with the right, or, finally, how to reconcile revolution with evolution. The triumph of nationalism was the triumph of simple (not to say simplistic) solutions over the logic of national thinking which was tired of its own contradictions and meandering. The nationalistic ideology represented in Poland (as in the rest of Europe) a form of non-thinking which in Poland fell on particularly fertile ground. This proved sometimes useful in political life, but always spelled disaster for intellectual life.

The Polish syndrome of incompleteness revealed with extraordinary force its positive and negative aspects at the time of Solidarity and thereafter of martial law. People of sober temperament must have watched the spectacle of the great Polish renewal with a certain sense of helplessness. And the scale of the renewal spectacle was greater than ever, as literally millions participated in it. It seems that it was only with the arrival of Solidarity that the Poles developed a full awareness as citizens (though not so full in the villages) and even then only of the type that was possible in Poland, which means that this awareness also remained paradoxical.

Stefan Kisielewski is one of those who, during the Solidarity period, wrote very little about it due to his temperament, or about political life in general. He displays a very good example of the sense of difficulty and constraint with which someone used to political thinking must have experienced watching the events taking place in front of him. Not because anyone could have foreseen what was going to happen, but because Solidarity, although it is a political movement as in Polish reality it must be, in 1980–1 on no account wanted to accept this for a fact; it did not want to be pushed towards a political stand. And it was right, because by its nature it was not a political movement. It fulfilled a political function but completely against its wishes and against the principle which united its rank and file. Therefore, when Kisielewski wrote, quite justifiably from his point of view, about the negative effects of Solidarity's lack of awareness of its purely political role, he wrote in a vacuum. Had Solidarity been aware of its political role, the whole movement would have lost its ethos, its ethos of citizenship. Solidarity was not fighting for power, it was fighting for the creation of a civil society, and to a large extent, no matter how one judged any particular move or any particular leader, it achieved its aim.

It appears that this fundamentally apolitical character of Solidarity has often been misunderstood by the commentators exclusively capable of political thinking. This may justify the Western commentators who are still of an opinion that Solidarity went too far, or the commentators in *Kultura*, in whose view it did not go far enough. But even if one keeps in mind the non-political character of Solidarity, one cannot suddenly abandon one's claim to be able to judge social phenomena in political categories. One cannot just confine oneself to moralizing, socially-minded exclamations, and sighing. Here again it is evident that the Polish syndrome of incompleteness and the paradoxical form of social life in Poland confront the mind with tasks which are impossible and shocking from a rational point of view. It transpired once again that either one had to offer one's mind in the service of social emotions or, putting the emotions aside, to fight one's way through the dangers of speculation far removed from reality. Neither way is satisfactory and there is no possibility of intermediate formulas. In this situation the position of an observer seems very tempting, but one cannot, and does not wish to, remain just an observer. Adam Zagajewski was perhaps too cautious when he contrasted solidarity with loneliness. In reality, it is our temperament and our personal talents which arbitrarily determine the character of our involvement. It is impossible to be truly in solidarity with others and at the same time truly lonely. It is equally impossible to adhere to one or the other alternatively in different periods of one's life: but in Poland one has to. The logic of the national spirit breaks down the barriers between faith and reason, common sense and emotion, morality and politics, faithfulness and loyalty – breaks them down and in consequence leads to situations in which nothing is complete, where no conclusions are ever fully drawn, where politics is not sufficiently political and where morality is not considered in terms of the individual, where social life still resembles a theatre. The costumes are changing, the audience is increasing, yet it is still the same performance that goes on on the stage. And I am not sure whether it is good or bad.

Translated by Irena Powell.

4

The Catholic Church, the Communist State and the Polish people

Jan Jerschina

Jagiellonian University, Kraków

The editors put the following question to me: how does the activity of the Catholic Church relate to Polish interests and national aspirations, and how does it relate to the interests and aspirations of the Communists? This is a very difficult question, which would require a whole book for an exhaustive answer. I decided nevertheless to make an attempt at such an answer in this essay, knowing that a synthetic handling of the problem would force me to raise the most important issues, and help to define my own standpoint more precisely. Moreover, I share the editors' judgement that anyone who wishes to understand Polish affairs cannot avoid the problem of the relations between Church, society and state. For it is indisputable, for reasons of long-gone history as well as a result of factors operating in more recent times and still operating today, that the fate of the Church and its activity are at the present time closely intertwined with the fate and activities of the Polish people. I was glad, therefore, to undertake this task, which is, as it were, an expedition into territory which, although it appears to be well known, nevertheless conceals more than one secret.

What precisely is the subject of this article? In the first place, of course, the role of the Church as an institution, with its hierarchy, intellectual elite, personnel and social doctrine. I will not go into detailed and exclusively theological questions, although this reduces the range of the analysis. It is true that the position of the Church on certain social questions is expressed in religious and theological language. However, despite certain opinions, it is often the case that the language of the laity, and even the language of science and politics, turns up in religious documents and in the language of the Church. Therefore 'codifying' the views of the Church hierarchy is not so complicated a matter as might be supposed. The revolution in the Church brought about by the Second

Vatican Council was accompanied by a real revolution in language as well. The introduction of Mass in the vernacular was only a small change in comparison with the opening up of the Church to contemporary social and political problems and its active participation in contemporary processes transforming the world. And this obviously entailed an enrichment of the language.

I shall try to reconstruct the ethos of the contemporary church in Poland. I understand 'ethos' in the sense in which it was defined in Poland by Ossowska, Szawiela and Goćkowski. Briefly: it is a certain system of values and a lifestyle corresponding to them, which is the property of some human community, movement or institution, or of all these simultaneously. Obviously, this will be a selective reconstruction, for reasons of space. I shall choose from it those features which are essential for comparison with the ethos of the state and the ethos of certain social groups.

I shall therefore compare the ethos of the peasant, the worker, the people in power, the intelligentsia, and the ethos of the Church. Someone perhaps may say that this is too ambitious, but it is worth trying, and the author of these remarks makes no claim to infallibility.

The inter-war period, 1918–39

We shall have to go back some way into the past, in order to consider how long the road is that the Church, together with Polish society, had to travel. In Polish writing there are two dominant, and conflicting, visions of the role of the Church in Polish history.

The first is an overly sympathetic approach. It serves to integrate believers. It is a vision which accentuates only the positive functions of the Church and its representatives. There is no doubt that Polish history can supply a great number of facts from which such an image can be created, just as it is obvious that such an image would be tendentious and incorrect.

The second vision is extremely anti-clerical. The Church, according to this vision, was first and foremost the most powerful landowner of the feudal era. When discussing the era of the partitions, it keeps silent about the participation of individual priests in the struggle for independence, and stresses the collaboration of the hierarchy with the representatives of the partitioning powers. The inter-war years, 1918–39, are viewed as an era when the Church 'co-operated' with the bourgeoisie. The primitive nature of this image needs no comment.

When Poland and the Church entered into independence after the First World War, they were closely intertwined. The fate of Poland during the Renaissance, and the history of the Reformation and the Counter-Reformation, decided that some 65 per cent of the citizens of Poland were Roman Catholics (a further 10 per cent were Greek Catholics). At the same time, a state was formed which was multi-confessional and multi-ethnic, in which the principle of tolerance clearly predominated over the principle of ethnocentrism. This tradition meant that, during the partitions, Catholicism as a religion and the Church as an institution could and did play the role of essential agents in the preservation of the Polish national identity. Furthermore, when the process of evolution of national identities began to gain momentum, in the second half of the eighteenth and in the nineteenth centuries, it was also when the Polish national symbolic culture was formed. Catholicism came so deeply into it that to this very day young Poles (including non-Catholics), going through the natural process of socialization and awakening to national identity by learning and experiencing this culture, form their cultural and social individuality under the influence of Catholic tradition. During this period the Catholic Church became the mainstay of Polishness, because by defending the religion of the Catholic peasant against the pressures imposed on them by the Orthodox and Protestant Churches, it defended them at the same time against Russification and Germanization. This defence, and also the participation of some priests in the uprisings, in underground independence movements, in cultural and social movements among the peasants, all this strongly integrated the Catholic Church and the Polish nation.

After the First World War, the Church had a great moral authority among Catholics, and had a strong link with all the social groups from peasants and landowners, to the petty bourgeoisie, the intelligentsia and the bourgeoisie. But this authority did not automatically ensure it a role in government. Throughout the formation of the new Polish statehood, the state apparatus, the elite of the state administration and the elite of the political parties were very mindful of their sovereignty with respect to the Church. Even the parties which stressed their Catholic character adopted this stance, trying their hardest, as the National Democrats did, to influence the Church through priests they had won over, so as to make the Church a tool for their own ends. On the other hand, even the parties with a Marxist heredity – like the Polish Socialist Party – tried rather not to come into conflict with the Church. It appears that the Church was rather on the offensive, while many a socialist, like the later Italian Communists, would walk in the Blessed Sacrament procession carrying the canopy over the priest. The only party with an anti-Catholic (anti-religious) and anti-clerical programme was the then Communist Party of Poland.

This was, however, a very small party, which had very little influence, in spite of the intense social and ethnic conflicts in Poland at that time (33 per cent of the population consisted of national minorities, of which the largest were the Jewish, Ukrainian, Byelorussian and German minorities).

We may note too that this was the party which had chosen – and not lightly – the name *Komunistyczna Partia Polski* (Communist Party *of Poland*) and not *Polska Partia Komunistyczna* (*Polish* Communist Party). The Communists disociated themselves from the socialists of the PPS (*Polish* Socialist Party), and thus stressed their internationalist character and pro-Sovietism. Moreover, a certain image of the Communists had by now become current in the public consciousness (and this image was carefully fostered at that time by government propaganda and the Church). This presented the Communists not simply as non-Poles, but as traitors and Soviet agents. The Catholics of that era were by no means just a crowd of zealots and bigots, led by the hand by the clergy. Peasant anti-clericalism, workers' anti-clericalism, intelligentsia anti-clericalism were not new phenomena, but were fairly deeply rooted in Polish culture. And this was not all. In the conditions of poverty, indeed of destitution, which prevailed over the greater part of the territories of the then Poland, in a situation in which it was necessary to think about integrating the territories and populations of the three zones of partition, there was a build-up of social and ethnic conflicts. The swing from democracy to the populist-dictatorship of Jozef Piłsudski in 1926 was intended, *inter alia*, to facilitate the launching of Poland on a course of modernization and of peaceful agrarian and other reforms. When, however, these possibilities began to take shape, the world economic crisis of the 1930s and the threats from the West and from the East delayed the realization of these aims. Throughout this entire period, the peasants looked for the help of the Church in their struggle to take over the land of the former landlords. The workers were ready to leave the Church if it proved to be not their defender but a partisan of the mighty. The tension built up. A situation developed which encouraged the Church to seek a new doctrine and new forms in its public, and especially its political, activity. The hierarchy of the Church and its intellectual elite applied themselves to this matter.

In this situation, the Church became involved not simply through members of the clergy taking an active part in various political movements (a great number were active in support of the National Party and some were with the populists), but it also aimed at organizing its own political movement and trade unions. These endeavours, however, basically came to naught. In that predominantly Catholic country – it is rarely noticed – there was neither wide popular support for the Christian Democratic Party, nor an auspicious climate for the development of trade unions based on the ideology of corporationism.

It was Stefan Wyszyński, the future Primate of the Polish Catholic Church, but at that time far lower in the hierarchy, who worked out a plan for new trade unions. As far as I know, this plan was based on the idea of solidarism, but differed considerably from the model of corporationism followed by the Christian trade unions of that time. This fact clashes with the view that the Church in the years 1918–39 was a monolith, which remained unchanging and dominating in the milieu of the Catholic majority, assured of the support of the state, which jealously defended its sovereignty and lay status, but which nevertheless favoured Catholics. This view is incorrect in so far as at this point, there was within the Catholic Church a search for a social doctrine and organizational forms which would allow the workers, peasants and intelligentsia to be won over. The view that the main social frame of reference of the Church at that time consisted of the propertied classes, landowners and the bourgeoisie, is, to say the least, questionable – though of course there was a strong conservative wing of the clergy which had close ties with these classes.

I recall this interesting fact from Wyszyński's life also because his studies of trade union problems and his drawing up of the aforesaid plan might have facilitated his abandonment of the stance of detachment and distance, which the hierarchy at first adopted towards the democratic opposition in the second half of the 1970s, when KOR and the other organizations opened a new page in the political history of post-war Poland.

The years 1939–70

The Second World War interrupted the initiation of probably funda-mental changes in the Church, changes which were evoked by signals of its diminishing influence, especially among the workers and intelligentsia. Nevertheless, this war to a considerable extent restored a high level of integration of the Catholic community and hierarchy, although in an unexpected manner. Two avalanches descended on Polish society – firstly, Hitler's armies on 1 September 1939, and then, under the terms of the Molotov-Ribbentrop Pact, the Soviet armies on 17 September 1939. Until a year and a half later, when war broke out between these two temporary allies, the territory of pre-war Poland was divided into two parts, in each of which the occupying powers implemented very similar programmes of the 'final liquidation of the Polish nation'.

In the first post-war years and during the Stalinist period, when a new wave of sufferings fell on the main part of Polish society, the Communists were also careful to ensure that the clergy remained a part of the suffering people. The well-known trials of Bishop Kaczmarek and other priests, and the house-arrest of Cardinal Wyszyński, left no doubt in society at large what the attitude of the authorities was towards the Church. I mention these facts in order to underline that this shared past of the Poles and the Church was not simply the kind of phenomenon summed up by the proverb 'When you're in trouble, seek God at the double' – it was a historical process which lasted almost twenty years

(1939–56). It was an educational process too, which to a considerable degree removed from the public memory the flaws and blemishes of the two inter-war decades.

The years 1945–56, however, were not simply a period of persecution of the Church, of its defence against liquidation by the Communists. Of course, the Church was under considerable threat, especially from 1949 to 1953. The Communists built up their authority not only by imposing it by force and rigging the elections. Their programme of economic and social reform included a number of important aims which were intended to achieve, and to a certain extent did achieve, the legitimization of their authority and the new social order. The mass media presentation of this programme was calculated to form in the minds of the Poles a conviction that it was the Communists (and precisely the Communists and not those people who cast aspersions on their honour and denied them their Polishness) who were bringing about historical and social justice. If the Church had adopted a stance which was uncompromisingly negative towards these reforms it would have been condemned as a reactionary and anti-Polish force. It therefore had to find an answer, in word and in deed, that was different. We shall discuss in detail only a few fundamental problems of that era and the way in which they were tackled, on the one hand by the Communists and on the other by the Church.

The first and most important trump of the Communists in their play for legitimacy was the fact that together with their coming to power ethnically Polish lands, as they were systematically called at that time, were returned to the possession of the Polish state. This was in truth a matter of great importance for Poland, and this was so not on account of some kind of nationalist aspiration. The acquisition of these lands as a result of pacts between the Allies and the actions of Polish Communists fulfilled several functions. First, the Recovered Territories (as they were called right up to the 1970s), after the expulsion of the Germans, became an area of resettlement for almost four million Poles displaced from the eastern territories of the pre-war Polish state. Second, Poland within its new boundaries was a territorial, economic and social entity, whose integration and development could be achieved more rapidly and more completely than the territorial-social creation which was a result of the First World War. It is not surprising that in the consciousness of modern Poles, irrespective of their political sympathies, this new homeland is their most natural, proper nest, and that they meet any doubt cast on this idea not only with hostility, but simply with astonishment. And third, in the light of the horrible awareness of injustice which Poles had (and still have!) after the war with its struggle for survival and struggle against Nazism, which did not, however, bring the hoped-for independent and democratic statehood, but which soon taught them to realize that the majority of the executioners – Nazis or Stalinists – got away scot-free, the possession at last of one's own proper nest, one's own proper territory, where one could manage one's own affairs, was and to this day is the only factor which can without doubt alleviate the pain, the only truly historical achievement.

The Church had an excellent understanding of this psychological, social and political situation, and in spite of a shortage of personnel, and political difficulties immediately after the war was over, it set to work in these territories and became an institution which played an essential role in the integration of society in these lands.

The Communists' programme also included other important ideas – agrarian reform, and the distribution of the lands of the Polish landowners and the estates of the formerly German territories. The indecision of the rulers of the inter-war years was a cause of the disenchantment of the peasants with the Polish state which arose from political oblivion after the First World War. The feeling of alienation from the state was so strong among the peasants that even years later, one of them, a former soldier in both world wars, who had marched under arms and unarmed across half of Europe, said to me: 'Sir, the state always exists in order to oppress the peasants, whether it is a Polish state or a Russian state or a Bolshevik state'. And so to the peasants, who for the most part either owned no land at all or else owned farms which on the average did not exceed three hectares, the Communists offered the 'masters' land'.

A reform of this kind made it impossible to establish large family farms which would be efficient and could make Poland self-sufficient in food production. But this reform was certainly not a mistake from the political viewpoint of the Communists at the time when they were consolidating their power. The peasants wanted to have land, even just a little bit of land of their own. And any government which gave them some would be a 'good government'.

With regard to agrarian reform, the Church adopted a stance which was very reminiscent of that of the socialists. While not denying the peasants' right to land or the need for agrarian reform, it did not maintain over-energetically that the existence of larger family farms must be guaranteed on economic and moral grounds. Such a stance could not discourage the peasants, but neither was it an acceptance of the reform which the Communists imposed.

The third important point in the reform programme of the Communists was the nationalization of private industry, trade and services. In this question, too, the Church could not and did not adopt a negative stance, although this was the nucleus of the communist programme of constructing the institutional basis of Communism. A very significant part of the large-scale industrial plant was property abandoned by the

Germans. What sense would there have been in defending the property rights of the Germans to the Silesian mines, to the factories where hundreds of thousands of Polish slaves had toiled to satisfy the military needs of Hitler's army? It was not only a matter of the choice of a vision of society based on private or state ownership; it was a question of the feeling of justice of the Poles who wanted now to enjoy the benefits of owning these assets. And with such an idea, the workers and technicians took under their charge, even before the formal nationalization, the mines and factories, in order to warm, clothe and feed themselves.

It was a different matter when it came to small-scale property, trade and services. Here the attitude of the Church towards the government's policy was decidedly negative. As we well know, within a few decades, the Communists reached a point where the rebuilding and development of this sector was seen as one of the most important factors in getting the Polish economy out of its profound crisis.

And finally one must remember the attitude of the Church towards the Communists during the time when they were consolidating their power. And here the problem was not as simple as it might seem. Only a relatively small part of Polish society was prepared to fight, work underground, and take up arms. Just after the war, the Poles were tired to death, drained of fighting blood, and many without housing or food. The Communists made them the proposition: don't fight, let us build up our country from the ruins together. Had the Church advocated an armed struggle it would have found itself in effect in the same boat as the soldiers of the underground, desperate and hunted down by the Soviet and Polish armies and the political police. Very soon it would have been isolated in this stance and would have perished in isolation. The Poles, although often with pain in their hearts, did not want to fight any more. This 'recognition of reality' at this time was perhaps one of the reasons for the ease with which, during the next few years, Stalinism penetrated into the communal life of a great number of Poles. One normally speaks discreetly about 'war-weariness'. But it was not simply war-weariness: it was also a matter of a moral and political choice. It seems that it is precisely this perception which is lacking in the otherwise penetrating analysis of Czesław Miłosz in *The Captive Mind* and *The Struggle for Power*.

In the years of Stalinism, the Church was divided within itself. Cardinal Wyszyński's decision to adopt a stance of normalization and formalization in the sense of legal Church-state relations was received in a negative manner by some Catholics, especially those among the intelligentsia who, under the new regime, lost their freedom; the petit bourgeois who had been dispossessed of their property; and the landowners who had been dispossessed of their land. But Wyszyński's decision was probably accepted with approval by the peasants who actually worked the land and who hoped to possess it. And what did those peasants from remote villages think, who went off to building sites and to factories in the towns, and who, in their own opinions, were bettering themselves? And the young peasants and workers who in their millions entered schools and higher-education colleges? We do not have precise answers to these questions. But it is significant that that was the time, the only historical era since the Reformation, when there was a mass exodus of believers from the Church. In the 1940s and 1950s the exodus took place even among those upwardly mobile young people from the villages (traditionally so religious) and from small towns, not to mention the new, young intelligentsia. In this situation, the Church's attempt at normalization, although it soon ended with the arrest of Cardinal Wyszyński, was the right response. In the long run, thanks to this, after 1956 the Church was in a position to carry out its service for the Catholic community.

The years 1954–6 were the end of the 'era of gradual Stalinization' of Poland, but not the end of Stalinism or post-Stalinism. From what had been created, if the word may be used without hesitation, by Generalissimo Iosif Vissarionovich Stalin, a great deal remained. Not only in political and economic institutions, but also in people's thinking and their system of values. The enormous totalitarian machine, designed to penetrate into every sphere, is still in operation at the present day. It shaped the mode of thought of hundreds of millions of people in the Communist countries and in the West. (Even today, a large number of western journalists are full of admiration for *perestroika*, as if without realizing or ignoring that it is intended to maintain the Communist dictatorship.)

Cardinal Wyszyński proceeded from the recently signed agreement between Church and state, which was not respected by the government, and from the status of a prisoner, to become the only *mediator* between Gomułka and the Communist Party on the one hand, and society on the other. This is a key word, one of the most important in the interpretation and understanding of the relations between the communist state and society and of the role of the Church.

Gomułka took on the position of party leader in the face of very strong opposition, first and foremost from the party leaders themselves. Most of them had been appointed by the people who put him under house arrest. They had cause for anxiety not because Gomułka represented some very different concept of how the party should function. They were worried that the new leader would build up his own political base in the party and threaten their positions. Second, there was the matter of the style of rule. Gomułka was an authoritarian, and his authoritarianism was not tempered even by a tendency to appeal to populist techniques of ruling. He was, however, opposed to large-scale use of the death penalty. He believed in the effectiveness of a repressive legal system, but also in the maintenance of legalism. He desired neither democracy, nor a return to private property. But he understood that the authorities must be *effective*, and he firmly believed that if reasonable food, clothing and modest housing conditions could be ensured, this would give the authorities legitimacy. He did not understand and could not bear the Polish intelligentsia. He had the prejudices of a man who was painfully and humiliatingly aware of the culture gap between himself and them. One cannot deny his patriotic motivation, which was very peculiar but none the less indubitable, if one wishes to grasp a sense of the history of Communism in Poland. He had in his heart a vision of a Poland with an autarkic and socialist economy, a Poland which would gradually build up a certain independence with respect to the USSR and have frontiers with Germany legalized at the international level. Like every fanatical Communist, everything which in reality conflicted with his vision of a developed communist society, Gomułka held to be a relic of the class-ridden past, a backward phenomenon. This outlook was not enough to win the allegiance of the majority of Poles for any length of time. But it was, however, a great deal in comparison with Bierut's programme and the ruling elite which he created.

Cardinal Wyszyński realized very clearly that in this programme the most important interests of the Poles were, to a certain measure, included. Their realization could push Poland in a direction which, while not the most desirable, would be at least closer to his religious, moral and patriotic ideals than that established by the former ruling elite. He therefore gave his support to Gomułka in 1956 and for some years afterwards. He also acted to convince Polish society that it was necessary to support the new communist rulers against Stalinists in the party and state apparatus. Those people who were adults or near-adults at the time understood this very well. It was not from fear that they welcomed this Communist who ten years previously with Bierut had savagely attacked many of them, all off his own bat, without any encouragement from Stalin, and sang *Sto lat* (the Polish equivalent of *For he's a jolly good fellow*) to him, and were prepared to forgive and forget. For the Stalinists he replaced were the most dreaded political murderers in the history of Poland. By this comparison Gomułka was a liberal. Moreover after many years they heard from the lips of this Communist words which rang true, that Poland was still an important matter.

This support was uncomfortable for Gomułka. He did not so much understand as sense a danger. He knew that to be the Father of the Nation, or at least his Vicar, is not simply to rejoice in the support of the populace, but is also a responsibility. Tomorrow these Poles could call him to account for how he was 'playing father'. And such an accounting, in his opinion and perhaps in the opinion of all Communists to this very day, was tantamount to sharing power. But one does not win power and possess it just to share it, to fritter it away. It is sufficient to read an eminent Polish communist leader and intellectual, Mieczysław Rakowski, to become convinced that this view is still the basic of the communist mode of thought on politics.

But in 1956, Gomułka had no other course than to appeal to the Church and the common people. By so doing, he began the *institutionalization of the role of the Church as mediator in relations between the Communist Party and society*. The Church, its intellectual and moral elite, its governing and directing leaders, accepted this role and, moreover, never let slip a chance *of creating for themselves situations demanding mediation*.

During the 1960s, Gomułka no longer wanted the participation of the Church in politics. He viewed any statement on the fundamental questions of the existence of the nation which did not issue from his lips as a usurpation of his authority. He was the boss. So it is hardly surprising that even in so delicate a matter as abortion, when the Church declared that it was against it, this evoked an attack full of fury from him. Even more important was the disagreement between the authorities and the Church regarding Church administration in the Recovered Territories. Here Gomułka demanded from the Church action totally subordinated to his policy and his propaganda. The Church, albeit it had fully assumed possession – through its work with the faithful – of the parishes and dioceses in these territories, aimed at a gradual and complete settlement of this question, on the basis of formal agreements and maintaining the superior role of the Vatican. There was probably too the issue of not creating still one more agent of discord between Germans and Poles, so soon after the war. It was well understood that not only must the Odra-Nysa frontier some day be legalized, and that not even a peace treaty (which we still do not have even today) can solve the problem of Poland's security and good relations with the Germans, but that there must also be *friendly* relations between the two nations.

Gomułka treated this stance as a betrayal of the nation. The 'Letter of the Polish bishops to the German bishops' which expressed this stance of the Church in a lapidary and principled manner, in the formula, 'We forgive and seek forgiveness', stirred up a furore among the Communists. This was a completely sincere furore, and had nothing to do with political games. Gomułka had accumulated around himself a group of Communist-nationalists. This group did not represent the kind of ideology imputed to them by Brzezinski or Bromke, but they were undoubtedly nationalists. It was, however, a peculiar type of nationalism, with, perhaps, the exception of Gomułka himself. It was found, for example, among Polish officers who had a feeling of outrage and insult to national sentiment if, after manoeuvres, Hungarian or Czech officers received greater praise from the Soviet field-marshal, on account of how well their troops were trained. They were ethnocentric, but it was still a long way from this to a mature modern national consciousness. With this stance and consciousness they were all too eager to believe in 'the eternal enemy' and in the idea that all foreigners must be enemies for ever, metaphysically, simply because they were foreign.

Polish society has remained ethnocentric and authoritarian to some degree to the present day. Its peasant heritage is a foundation for maintaining this kind of outlook. Its history has not educated it in the spirit of other outlooks. In the face of the fresh experiences of the Second World War, it is no exaggeration to say that a considerable proportion of Poles received the words of the 'Letter of the Polish Bishops' with mixed feelings. The letter forced them to think in new categories. It told them to recognize the *sufferings of the Germans*, when they were accustomed to look on them only as those who inflicted suffering. It told them to think about the distant future, about their own history – and they were quite unaccustomed to this. This had always been the business of the 'masters'. And if today Polish society is very different, if it contains less ethnocentrism, less prejudice concerning the Germans, and sometimes even exaggerated and ostentatious protestations of friendship and esteem, then the beginning of all this was surely the bishops' letter.

The fury of Gomułka and the Communists in general had a quite different origin. The Catholicism of the majority of the Poles was something which they and the Soviet elite knew well and accepted as a fact of life. They wanted to destroy it, to wipe it out, but they accepted that 'this would be a long process of education'. However, they would not accept any *pro-western attitudes* on the part of the Poles. That was treated, and is still treated to this very day, as an evil of the greatest magnitude. And for obvious reasons. Could anyone trust an ally which was supposed to struggle against the West, but which revered the West, and considered itself to be part of it? To be part of that very enemy?

The struggle against these trends was always very difficult, especially since they were not simply specific to the intelligentsia. The Polish peasant and his children were pro-western, whether they stayed on the land or moved to the town. They were pro-western for different reasons from the intellectual. There were three main reasons: First, because millions of Polish peasants had emigrated to the USA, to France or to Germany, and these were for them countries of higher pay, freedom and democracy. Second, because these were countries where no one confiscated one's land. And third, because these were the countries which had kept free or liberated themselves from the Nazi yoke.

This explains conclusively why the communist propaganda which has to do with the 'hopeless complex of the West' has always made an all-out effort to evoke Polish hostility towards the Germans. It has to show to the West that the Germans are the *metaphysical enemy and the USSR is the metaphysical friend* – enemy and friend *from the very nature of their being*. This persists to this present day, and whenever successive presidents of the USA have wanted to visit cemeteries of the Wehrmacht and SS and to lay wreaths on the graves of valiant foes, nothing could be imagined that would be better for this propaganda and its aims.

It is obvious that a change in the Poles' attitude towards the Germans, and the Germans' towards the Poles, constitutes a deadly threat to these plans of educational integration into the Warsaw Pact. It is not surprising therefore that the language and ideology – the ideology which from the time of the bishops' letter the Church inculcated into Polish society – was received with the greatest hostility by the Communists. The symptoms of this hostility, which were not concealed, turned out to be counterproductive. (My own research has confirmed this, and has made me totally distrustful of the very different conclusions which have been produced by the party-government public opinion survey centres.)

The final moment of the Gomułka era – if we are talking about his struggle for the soul of the nation – was 1968. Gomułka was coming to grips with the growing opposition, not so much within the Party itself, which was only a reflection of a wide spectrum of factors. The main opposition came from a great, newborn force made up of managers of large-scale industry, the technocracy and its large infrastructure. This group, the core of which was the technocracy of Silesia, found allies among the ambitious leaders of the political police (Mieczysław Moczar) and the political apparatus. This is not the place to describe the cunning manoeuvres of these people, which were aimed against the authorities. Their launching of a campaign of anti-semitism was a push 'on three fronts'. Their anti-semitism was aimed first and foremost at the group of Polish Communists of Jewish origin. These Poles were politically differentiated. Some of them supported Gomułka's regime, some of them owed their careers to the Stalinist period. In any case, they occupied influential positions and were obstacles on the road to advancement of ambitious careerists in the Party, state and military apparatus, the mass media, science, culture, etc. The anti-semitism of 1968 was also calculated to awaken anti-semitism among the peasants. This was the second front. For the Polish peasant the Jew still is not only the victim of the Nazis but also a cultural and religious stranger. And finally, it was a matter of getting rid of a party leader who in his time had had the support of the people. The new groups aspiring to the leadership for whom Polishness and national interests were only of secondary importance (there is no room here to discuss the connections of some of the leaders of this group with the Soviet security police, dating back to before the war) decided that it would be useful to create for themselves the image of being real representatives of national interests and sentiments. To this end, by making the Polish Jews responsible for all the economic shortages and repressions, they found a scapegoat. Rightly or wrongly, they counted on the support of society, if the latter was told that it was not the entire party which was responsible for the material and political destitution of the country.

I think that Gomułka lost his way in these intrigues which were being carried on by cunning players. His counter-attack was based on the assumption that it was necessary to compete for the 'support of the people'. He proceeded from a muddled position, full of murky expressions about Zionism, with attacks on the intelligentsia thrown in. His prejudices sprang to life in full force at a moment of threat, and his political acumen fell into a dead sleep.

The Church's part in the events of 1968 was only indirect. In this dispute the Church could not mediate; it supported no one in the Party, although Moczar made considerable efforts to woo Church circles and the priests. The clear statements by the Church expressed its disapproval of anti-semitism and all it entailed, and sympathy for the persecuted, who belonged to the circles of the real opposition, to groups of scholars and workers in the arts. This and the frequent statements defending these people by members of the Polish intelligentsia made it impossible for Moczar, Olszowski and Gomułka to set themselves up as the representatives of the nation. The damage which Poland suffered was enormous. She lost a huge company of distinguished intellectuals and specialists in different fields, who nevertheless still preserve strong links with Poland to this day. And she lost a great deal of her good name, as it is difficult for people in the West to distinguish between state and nation.

Gomułka's policy had a number of features which were bound to lead to a crisis. More precisely, it was not so much Gomułka's policy as the economic and political system. The centrally directed economy, the lack of market competition, the continuation of the development strategy shaped during the cold war; all this was a brake on the process of improving living conditions and a blockage in the channels of social-professional progress. There is no room here to enumerate all the spheres of life about which the Church made pronouncements, either *ex officio*, from the lips of the Primate and in the documents and letters of the episcopate, or from the lips of its priests. All these pronouncements had a certain common denominator: *the needs of the working people and the development of the nation – the economy and culture.*

How should we sum up our deliberations on this past? The Church, as a result of historical developments and first and foremost of its work and the strategic thinking of its religious, moral and intellectual leaders, was transformed from a *victim* into a *mediator*, and so into an actor in the politico-historical processes, a co-creator of change in society, its consciousness and its bonds with pre-war Poland. As circumstances developed, by continuing this role of mediator it became ever more and more the *partner* of the authorities. I am not afraid to use this word, although it entails grave consequences. What these were, however, we shall consider later.

The Church and the authoritarian-populist socialism of Gierek, 1970–80

The turning-point of 1970 is usually viewed in a fairly shallow manner. This crisis had very deep foundations, the understanding of which is important if one wants to grasp the situation in which the position of the Church was shaped and its role realized in the decade 1970–80. Gierek was not a puppet, but he was not far short of being one. His predecessors had wielded power in a sphere in which Gierek did not. However, we may speak of what 'Gierek did', if we remember that this is a metaphor.

In 1970, the Church gave him its support. Cardinal Wyszyński once again played a part, calling on the workers to keep calm and to cease their struggle once the party had got rid of the now-hated Gomułka. He spoke out against bloodshed, took part in the defence of the suffering, and appealed to the conscience and the national sentiments of the authorities. No one could have any doubt that this voice was as influential on how things developed in 1970 as in 1956. The situation was a threatening one. Party committee buildings were set on fire, and the feelings of bitterness and desperate fury were so great that it is doubtful that anyone gave any thought to the people who might have been burned in these buildings. The Party was completely alienated. The workers organized themselves. Only in the Solidarity era was it openly acknowledged that the first free trade unions since the Second World War arose then, in Gdansk and Gdynia, in 1970.

In spite of the fact that the storm which had been let loose posed an immeasurable threat, the system nevertheless had important sources of legitimacy. Gierek fairly quickly won over a considerable number of workers and intellectuals by his policy of raising the standard of living of the population. He promulgated an ideology that was naïve but attractive – the linking of technocratism and patriotic slogans – both being rather primitive, but appealing to people who were hungry for something more optimistic. This was all linked to consumerism. The aim in life for a worker, and especially for an intellectual, was supposed to be a cheap car, or a bigger and better apartment. One must not, however, minimize these changes. A modern refrigerator, a television set, the possibility of travelling abroad – to socialist countries on vacation and to the West on business – all this sounds very modest, but in Poland in the 1970s it seemed to be a revolution in the normal way of life. All the more so, in that everyone was offered some kind of 'extra'. The peasants could deal more boldly on the free market and the countryside began to build itself up more rapidly than in any other period in the history of the Polish People's Republic. The workers did overtime and bargained with the foremen and enterprises over the efficiency of their work and their pay. Scientists had access to more resources for their research. The results of this research were hardly ever used. Nevertheless this was a fairly clever system of corrupting them: they could delude themselves that they were doing something, that something would come of it, and that authorities would eventually make use of it. The paradox of those years was that rampant parasitism and corruption (although occasionally this was written and spoken of with a certain distaste) became in part an effective way for the authorities to legitimize, in a predominantly Catholic and pro-western society, a socialist and corporate system of communist technocrats.

In the face of these phenomena the Church adjusted its stance fairly rapidly. It very swiftly launched an attack on consumerism. However, after a period of improvement, the economic situation began to deteriorate again, and there was no need to proclaim that the pursuit of material things and earthly goods at the expense of spiritual values was evil. The vices of the economic system were now stigmatized, and the demoralization of the workers by the system was said to produce corruption, lack of dignity, poor relations with the authorities, etc. This moralistic approach may not have been too effective in the beginning, but it caught people's attention. The richer its content of economic, sociological and politological theory, the more universal it was, and the more that people asked why was everything so bad if they'd never had it so good, the more seriously was the voice of the Church taken.

The 1970s are often described as the period of development of the democratic opposition. In reality, it began in the 1960s. The 'Letter of the 34 intellectuals' in defence of culture was the first occasion when a dignified and integrated group of intellectuals protested to the authorities. The 1970s were the period when the democratic opposition matured and developed, especially after 1976, after the strike at Radom and the foundation of KOR. But far far earlier, beginning, roughly, in 1956, there had been constant practical and constructive work on the part of the Church. This had a number of levels, and it was carried out in accordance with the religious and moral ideals which would later become embodied in the decrees of the Second Vatican Council. Certainly this movement in the Polish Church owes a great deal of gratitude to Cardinal Wyszyński, but its inspirer, organizer, moral and intellectual leader was the then Bishop, and subsequently Cardinal and Pope, Karol Wojtyła.

This was multilateral work, but it was planned on clear strategic principles. It patiently increased and raised the quantity and quality of intellectual training of the clergy. It built up and renewed the intellectual elite of the Church. It gradually increased its publishing work. It won over artists and intellectuals in the universities. It paid careful attention to work with young people and families, basing it on careful and substantial preparation. It adopted new and updated methods of teaching religion, which were free of the old authoritarianism and formalism and filled with concepts from modern psychology, pedagogics, sociology, etc. Different approaches were developed for the teaching of religion in different milieux, and in some cases it was brought up to an excellent level, for example, in the academic settings of Warsaw and Kraków. The idealistic, cognitive and moral content of this teaching was enriched in an attempt to reach out to different professional milieux. A formula was worked out, in which, due to its appeal to personalistic philosophy, there was room for the idea of the individual, the *individuum*, and the idea of the community. This ideology was integrated with the idea of the nation as a sociocultural community and as a maker of history, which has the right to create its own history and to possess a democratic and sovereign national state. This well-thought out and well-founded ideology harmonized with the ideas of the movements which were coming to life in Poland during the 1970s – with the ideas of the movement for human and civil rights, with the ideas of political pluralism voiced by the democratic opposition and with – at least some – of the ideas of the neo-nationalism of the Confederation of Independent Poland. The Church proposed an ideology which was broader, philosophically and morally richer, and also more profound, being rooted both in the national traditions of Poland and in the culture of the West. The 1970s, instead of being the years of victorious secularism, appealing to the consumerism of the urban population, became instead years of religious revival. This was not an obvious development; it did not come about simply because 'the Poles were, and always have been, religious and Catholics'. It came about as a result of the work of the Church and the integration of that Church with the development of the non-material (higher-order) needs of the Poles.

In the years 1945–60, as I have said, a process of secularization took place. This created the expectation, in the minds of politicians and researchers, that things were going the same way as in the West. Secularization was regarded by many of them as an irreversible developmental property of Western societies. It was considered that the process of secularization of society in Poland would take place in step with the processes of urbanization. The researches of Stefan Nowak, a scholar who had no personal commitment to this view, published in 1961, confirm that at that time approximately one in four of the students in Warsaw were non-believers, and another half betrayed fairly profound symptoms of non-involvement. This process slowed down during the 1960s, and reversed itself during the 1970s. The laws of sociology governing the West did not work in Poland. During the 1970s a young people's movement of religious renewal took shape and developed rapidly, under the protection of the Church, but with considerable autonomy, spontaneity and pluralism. This movement shaped the outlook of hundreds of thousands of elementary and secondary school pupils, students, young workers and intellectuals. It began to penetrate into and influence the functioning of schools, universities and workplaces.

What does it mean, however, that the activity of the Church was integrated with the process of development of the non-material needs of the Poles? That is a whole subject in itself and one can barely sketch out an answer. We must return again to our starting-point, to the issue which a great many modern intellectuals ignore, partly due to a lack of systematic sociological knowledge. It is a matter of the peasant nature and the poverty of post-war Poland. Firstly, one has to realize from what depths of destitution the greater part of this nation had emerged. The development of the needs of civilized society and learning how to satisfy them have been a significant factor in Polish history only for the last forty years.

Secondly, in parallel with material progress, although trailing it somewhat, there developed a taste for non-material needs and a concept of the value of quality of life in the individual sphere. The workers and intellectuals of the 1970s and 1980s were no longer satisfied with the fact that they were urbanites and that they had professions and jobs, that they had bettered themselves. They began to be concerned about the conditions in which their personalities, especially their professional personalities, could develop properly. It became ever more painful to endure that much of their work was fruitless, that they could not work as well as they wished, that their educational achievements and good will went for nothing. This attacked their dignity and blocked the development of their talents. With the passage of time, their dissatisfaction became ever stronger, and moved from individual to group protests. In the end it developed into an awareness that the misfortunes of everyone, of the whole nation, were the result of the colossal waste of the potential of the entire nation. This stimulated the development of a modern national consciousness.

Thirdly, in 1945 a very large proportion of the then peasant society had no national consciousness in the modern sense of the word. The Polish intellectual habitually fears to admit this fact lest someone questions the existence and age of his nation. But the truth of it is that in 1945 the Poles were a nation at once both very old and very young. The very old nation consisted of the strata of the landowners, the intelligentsia, and part of the petty bourgeoisie. But the workers and peasants started to become a nation, in the sense of being a cultural, historical and ideological community, only at the end of the nineteenth century. Chałasinski got to grips with this problem, when he wrote about the birth of the personality of the peasant Polish citizen during the twenty years between the wars. The war may have hurried this process forward a little, but it certainly did not bring it to completion. Socialism in its first period – that of Stalinism – associated with the mass advance of the peasants to become workers and intellectuals, may have moderated or even hampered this process.

A number of additional factors, apart from those mentioned above, affected the development of the national consciousness and national aspirations of the new workers and new intelligentsia. Particularly important is that the educational revolution produced a major homogenization of the Polish language, which favours the participation of all groups in the same community of national symbolic culture. Of great significance, too, was the fact that *the Church took part in this process* of developing the non-material needs and the awakening of national consciousness in the ordinary people – peasants, workers and the 'new intelligentsia'. In the homilies of Pope John Paul II to the Poles, he stresses the importance he gives to the development *of historical awareness and the development of political and national aspirations*. Without this change of approach the reception of homilies of the Churchmen would be much colder today. The Church, which was once an authoritarian leader, must today appeal to the imagination and meet the newly developed needs of the faithful.

The 1970s, which were meant to be a triumphal march of the developing socialist welfare state, conducive to the decline of the Church, turned instead into an era when the Church's significance flourished. When towards the end of his reign Edward Gierek sought the backing of Cardinal Wyszyński, there were several reasons: the difficult economic situation of the country and political problems of the state, and a major erosion of communist ideology. This erosion removed the influence of the Party on the outlook of the Polish people but left that of the Church virtually untouched. The election of Cardinal Karol Wojtyła as Pope and his visit as John Paul II to Poland in 1978 led to a considerable increase in awareness of the community, value and strength of the Polish people, hastening this process still further.

The Church during the struggle for the reform of the trade union system

The events of the years, say, 1976–85 are well known from the famous books of Micewski in Poland and Garton-Ash in Great Britain. The first traces the history of Cardinal Wyszyński and the Church in Poland up to the Cardinal's death. The second is a vivid account of the history of Solidarity and the participation of the Church in it. I shall concentrate rather on the later years, even omitting the first years of the 1980s, the period of martial law.

The Communist system, by the end of the 1970s, entered into a phase of stagnation and crisis from which it could escape only by means of a very profound economic and political reform. The further existence of an economy of waste and a centralist authoritarian state had, in Poland, a large question-mark after it. Of course, there was the alternative that all the millions of Poles who could not endure the conditions of life in Poland could have emigrated. But this macabre possibility was, however, extremely unlikely. On the other hand, internally things had gone too far. The Polish Communists had committed the 'grave error' of permitting or even facilitating the development of a modern national consciousness and the awakening of citizens' political aspirations. They had not managed to destroy either the Church or the independent political movements.

It is hard to say how far the Church leaders foresaw and now perceive this state of affairs in all its complexity. Certainly in the 1970s they foresaw a considerable proportion of what today is reality. But maybe they did not foresee that it would come to pass so quickly.

Already in the first years of martial law the Church faced difficult problems. In the prevailing conditions, the democratic opposition took shelter under the mantle of the Church. Churches began to function as tranquil and safe meeting places and assembly points before demonstrations. Masses took on the significance of demonstrations. The opposition movement, not excluding, of course, the independent self-governing trade union Solidarity, was weakened, but nevertheless endured, institutionalized itself, and differentiated itself internally. Every one of its groups found in the Church psychological and material help when the authorities applied their usual penalties: imprisonment, fines, beating with truncheons. Nevertheless, all these groups preserved their independence and identity.

The role of the Church today consists to a considerable extent of the strengthening of optimism, counselling young people to remain in Poland, and working to raise national morale. This is difficult work, since the Polish people are raising themselves only slowly from feelings of despair. But it has not been fruitless work, especially since 1985, when martial law formally came to an end. The process of reform is moving very slowly in Poland. Basically, since 1981, the authorities have wasted almost all their time looking for a way to change the system that would not change its essence. But they have had no success: there have been neither political nor economic improvements. So far, no reform has proved a source of hope. [Eds: This text was written before the reforms of Spring, 1989.]

But these years have not been a total loss, however. The authorities are learning slowly, but they are learning something. At the beginning they repudiated the idea of political reforms completely; now they are trying to introduce them. Of course, these are surface changes only, since it is impossible to promise substantial democratic reforms without paying the penalty, and this they are not prepared to do.

Nor were these years entirely wasted for society. After a period of shock, in which it sought a refuge under the wing of the Church, Polish society is returning, as it were, to seeking new forms of action separate from the Church. Today the Church is again playing the role of a mediator and partner with respect to the communist state. Although against its will, the state has to call on the help of the Church in order to maintain social calm. This does not mean in the least that the Church acts as a prop for Communism. It continues its work of preparing the people to change, reshape, and ultimately to reject this system. For at the root of the historical vision of the Church seems to lie the conviction that such transformation is possible, but that it will take the form of a long process of evolution.

Translated by Vera Rich.

5

Solidarity's adventures in wonderland

Jerzy Holzer

Institute of History, Warsaw University

Poland in the 1970s

The beginning was extraordinary. The system of the dictatorship of the proletariat, of the working class ruling through its representatives – through the Communist Party – is part of communist theory. But since, according to Marxism, the state is an instrument of class rule and it is intended to restrain hostile classes, anyone attacking Communism is by definition an enemy of the working class. Thus the events of December 1970 in Poland, although carried out by workers, would be considered as being anti-working class. This idea would be consistent with the principles applied many times to strikes and protests in communist countries. In fact, there had been only one exception to this rule, one which had also happened in Poland – the way the events in Poznań in 1956 were evaluated. Then the authorities first of all struck with an 'avenging fist of justice', only to reverse its policy when it recognized the extenuating circumstances a few months later and reprieved those individuals and groups sentenced.[1]

It was different in December 1970: no one could have any doubts that it was the workers from Gdańsk and Szczecin (and the workers of all Poland with their ominous silence) who overthrew the ruling group, although it was not they who appointed the new one. The Communist Party's mandate to rule in the name of the working class had been questioned. The ideological legitimization of the authorities had suffered a blow when it was admitted that the party could not have been representing the interests of the workers.[2] Ideology needed to be backed by a public show of consensus: Edward Gierek asked, '*Pomożecie?*' ('Will you help?') not rhetorically, as by other communist rulers to a carefully chosen group of people, but to a public meeting. '*Pomożemy!*' ('We will help!') the Gdańsk workers answered him. This took a weight off

97

Gierek's shoulders, but was to hang another round his neck ever after and to pull him down.

December 1970 softened the foundations on which the communist system in Poland was based, but Gierek's group soon seemed to have forgotten this after a temporary shock. Substantial changes, including the replacement of officials, were promised in the trade unions, but it was soon apparent that they were maintaining their bureaucratic ways, and the new leaders produced by the events were either intimidated, bribed, or got rid of in various ways (there were even several mysterious deaths). The slogan of consultation with the working class was widely applied, but it was the party's own apparatus – either party or union – that negotiated with the authorities. Gierek and his collaborators enjoyed the feeling of power, as if they did not realize that they were deluding themselves.

It was the Polish 'economic miracle' of the years 1971–4 that helped to build these illusions. Polish Communists propagated a new economic policy: they tried to achieve technological modernization through contacts with the West, and to embark on a second industrial revolution by an enormous industrial programme and by developing consumption as a way to increase people's qualifications and efficiency. Yet these new trends went together with the old conservative economic structure, the maintenance of authoritarian management methods characteristic of the previous period, and a lack of flexibility. These contradictions had several consequences. First of all, generous Western credits became an important element in financing modernization. Debts mounted up, and it became more difficult to repay them, as the Polish economy did not become noticeably more capable of foreign expansion, of reacting quickly, nor of improving the quality of its products. The 'economic miracle' was therefore a relative one, as no miracle is needed to invest and spend someone else's money. Second, the amount of money put at the disposal of the bureaucratic apparatus stimulated corruption at all levels of the Party, administrative and economic hierarchy. Thirdly, reluctance to halt the mounting debt, together with the deeply entrenched bureaucracy and the growing corruption, led to random decision-making, contradictions and a lack of coherence in the economy, and, finally, to growing costs and declining productivity.[3] For a long time Western economists and politicians could not believe that modernization could result in a decline in economic efficiency. But this was one of the strange aspects of the 'economic miracle'.

Gierek's clique had come to power through the workers' rebellion, and accepted the reasons for their protests. Yet when its economic policy failed, it repeated its predecessors' mistakes with even less concern.[4] Gomułka never promised to seek the advice of the working class and to discuss his ideas with them. On the contrary, he always stressed the superiority of the well-informed and intelligent ruling party, compared with Polish society which lacked political consciousness. With Gomułka one could see the way the workers' and other groups' opinions were denigrated. Gierek can be accused of deliberate cheating, even if it was that of a petty provincial magician with shaky hands, rather than that of a great illusionist. He announced pseudo-consultations, which were really instructions. He tried to raise prices in June 1976 on a much larger scale than had been attempted five years earlier, and he reacted in a very traditional way to the next workers' rebellion (although moderately, in that guns were not used). It was dealt with by baton charges, tear gas, arrests and sackings from factories, police lynch-law in gaols and a mockery of court proceedings, but, above all, with an outrageous propaganda campaign stigmatizing those who claimed to be workers as hooligans and criminals. Gierek and his collaborators seemed to forget that they had tried to legitimize their power not only by the dogma of the dictatorship of the proletariat but also by the public support of real workers and of real Polish socialism. Now they abandoned the Gdańsk slogan of 'We will help', but did not thereby regain their communist purity.

Unless the decisions of June 1976 were a sign of inexplicable stupidity on the part of the ruling group, then there can only be one other argument in their defence. The standard of living of all society, including the workers, had improved in the early 1970s as never before under communist rule (except the very first years after the Second World War).[5] Gierek's group seemed to believe that the masses would be ready to make relatively small sacrifices compared with the benefits they had gained. This might have proved correct save for the pressures from the result of two simultaneous ideological and propaganda ideas – both produced by conscious policies of the communist rulers. These ideas were contradictory, the one older and entrenched, the other coming with Gierek's innovations. Instead of neutralizing one another, they simultaneously attacked the weak foundations of the decisions of June 1976 from opposite directions.

Egalitarianism was a traditional propaganda weapon. According to this, Communism was to remove poverty as well as excessive wealth. In spreading this idea of egalitarianism the Communists in Poland won one of their few ideological and propaganda victories. As Gierek's group dared not directly condemn egalitarianism, it began to promote consumer-orientated and non-egalitarian ideas. These were not only intended to increase economic expectations but also to alleviate the frustrations which were previously expressed in fierce social unrest. The aim was to create a society obsessed with making and spending money, and divided into small families, and to deprive people of any ideological or intellectual aspirations. Consequently the indoctrination model had to be changed. Television was to be its main instrument: it was intended to keep millions of people stuck in front of the screen, to stuff them with propaganda about the government's success as well as with cheap entertainment. The consumer-orientated ideas were also welcomed by the administrative apparatus. The latter had always been preferentially treated in communist Poland, but the prevailing egalitarianism had forced them to conceal this and to pretend to live modestly like ordinary citizens. The 1970s saw the emergence of ideological support for legalized privileges, and thus enabled many not to deny themselves various luxuries. Consumption was also a useful façade to use to hide corruption, acquisition of public property, and using one's position to gain benefits for oneself and one's family.

The events of June 1976 and then increasing signs of economic crisis led to social resentment, caused by a strange mixture of both egalitarianism and consumerism. The ordinary citizen queued for hours to buy necessities, and could wait decades for a flat or a car paid for in advance. Participation in the workings of the state apparatus, or contacts with those in power, enabled one to acquire everything that the ordinary citizen only dreamed of. Modernized Communism brought less egalitarianism than the traditional form, but did not provide the chance of meeting the newly awakened consumer appetites even if people had earned enough money.

Even one of the Gierek group's potentially strongest cards turned against it. The policies of 'peaceful coexistence', widening contacts with the West, had been interpreted much more freely in Poland than in other communist countries. This was the result of the new economic policies, attempts to acquire western credit, the problems associated with paying this back later, and requests for aid and other special concessions. In return Poland was expected to be a model (communist) country putting into effect the Helsinki agreement on human rights. Yet these reasons alone do not explain the enormous number of Poles (four million) who went on trips to the capitalist states in the 1970s. Freedom of contact and travel acted as a safety-valve for young people who wanted to visit other countries. They were also a way of meeting the demands for consumer products from the more enterprising Poles, who took up various jobs in the West, or profited by various trade exchanges. The opening of Poland to the West allowed many Poles to profit materially and spiritually. It also allowed them to become aware of the inefficiency of the communist economy, and to discover the workings of democratic societies, what rights they had, and the extent of public criticism, and of control over the authorities.

As if this was not enough for Gierek and his supporters to worry about, in 1978 the Poles acquired a new focus for, and representative of, their hopes and interests, independent of the authorities. This was the election of the Archbishop of Kraków, Karol Wojtyła, as Pope. Relations between the Communists and the Catholic Church had never been better than in the 1970s during Gierek's rule, although Polish Catholics still experienced various restrictions and the irritating, if ineffective, attempts to promote atheism. There had been many reconciliatory gestures and concrete concessions. The election of John Paul II not only caused unprecedented difficulties in restricting the Church's activity in what was the communist state which had the most liberal policy towards it, but also led to a great upsurge of religious fervour and made Polish society more than ever independent of the Communists. The Polish people now turned to the Pope rather than the state for guidance on morality. Finally, the Pope's visit to Poland in June 1979, both a pilgrimage and a state visit, instead of bolstering Gierek as a partner of the pontiff, resulted in a further decline in his popularity. The authorities, unable to accept that their efforts to gain total control over society had collapsed, tried ineffectively to play down the effects of the Pope's visit in the media, and at the same time equally ineffectively stressed their own contacts with John Paul II.

All these difficulties of the government were also characteristic of its policy towards the opposition. In 1976, when the first opposition organizations were founded, especially the *Komitet Obrony Robotników* (Committee for Defending the Workers) (KOR), set up by intellectuals of different generations to defend those workers punished after the June events, the authorities lacked any clear idea of what to do. Members and sympathizers of KOR, who acted openly and illegally, were stopped and beaten up by the police, sacked from their jobs, and denigrated in the press and at public meetings. Yet these were minor actions, compared with the known practices of earlier periods of communist Poland's history, still being used in other countries of the eastern bloc. The opposition was not purged from society, its members were not given long prison sentences or sent to psychiatric hospitals. There did seem to be a return to the old practices with the mysterious death of the Kraków student Stanisław Pyjas in May 1977 and the arrest of KOR activists after protests over this tragic event. But by July an amnesty was declared, all opposition members were released, as were those workers still in prison from June the previous year.

The situation therefore returned to where it had started. Poland remained the most liberal state in the Soviet bloc, and therefore (but not only for this reason) opposition increased there. The opposition was persecuted enough, however, for it to wear the mantle of martyrdom. By the late 1970s, contrary to all the principles of the communist system, opposition had become a permanent element in the country's life. Underground publishing activity became extensive enough to influence opinion in wider social groups than its own immediate supporters.

The form of the opposition was as strange, given the background of the

Soviet bloc's and Poland's previous experience, as was the attitude of Gierek's group towards it. It seemed that all possible kinds of opposition had been tried before: an insurrection or revolution in East Germany in 1953 and in Hungary in 1956, and, to some extent, in Poland in 1970; revisionism in Poland in 1956 and in Czechoslovakia in 1968; and the minimalist attempts of various groups of intellectuals or Catholics, especially (but not only) in Poland in the 1960s and 1970s. Now a new concept emerged, in various shapes but similar enough to be covered by the formula expressed by Adam Michnik as 'the new evolutionism'. The strangest fact was that the various opposition groups, large or small, soon stressed their differences, as if unconcerned about the presence of their initial, and much more dangerous enemy, the communist system.

Yet what all these concepts shared was the idea of inspiring and creating organizations in the community independent of the authorities. They wanted to exert external pressures on the structures of the communist system, not intending to push them to act in a specific way, but rather to persuade them not to interfere with their own activities. KOR only alluded to future sovereignty for the Polish state; it was the *Ruch Obrony Praw Człowieka i Obywatela* (The Movement for the Defence of People's and Citizens' Rights), and especially *Konfederacja Polski Niepodległej* (Confederation of Independent Poland) after it separated from it, that stressed this point explicitly. Yet even the leader of KPN, Leszek Moczulski, called like other opposition activists for the creation of independent Polish institutions by the side of the existing ones, and only after the expected 'revolution without a revolution' were they to establish a government in an independent Poland. Moczulski did not, however, specify how and when it was to take place, and because of silence on this point, the independence programme provided more of an inspiration than a plan for action. The most moderate group, *Konwersatorium Doświadczenie i Przyszłość* (Experience and the Future Discussion Group), was closer to revisionism. Nevertheless, its appeals to the authorities for reasonable reform were accompanied by calls for independent social action.

As the opposition could not argue over the ultimate direction of its activities, it was ideological and personal issues which gained in importance. These were related to the past and to personal backgrounds since contemporary differences amounted to little. The latter were carefully concealed, as they did not fit in with the debate over principles undertaken against the Communists, the fundamental reason for the opposition's existence, i.e. the principle of freedom as against oppression, diversity as against uniformity, truth as against lies. At a time when ideology had become of little importance both in West European politics and in the politics of the Communist Parties of Eastern Europe, it appeared to gain the upper hand among the Polish opposition. Yet this was only a matter of outward appearances. Some opposition groups adopted the nationalist tradition, although without authoritarianism or chauvinism with its radical anti-semitism. Others considered themselves heirs of the socialist tradition, although with complete acceptance of democracy, without class theory, and with a definite opposition to Communism. Finally there were those who adopted Piłsudski as their idol, not the dictator of 1926–35, but the pre-1914 socialist and fighter for Polish independence, creator of the independent, democratic state of 1918. Potted history and potted ideology removed previous differences, and almost met on the same level: respect for the people's rights and political democracy, national solidarity, and acceptance of values derived from Christianity and western culture. The ideological debate was reduced to invective on the one hand, and to subtle attempts to conceal differences on the other.

These internal disputes were unknown to wider circles of society, even if they knew of the existence of the opposition. People who opposed Communism were sometimes admired, but more often treated cautiously as if they were desperadoes. They might be listened to, asked to correct information about the present and the past, but hardly anyone was ready to follow them. The opposition found support mainly among the intelligentsia and students, and nothing seemed to point to the existence of organized mass activity of the workers. It was only in Gdańsk that these groups had a relatively greater importance, and these pretentiously called themselves *Wolne Związki Zawodowe* (Free Trades Unions). What were more feared were spontaneous riots like those of December 1970 and June 1976, when the masses took to the streets, burned party headquarters and clashed with the police. In its *Karta praw robotniczych* (Charter of Workers' Rights), published in August 1979, the opposition saw the creation of larger-scale independent trade unions as a distant aim. Their tasks were set out very moderately. Current workers' problems and the idea of activity within the framework of the official union were stressed.

The self-limiting revolution, i.e. the social compact between the government and society

The summer of 1980 and its events surprised both the authorities and society. It is even harder to understand what Gierek's group wanted to accomplish at this time, than in 1976. It began with a furtive attempt to introduce a limited rise in prices, so as to prevent, at least temporarily, a crash of the market, especially the food market. Yet the whole undertaking lacked a far-reaching plan, even though these were the proper, if instinctive, actions of a drowning man. When these led to an unexpectedly large wave, the drowning man completely lost his senses.

103

The first strikes at the beginning of July 1980 produced a conciliatory reaction and wage rises for the protesting factories. Perhaps it was assumed that news of this would not spread, but in a country the size of Poland, and with foreign broadcasts transmitted in Polish (despite attempts to jam them), this was an illusion. Thus the number of strikers grew, while Gierek's group, as if forgetting its initial intentions, proved willing to swamp Poland with paper money and the inevitable inflation in order to get the workers to give up their political ambitions. It led to further strikes. If all the workers received increased wages because of the strikes, the country would explode: either the authorities would have to raise prices again, or the workers would end up with worthless pieces of paper.

The opposition, especially KOR, which attempted to collect and disseminate information, to contact their supporters in factories and to formulate demands, showed signs of activity from the very beginning of these events. The need for an independent trade union was only mentioned timidly in their demands, although workers were advised to elect their own representatives in factories. But it was more the problem of economic reform that was stressed, followed by demands for the end of political repression. Even on 18 August 1980, when it was known that the *Międzyzakładowy Komitet Strajkowy* (Inter-factory Strike Committee) had sprung up in Gdańsk, KOR still did not seem to believe in the possibility of formulating political demands and getting the government to accept them. Instead it insisted on discussion of bonuses, and free debate on the economic reform programme with the authorities. Even in Gdańsk the intellectual advisers of the striking workers hesitated over whether to back the demand for the creation of an independent trade union, as was being demanded by the workers.

The authorities resisted making political concessions, but the opposition itself did not believe in the possibility of forcing them through. The workers, who neither took to the streets nor burnt Party headquarters, still remained an unpredictable element. Organized in striking factories, they at the same time made spontaneous demands which ignored the unchangeable realities of the communist system. And it was they who succeeded in getting the August agreement signed with the authorities, an agreement which allowed the creation of free trade unions. After the blow suffered by the authorities' legitimization of workers' protests in 1970, this was a complete defeat. The workers wanted an institution separate from the Party to defend their rights. In 1970 it was acknowledged that the Party could not represent the workers in all situations; in 1980 it was accepted as a rule. The recognition of the leading role of the Party by the Gdańsk agreement, but only in the state, not in the community, confirmed a division into Party and state on the one side and society on the other.[6]

The victory of the striking workers over the communist system took place despite the opposition's previous political ideas. According to the 'new evolutionism' the emergence of an independent society was to take place slowly and gradually. The communist government apparatus was to be opposed, squeezed strongly enough from the outside to force it back, but gently enough so as not to frighten it too much. Neither following the Party line nor challenging it was the essence of the 'new evolutionism'. In reality the birth of a free trade union, the birth of Solidarity, was the greatest upheaval in the history of Poland's communist system, and as it questioned the foundations of the system, it was, at the same time, a challenge to the authorities. The period of the legal existence of Solidarity turned into a spasmodic effort to reconcile two contradictory elements – the political ideas of the opposition and socio-political realities. To solve those contradictions a new concept of 'self-limiting revolution' was added to 'new evolutionism'.[7] These theoretical considerations were accompanied by hopes of avoiding confrontation with the physical strength of the state apparatus represented by the police and the army.

As early as August 1980 the outlines of the play had been sketched, but an ingenious director could have filled in or erased a lot. The instinct of self-preservation pushed the authorities to destroy Solidarity. There was never any question of coming down on the side of a free society rather than on that of Moscow's conservative ideas. From authority's point of view it made no sense to present the choice to 'accept or not to accept the existence of Solidarity'. It was merely a matter of 'how and when to destroy it'. There were different ways of achieving this. They could try to control elements within Solidarity by using people as agents, by corrupting or blackmailing them or by playing on their ambitions. Attempts at this were begun early on in several places at the same time, but on an especially large scale at the Upper Silesia coal-mining centre of Jastrzębie. It was also possible to resort in turn to concessions and pressure, so as to provoke inner tactical and personal conflicts, which would lead to one group being brought under control and another destroyed. This is why Wałęsa was praised for his reasonableness, while at the same time the leaders of the pre-August opposition, Kuroń, Michnik, Moczulski, and activists close to them, were attacked.

When this failed, two more approaches remained: either to use domestic armed strength or to ask for direct Soviet intervention. The only surprising factor was that the onslaught on Solidarity was carried out by the most flexible Polish communist rulers. Those more hidebound by ideological dogma, or more impatient and afraid of losing power, had been eliminated earlier on, either through direct or indirect pressure from Solidarity.

Solidarity played the main role in the spectacle, but, as in a Greek tragedy, fate directed events. Nothing could prevent it, as every success brought Solidarity closer to final defeat just as much as every failure. When it was not on the offensive, it was forced to defend itself. This is what happened after the registration court hearing of 24 October 1980. An attempt was then made to ridicule the barely established trade union by adding a formula about the leading role of the Party in the state to its statutes (although this was accepted in the Gdańsk agreement, it was completely senseless as part of Solidarity's own statutes). This is what happened, when in the second half of November 1980, the public prosecutor general's guidelines, '*Uwagi o dotychczasowych zasadach ścigania uczestników nielegalnej działalności antysocjalistycznej*' (Notes concerning previous principles for prosecuting participants in illegal anti-socialist activities), prepared for provincial public prosecutors, became known, and thus betrayed the government's preparations to suppress all persons it considered dangerous. This is what happened, in the most brutal way in Bydgoszcz on 19 May 1981, when police action led to several Solidarity activists, including the regional president Jan Rulewski, being beaten up.

The nonsense of defensive action was realized earlier among the originators of Solidarity's political ideas. In September 1980 Adam Michnik wrote:

What does all this show? It is evident, that every attempt to rule against the wishes of society has to lead to a catastrophe; it is also evident, that every attempt to overthrow communist rule in Poland is an attack upon the interests of the USSR. Pluralism in all spheres of social life is possible, liquidation of the preventive censorship is possible, rational economic reform and just social policy are possible, a competitive press and television speaking the truth are possible, freedom of science and autonomy of universities are possible, social control and organised defence of consumers' interests are possible, independent courts and police stations, where people are not beaten, are possible. . . We have to wrest and extort these from the government, as no nation has ever been given its rights as a present. Yet while wresting and extorting, let us remember not to tear apart what makes the Polish state; not a sovereign independent one, but a state, without which our lot would have been far worse.[8]

But these excellent words had a lot of wishful thinking about them. Could the movement which worked to 'wrest and extort' remain within the limits set out by Michnik? When would it be so organized and disciplined to be able to call a halt, when facing a retreating enemy? Moreover, could the aims pronounced by Michnik have been reconciled with the state interests, political, ideological, and, consequently, military, of the Soviet Union? In fact the aims meant the destruction of the whole communist system in Poland, and if Moscow tolerated them they would be a disastrous example for the whole Soviet bloc, and lead to the dissolution of the system in each member state and of the whole international communist system.

If defence was a nonsense, attack was equally absurd, as the principle of the 'self-limiting revolution' always tended to minimalize the use of the consequences of success. The amount of energy expended was not worth the results, especially because of the continual awareness of the government's physical superiority, enabling it to choose the right moment to destroy Solidarity at one stroke. The attacks (or counter-attacks) yielded fewer and fewer results in any case. When Jaruzelski's group achieved power, the authorities themselves started to exploit the principle of the 'self-limiting revolution', pushing every conflict almost to the point of a direct clash. This happened first during the Bydgoszcz conflict, was repeated a number of times, and reached flashpoint on 21 November 1981: the Warsaw police attacked the building of the Fire Brigade Officers' School, which was on strike. In doing so they ignored the risk of a general Solidarity strike in Warsaw and the whole Mazowsze region.

There were other factors which made Solidarity's situation hopeless. On the one hand the experiences of 1956 and 1970, and on the other the Czech experience of 1968, created a feeling of disbelief in the possibility of real changes within the Party. Either the Party's activities could be simulated by a democratic mimicry, in other words they were fraudulent (manipulation was one of the popular notions of that period). Or, if the Party really reformed itself and Poland, then it would cease to act as a safeguard against Soviet intervention. It was Jan Józef Lipski, one of the outstanding representatives of KOR, who expressed the views of many of Solidarity's activists and advisers in an open letter to the Party in November 1980: 'It seems that the reforming elements within the PZPR, especially among the ordinary members, do not always realize what should be the methods and limits of the necessary reform within the Party.' He went on to claim: 'The PZPR should not only remain here and now, today and tomorrow, holding political power, but it remains one of the necessary conditions for the security of the state. Its conservatism and the self-limiting of its reform projects are such a condition as well.' Finally Lipski put forward his strongest argument: 'The country's welfare demands it.'[9]

Lipski's opinions were shared by many in the leadership of the Party. Memories of the fate of Dubcek and his group prevented any inclination to adopt risky political measures. Only the members of some university and workers' Party groups proposed more determined reform ideas, including that of changing the Party from inside by creating so-called 'horizontal structures', agreements at the lower levels, which would ignore the Party hierarchy and its apparatus. Yet these 'horizontal structures' soon found themselves in a blind alley. They were condemned and attacked by the Party authorities, distrusted or despised by Solidarity, and were unable to play any important role. Other processes in the Party were more important, such as the mass resignation of those members who felt themselves closer to Solidarity. This took place above all in 1981, when over 400,000 members, about 13 per cent, left the Party. Even these figures are probably too low, as many Party members stopped being active, but did not resign formally. They constituted a large part of the further 350,000, who, according to official figures, resigned in 1982.

The most active and independent-minded members of the Party had therefore purged themselves from it. The Party leaders could have made the 'horizontal structures' harmless, because they had decided to use democratic rules in the discussions and elections of deputies before the Party's IX Congress, which took place in July 1981. Although in fact it was mainly the employees of the apparatus and representatives of the so-called 'party-concrete' who lost in the elections, the reformers fared no better. The result was that this, the most democratic Congress in the PZPR's history, elected a Central Committee with no outstanding personalities, but instead rather harmless characters who, as the future was to prove, were conformist and ready to accept without protest such a major change of policy as the introduction of martial law.

Solidarity's paralysis was apparent from summer 1981, and the reaction to this was growing aggressiveness. This was expressed in two, equally unproductive, directions. The first was growing controversies within Solidarity itself. And, as in the late 1970s, the differences of opinion were hard to define precisely. Wałęsa and his advisers were accused of being too conciliatory, yet positive solutions were not that easy to find, and were hardly convincing. There were also accusations of a more personal character: Wałęsa was accused of leading in a non-democratic way and some of his advisers of acting underhandedly. More dangerous was the stirring up of mass hatred. The emerging anti-intelligentsia tendencies can easily be linked with a populist demagogy (often provoked by other members of the intelligentsia, who tried to use them against Wałęsa's advisers). Nationalist demagogy went even further: rivals were accused of lacking patriotic feelings, and these accusations were often accompanied by recalling real or supposed sins from the past, for example of collaboration with the Communists. Hidden behind all this one could find anti-semitic feelings which, directed against several members of the former KOR, or Wałęsa's advisers with Jewish origins, tried to discredit both groups. The nearer the December catastrophe of the introduction of martial law came, the more one could witness antagonisms, even absurd ones, within Solidarity.

The second way in which the unproductive aggression was expressed was spoken and written attacks on the communist authorities, accompanied by praise for Solidarity's own supposed strength. Even though

Solidarity had practically stood still from summer 1981 and had lost several minor disputes with the government, the tone of its declarations appeared more and more self-confident. In fact it posed no real threat to the authorities, but actually helped them, to some extent, to consolidate their own position. No actions of any note followed the declarations on the part of Solidarity. A favourite way of attacking the government by the written word was in publications about Polish-Soviet relations, and in others showing hostility to the Soviet Union. The opposition had already tried in the 1970s to tell the truth about contemporary history, and in doing so it did not shirk discussing the issue of the Soviet aggression against Poland in September 1939, repression of the Polish population and the crime of Katyn, which were taboo subjects as far as Moscow was concerned. But the opposition never focused their attention on these matters. Late in 1981 it might have appeared that the issues just mentioned were crucial ones and that the future of the country depended on resolving them. It is characteristic that during the last meeting of the national Solidarity Commission, on 11–12 December 1981, several speakers stressed the need to stop the manifestations of anti-Soviet feeling, while Kuroń declared they should not 'stamp their feet without reason', and not resort to demagogic slogans like 'Moscow will be ours tomorrow'.[10]

For a historian the last months of Solidarity's legal activity provide a very interesting example of how contemporaries interpret events to fit their own expectations of what will happen and consequently fail to work out alternative strategies. Although preparations to introduce martial law were not made openly, they were not done in total secrecy. Some leaks about these preparations could have been interpreted as intentional attempts at intimidation, but the government's resolution of 23 October 1981 about setting up military operations groups were of a different order. At first these groups operated in small towns, and provincial administrative areas, but from 23 November they began to operate in larger towns as well. Information available several days before the introduction of martial law provided an even clearer warning. On 10 December Solidarity's regional committees received information from the national committee about plan 'W' – the state of war – being put into effect in the army. On 12 December telexes reported movements of military and police forces. Waldemar Kuczyński, assistant editor of the weekly *Solidarity*, recalled conversations on the evening of 12 December in the Mazowsze regional headquarters: 'I came across several girls. One of them greeted me with a question: "Are you also in a panic because of the military and the police movements?". . . Under a collective pressure the political environment liquidated its own vigilance.'[11]

General Jaruzelski's Poland

On 13 December Solidarity had no idea what the communist authorities intended to do, while the General's clique knew very well what Solidarity would do. The great majority of Solidarity's members and activists wanted to believe that the union was safe from attack, and believed they had reliable defensive weapons in strikes and occupations of the large factories. It is usually generals who imagine future wars will be repeats of previous ones. Similarly, Solidarity, throughout the sixteen months that it functioned legally, organized itself to be able to conduct passive, non-violent resistance within the factories. In only a few days the weakness of this concept was very apparent. Solidarity proved an easy prey for the relatively small, but well-trained, highly mobile police forces with excellent equipment. It was dispersed and divided, lacking any means of communication once the telephone lines were cut, a curfew was imposed and striking factories blockaded.

Yet the successful organizational measures of Jaruzelski's group were not accompanied by any far-reaching political concept. Physical force was its decisive argument, and its actions could well have been interpreted at the beginning as a campaign to cow society. Even though there were comparatively few victims of the introduction of martial law in December, this was put down to Solidarity being unprepared to resist rather than the authorities' intention to avoid brutality. Moreover, the whole action did have its brutal aspects. Tanks forced their way into factories; strikes were broken up with tear gas and baton charges; and, when this proved insufficient, miners were killed in the Wujek coal-mine in Katowice. No less brutal was the ideology set out frankly by the government's minister for press relations, Jerzy Urban, when he said: 'The government will somehow manage to feed itself'. Martial law therefore awakened the worst fears. Later on there were forecasts of a milder version of the Stalinist purges or at least a more severe form of the Czech 'maintenance of order'.

Even though after the introduction of martial law General Jaruzelski was represented in Poland and abroad with blood on his hands, he did not become a Polish Pinochet or a bloody dictator. It must be admitted that such an image was a logical interpretation of the process initiated with violence and terror in December 1981. Jaruzelski's supporters have committed a large number of sins – thousands of people have been suppressed in one way or another by internment, arrests, imprisonment, beatings, murders, dismissal from jobs and so on. Despite all this, it has to be said that today, in the final analysis, the kind of communist system imposed on Poland by this group has been the least politically repressive since the emergence of the system itself.

The attributes of Jaruzelski's system, beside the limited nature of political repression, have been to allow more freedom of speech in the media, far-reaching freedoms for artists, academics and scientists and almost complete toleration for the Catholic Church. Yet this variant of Communism is still a repressive one. When the authorities gave up the idea of breaking the resistance of the reluctant majority of society by force (after the initial surprise, the use of force only stimulated further resistance rather than prevented it), they tried to seek a compromise on their own terms. The early pronouncements about trying to restore a legal Solidarity, and the amnesties, can both be interpreted in this light. Solidarity itself after the experience of December could not accept a compromise as this would merely have been an admission of its weakness. It would not have had the support of the more conformist or frightened people, and, at the same time, such a compromise would have been condemned by the more radical elements, who would have interpreted it as surrender.

In any case, a compromise which would have been acceptable to Solidarity was, until 1989, rejected by Jaruzelski. We have no way of knowing why. It could have been political considerations of his own, the Polish government apparatus even being afraid of Solidarity's shadow, or Moscow's instructions fully to condemn the Polish counter-revolution, personified by Solidarity, in case it provided an example to the whole Soviet bloc. The variant of Communism that emerged was less sensible than the rejected alternatives of ruling by force or legitimizing the government through a real national agreement. What emerged was a collection of gestures by which the head of state, after forcing himself on the nation, tried to take on the role of a father-figure. History, however, has reserved paternalism for popular and accepted individuals, backed either by the divinity of their office or by personal charisma.

Over the past few years Western observers have sometimes asked why Polish society does not finally recognize Jaruzelski's group, at least as a necessary evil, or even as the best solution in the reality of Eastern Europe. This question is as naïve as those posed at the end of the 1970s and in summer 1980, when they were surprised by the growing discontent with Gierek's regime – at that time the most liberal in the communist bloc. The answer is simple in both cases: the new ruling groups took on the responsibility for overcoming the Polish crisis, and could not cope with it. The issues of this crisis were not whether Polish intellectuals had, or did not have, the right to speak and write freely on history, sociology, philosophy or economics. They were also not whether the Catholic Church could, or could not, build a few hundred churches or broadcast to the masses over the radio.

The method applied by Jaruzelski's group could be called healing through sleep. If the crisis had been mainly a political one, then the country would have slowly settled down and social and economic life would have returned to normal. Yet the essence of the problem lay in the fact that, if we consider the pre-August 1980 situation as normal, then already at that time it was a 'crisis normality'. Jaruzelski's group was clear about this fact, since they declared the need for a profound change in both the economy and society. The transition from an economy of directive management to a market economy had to be followed by a shake-up in society, which is largely determined by participating in the governing apparatus, and through it in the disposition of national wealth.

Specialists will have to judge the value of the economic reforms suggested by Jaruzelski's group as a programme for tackling the crisis, yet this type of programme is useless unless it is accompanied by an analysis of society and its reactions to it. A programme for reform which will affect the interests of the representatives of the ruling elite, and uses the same elite to effect it, while other social groups remain passive, is hardly realistic politics.[12] Moreover, removing other groups from participation in forming and carrying out decisions, leads to their acting only if the reform programme directly threatens their own interests. As the reforms will reduce the egalitarian tendencies in the distribution of the national income, tensions will inevitably increase between the low and high income groups, between the employees of more and of less profitable factories and trades, between those employed in private and in state enterprises, co-operative and communal ones. It is equally inevitable that resentment will be directed against those responsible for drawing up the reforms. It was the resistance of the ruling elite and fear of too great social tensions, that paralysed the actions of Jaruzelski's group for five years. The energetic new attempt to carry out economic reform in autumn 1987 affects the same configuration of social forces which effectively blocked previous attempts. Thus the economic reform still has built into it a self-blocking mechanism.

The authorities' biggest success was weakening Solidarity. Ten years earlier the representatives of the 'new evolutionism' could not have dreamed of the political opposition of the 1980s being rooted in many parts of the country and in all social groups, of the hundreds of the illegal periodicals printed, and of millions of people (although not the whole of society) losing their fear of speaking their opinions out loud. They could not have dreamed such far-reaching limiting of political repression, lifting of censorship, introduction of rudimentary workers' self-government and the partial relaxation of the bureaucratic management of the economy. Changes (or should one prefer the word reforms?) introduced by Jaruzelski were without doubt carried out because of pressure from 'independent society': one could argue if this was direct pressure from post-December underground Solidarity, or indirect from the memories of the experience from the period when Solidarity existed legally.

Solidarity achieved too much after August 1980, and it also lost too much in December 1981, for the ideas of the 'new evolutionism' to achieve broader social approval. Success came to be thought of as the restoration of the pre-December situation, which had been produced by a single outburst of discontent, rather than by a slow evolutionary process. The political ideas of illegal Solidarity, of its leaders and advisers, became (even more than in the period of legal activity) enmeshed in insoluble controversies. The demands for restitution had wide implications since the restoration of legal Solidarity (after it had once been liquidated) would have been a contradiction of the whole communist system, greater even than of its existence between August 1980 and December 1981. All these demands were accompanied by renewed declarations about the need for seeking compromises, and about the need for caution in formulating demands and in actions undertaken by the opposition.

To overcome a crisis the size of the Polish one required actions of an exceptional nature, agreement between all the basic political and social forces, and a common willingness to make sacrifices. What would have been required was a realization in peacetime of a *Burgfrieden* or sacred union, as it had not been decided to carry out the kind of political repression, further bureaucratization of socio-economic life, and an indoctrination offensive. It had probably been correctly judged that that way could only be successful in conditions of 'cold war' mobilization, contrary to the general policy being adopted at the present time by the whole communist bloc. [Eds: This was written before the Round Table Agreements of 5 April 1989. For a comment on the Agreements, see our Afterword, p.261.]

Thus the rulers of Poland have no chance of overcoming the crisis in the foreseeable future, unless they can find a partner whose co-operation would ensure nation-wide agreement, or at least very wide support accompanied by a willingness to make sacrifices. Jaruzelski's group seemed to regard the Catholic Church as such a potential partner. The partnership was to be based on the Church lending its authority, while decision-making was to be left to the organs of the communist state. It would be oversimplifying matters to believe that the government thought in terms of a straight exchange: the Church's backing for Jaruzelski's political initiatives in return for unlimited freedom for the Church's widely accepted pastoral activities. More probably the government assumed that the Church felt so deeply responsible for all national life, that it would back these initiatives unconditionally for the sake of saving Poland from economic, moral and cultural decline.

But neither the contemporary world-wide acceptance of the principles that the Church should participate in political life, nor the state of mind of the Polish clergy and laity entitled the communist authorities to such far-reaching expectations. It was but another example of a false interpretation of reality – one in accordance with their own plans rather than with genuine observations. As an institution, the Church can calm social tensions by appeals for quiet, by charitable actions, or by declarations calling for national agreement. The Church can also actively try to stem the flood of alcoholism, dishonesty and brutality, although in these fields its successes in Poland have so far been limited. It is, however, hard to imagine that on the eve of the twenty-first century the Church should appeal to the nation from the altar to back the country's rulers; it is even harder to understand why it should give such a blank cheque to a communist and essentially atheistic state.

In reality it was Catholic activists, not the Church as an institution, who became potential partners. The Church itself neither could, nor wanted to, persuade these Catholic activists to co-operate unconditionally with the authorities, just as it could not, and did not want to, object to such co-operation undertaken by various groups. Yet such co-operation proved relatively worthless without the Church's blessing. A group of Catholic activists was involved in various official institutions – *Patriotyczny Ruch Odrodzenia Narodowego* (Patriotic Movement for the National Revival), the parliament's, *Rada Konsultacyjna* (Consultative Committee) – but always on their own account, without the total backing of the Church and a broader response in society. Often the people concerned were of great intellectual and moral stature, whose good intentions one cannot doubt, but all these activities were politically nugatory: despite many strange Polish absurdities, good intentions play a relatively small role in the effectiveness of politics on the banks of the Vistula.

And so, as time went by, it became more and more clear that Solidarity, despite its weakness and passivity, remained the only recognized symbol of the independence of society. This was confirmed during the Pope's last visit to Poland, not only by hundreds of banners displayed at rallies attended by him, but also in the applause given them by the crowds and the anger shown when the police intervened. Jaruzelski's group may well destroy Solidarity, if it sentences it to a longer period of inactivity, and thus neutralizes its ideas. However, the true paradox of the Polish situation lies in the fact that the defeat of Solidarity is also a defeat of the communist authorities. Besides the kind of compromise with Solidarity rejected in December 1981, only two others now seem possible: either a further crisis and Poland's humiliation in the world, as well as in the communist bloc, or a spontaneous rebellion, the catalyst of which may well be the young workers from the big towns, but which will probably result in a further crisis.

The wonderland which Solidarity's Poland was, has become a repulsive land. Poland's revolution did not end in blood but in a state of hopelessness and torpor.

Notes

1 Cf. Hiscocks, R. (1963) *Poland, Bridge for the Abyss. An Interpretation of Developments in Post-War Poland*, Oxford: Oxford University Press, 202.

2 This was noticed by Ascherson, N. (1982) *The Polish August. The Self-Limiting Revolution*, London: Harmondsworth, 104.

3 Pawel Bozyk, chairman of Gierek's team of economic advisers, wrote about it afterwards as if it was obvious; see his *Marzenia i rzeczywistość, czyli anatomia polskiego kryzysu* (*Dreams and Reality, or an Anatomy of the Polish Crisis*), Warsaw: PIW, 1983, 200–1.

4 This was seen immediately by Osadczuk, B. (1982) *Weisser Adler, Kreuz und rote Fahne. Chronik der Krisen des Kommunistischen Herrschaftssystem in Polen, 1956–1982*, Zurich: Ferlag Neuer Zürcher Zeitung, 88 (28.6.1976 text).

5 Cf. Sanford, G. (1983) *Polish Communism in Crisis*, London: Croom Helm, 29.

6 This was well observed by Ash, T.G. (1984) *The Polish Revolution: Solidarity*, New York: Scribner, 89.

7 Various problems with the interpretation of this concept of 'Self-limiting Revolution' are discussed by Touraine, A. Dubet, F. Wieviorka, M., and Strzelecki, J. (1983) *Solidarity. The Analysis of a Social Movement: Poland 1980-1981*, Cambridge: Cambridge University Press, 64–79.

8 Michnik, A. (1980) '*Czas nadziei*' (Time of Hope), *Biuletyn Informacyjny* 6(40), 4.

9 Lipski, J. J. (1980) '*Zamiast listu otwartego do członków partii*' (Instead of an Open Letter to the Party Members), *Biuletyn Informacyjny* 7(41), 77.

10 *Komisja Krajowa NSSZ 'Solidarność'. Posiedzenie w dniach 11–12 grudnia 1981 r., Archiwum Solidarności. Seria Dokumenty* (1986) ('Solidarity's' Country Committee. Mceting on 11–12 December 1981, Solidarity's Archive, Documents Series), Warsaw: Nowa, 111.

11 Based on manuscript owned by the author; Waldemar Kuczyński's memoirs were also published in Poland and abroad.

12 As Peter von der Lippe wrote: '*Was als offene Reformsdiskussion begann, an der alle Kreise der Bevölkerung beteiligt waren und als Reform gedacht war . . . ist zu einem Machtkampf zwischen verschiedenen Fraktionen der Burokratie geworden*', '*Die Wirtschaftspolitik der Regierung Jaruzelski 1982–1984*', in Bingen, D. (1985) (ed.), *Polen 1980–1984. Dauerkrise oder Stabilisierung. Strukturen und Ereignisse in Politik, Gesellschaft und Wirtschaft*, Baden-Baden: Nomos, 307.

Translated by Jakub Basista.

Part II

Culture and political economy

6

The incompatibility of system and culture and the Polish crisis

Wiktor Herer and Władysław Sadowski

Institute of National Economy, Central Planning Bureau, Warsaw

During the early 1980s Poland's economy suffered a collapse on a scale which no other European country had experienced since the end of World War II. In 1982, the national income produced was 25 per cent lower than in 1978, and although some recovery occurred during the years 1983–8, the per capita income in 1988 was, according to usually optimistic official statistics, still 10 per cent lower than in 1978. Perhaps even more significant than the statistical dimensions of the economic collapse is the fact that a question mark has been put over the whole future of the country. For this collapse, unlike an ordinary cyclical depression in a capitalist market economy, is not activating automatic mechanisms for recovery, but instead it appears to block the ways which may lead to improvement.

It is possible to point to manifestations of economic failure in the other socialist countries, but the effect there has been much less intense. This fact raises some important questions about the collapse of the Polish economy. Why was it so severe? Why did it take place in the early 1980s? To what extent were these events influenced by general factors relating to the economic and political system, and to what extent by factors relating specifically to Poland? Although the answers to these questions lie in the present, one must look first to the past for a clearer perspective.

The years between the wars

Poland's history since gaining independence in 1918 may be looked upon as the scene of a dramatic struggle against economic backwardness waged by a country which, despite a shared western European cultural heritage, and despite its ambitious economic and political aspirations, has not succeeded in achieving western European standards of economic management or prosperity. The aspirations of Polish society and the possibilities afforded by the Polish economy have proved to be fundamentally irreconcilable.

While emerging from over a century of political non-existence, Poland has managed to create a modern state apparatus as well as a rail and postal network, both highly efficient. In addition, a network of excellent universities, polytechnics and secondary schools was set up. However, within the economy there were only small pockets of modern industry, which, while often as good as any in the world, were generally immersed in a sea of technical underdevelopment, backwardness and stagnation. In 1938, steel and coal production was lower than in 1913. The urban population was afflicted by unemployment and often desperately bad housing conditions. Agriculture was excessively comminuted and badly under-resourced. Around 50 per cent of the people were economically active in agriculture, that is 33 per cent of the country's total workforce, were unemployed. In the 1920s and 1930s, Poland was thus a country in which modern standards co-existed with what is nowadays only a mass phenomenon in the Third World. This made the country an oddity within Europe.

The twenty-five years since the Second World War (1945–70)

The years immediately after the war were a turning-point in Poland's history, in the sense that even the most underdeveloped regions could no longer be termed Third World enclaves within Europe. Mass malnutrition was eliminated, the rural population was clothed and shod, every child went to school, and infant mortality decreased at a phenomenal rate. The war had caused devastation and population displacement on a scale hitherto unknown in the history of twentieth-century Europe, but despite all of this, the reconstruction programme in Poland was more successful (particularly in 1945–7) than that of any other European country, capitalist or socialist, affected by the war.

To some extent, the foundations for these achievements had been laid during the inter-war years when valuable human resources in terms of qualifications and motivation had been created throughout all sections and classes of society. There is no doubt that the redrawing of Poland's national boundaries was also a significant factor in the economic successes of the post-war period, since the country's economic potential was thereby substantially increased.

The new socio-economic order had been imposed from outside as an outcome of the war. Nevertheless, during the early years of post-war reconstruction, it brought with it a number of valuable and specific features which justified the term then used officially to describe it, namely the 'Polish road to socialism'. Although the state-owned sector in industry was immediately organized according to the Soviet command system of enterprise management, it was still a far cry from the hypercentralization and bureaucratization that was still to come. More significantly, the conditions of that period meant that the command system had considerable support within society. People were war-weary and eager to start producing. For the most part, they had little confidence in the new political authorities, and many were openly hostile. However, they did largely identify with the authorities' economic programme of national reconstruction because, in addition to helping themselves, they wanted to help their devastated country. As this attitude was common, it was probably a successful substitute for purely economic market pressures to work well and efficiently. There was therefore a singular meeting of patriotic fervour and good market traditions (still present at that time) with the new political structures, ensuring that resources were concentrated on the important and relatively simple investment programmes of the time.

This set of conditions, which gave rise to the rapid economic successes of the first post-war years had, however, begun to be corroded by the end of the 1940s. The advent of the 'cold war' resulted in a wide-ranging Stalinist standardization of economic, social and political relations in Poland. Political discrimination weakened the Polish intelligentsia's motivation for work, fear of collectivisation paralysed the peasants' production effort. State sector enterprises changed over to the working methods laid down by the Soviet command system. For the next twenty years, the changes taking place in Poland would be dictated by what was going on in the USSR.

The shockwaves sent out in the communist world by Khrushchev's famous denunciation speech at the 20th Communist Party Congress coincided with the strike of Polish workers in Poznan (June 1956). These events resulted in both a change of political leadership in Poland and the first attempt at reform, commonly known as the 'Polish October of '56'. These first attempts led to a series of significant social gains. However, these gains were limited to alleviating the more repressive aspects of the system and liberalizing relations in cultural and academic life. Within the economy, the only real and lasting changes affected agriculture where enforced collectivisation was abandoned for ever (in contrast to Hungary, where it was reactivated in 1959).

In all other sectors of the economy, the imposed command system was maintained without significant change until the 1980s. During the first fifteen years after the war, this system succeeded in developing much-needed industrial capacities drawing on reserves of unemployed or partially employed labour and cheaply exploitable raw materials (mainly coal). However, as time went on, the economy changed and its needs became more complicated. The importance of the more diverse and technically advanced branches of industry grew, but they were ill-suited to centralized management. The lack of authentic market links amongst enterprises, as well as between national production and the world market, was, along with the growing complexity of the economy, the source of its poor efficiency. Informed decisions concerning investment became more and more difficult. The new circumstances presented the central economic policy with a task which was increasingly complicated and intellectually demanding. Meanwhile, the highly bureaucratized system of planning and administration meant that key economic decisions were made in an arbitrary, often downright incompetent way, and that the operations of enterprises were inhibited by a strait-jacket of administrative directives and central allocation. The system therefore became more and more unsuited to the requirement of a diversified economy which was increasingly difficult to control centrally. This fact in turn was reflected in the demoralizing influence the system had on society as well as on people's attitudes towards issues connected with the national economy.

The command system and the policy of central allocation handed the economy over to the bureaucrats. By transforming enterprises into offices for production, it killed initiative, destroyed the spirit of enterprise and discouraged people from thinking in terms of economic realities. Its main thrust was *discipline, hierarchical submission and blind obedience* – in other words, *everything that was alien to the Poles*. It might have succeeded in other countries, but not in Poland. The result was that the weak and the cynical gravitated towards opportunism and conformism. Meanwhile, the majority felt increasingly alienated from matters concerning the national economy, perceiving them as the exclusive domain of an omnipotent bureaucracy forcibly imposed from outside. The restrictions on self-government and democracy in all spheres of public life resulted in an increasingly dangerous conflict with the aspirations of the younger generation in particular. Negative selection in managerial appointments began to take its toll. The cadre from the 'heroic age' in the nation's economy – the generation which rebuilt Poland – were beginning gradually to shuffle off the stage. Their place was taken by new people, and in a system where obedience and toadying were valued more highly than professional and moral qualities, it was the clever, cynical mediocrities who had the smoothest ride to the top.

In the 1960s, the Polish authorities were no longer in a position to support the system with repressive measures. The deployment of such measures on a wide scale had ceased to be possible following the events of October 1956. With neither popular support nor the option of repression to fall back on, the increasingly anachronistic system became less and less workable, and it was becoming clear that it was seriously inhibiting the development of the economy.

By the second half of the 1960s, the Polish economy was not in a position to satisfy consumer aspirations at all or to provide decent housing for the rapidly increasing urban households. Consequently, the social tensions intensified, leading eventually to an uprising of the working class in December 1970 and a change of the country's political leadership.

The economic collapse – why was it so severe?

During the early 1970s, the new government team of Edward Gierek (the First Secretary) and Piotr Jaroszewicz (the Prime Minister) was faced with the same basic challenge which economic development had posed back in October 1956. The pressure of time, however, made it all the more urgent. The reserves of cheap labour in agriculture were all but exhausted. Wasteful employment practices in the non-agricultural sectors of the economy became costly in terms of extra expenditure for investment and materials directed to agriculture in order to substitute for the labour force migrating to industry. Cheaply exploitable reserves of minerals and raw materials were also gradually being exhausted. Wastefulness with regard to materials and energy therefore became particularly costly, restraining the growth in industrial production and beginning to destroy the natural environment.

There were also significant changes in social attitudes. It was not only the reserves of cheap labour and raw materials that were being gradually exhausted. The reserves of patience of the working class, and indeed the whole of society, were also running out fast.

Outside Poland, great changes were taking place. The years 1956–70 were a period of rapid economic progress which increased the technological links between the economies of different countries to a hitherto unknown extent. For Poland to be able to change its industrial structure and update its technology in all sectors of the economy, it had to increase its exports to the West in order to pay for the necessary technological imports.

What should have been done in this situation? First of all, there should have been a radical reform of the system to curb the waste of materials and labour in nationalized enterprises, and to decentralize and rationalize the way in which investment decisions were made. Only then, under the protective umbrella created by solving these two key problems, and with the backing of a sensibly constructed long-term economic programme, could the problem of undertaking new wide-ranging investments be tackled.

In fact, the new administration of Gierek and Jaroszewicz did exactly the opposite and staked everything, as in former years, on increased investment and employment against a background of unchanged conditions. They did, however, come up with one significant new idea. They realized that economic growth could be stimulated swiftly with foreign loans, obtained for the most part from western Europe. Exploiting the credit option was not necessarily erroneous, but the administration used these loans during the 1970s to finance an expansion which was unusually fast, badly thought out and uncoordinated. In the face of extensive opportunities for drawing from external sources, central planning underwent an almost total disintegration. The economy was effectively developing with neither central accounting nor central five-year plans, since those plans which did exist were not in practice binding upon anyone at all. Yet it should be noted that neither were there any regulating market forces in operation. The nationalized enterprises were functioning without any hard financial constraints which would limit and rationalize their demand for current inputs and investment. There were in particular no interest and exchange rate rises to signal a ceiling on investments and imports. Many new investment projects were undertaken on the assumption that everything that was needed for them could be bought on foreign credit.

The credit-financed investments were undertaken in the hope that they would stimulate the exports necessary for the servicing of the debts incurred. However, because of the immense scale of the economic expansion and the scale of the debts incurred to finance it, these calculations were based from the start on wildly unrealistic assumptions of the export potential of the country. As a consequence, record levels of investments in Poland between 1972 and 1980 were accompanied by a debt to the capitalist countries which grew at an equally record speed. The quality of the decisions regarding investments completed the picture. New production capabilities were concentrated too heavily on the final phases of the technological process, at the expense of developing supplying industries. This led to the emergence of a production apparatus which was not only incapable of producing sufficient exports to pay off the debts, but was also dependent on imported inputs to an extent never previously experienced in Poland's post-war history. An economy endowed with such a defective production apparatus could function only as long as it was constantly supplied with fresh credits from abroad. Any loss of this artificial support threatened a sharp decrease not only of investments but also of output.

Meanwhile, in 1980, the servicing of debts incurred in the capitalist countries exceeded the value of the whole year's exports. The country's gross national income dropped for the second year running. In the same year, the rate at which borrowed money was flowing into Poland decreased radically, and during the years 1981–2, it stopped altogether. The sharp decrease in the national income over this period was, under those conditions, the economy's inevitable reaction. The immediate answer to why the collapse of the Polish economy was so unprecedented and so severe lies thus in the fact that its economic expansion was based on foreign loans which were far too great and which were grossly mismanaged.

Why Poland in particular?

It is worth considering why events developed in the way they did during the 1970s in Poland. Why were such dangerous policies adopted in Poland in particular? Was it merely an accident? Was it just Poland's misfortune that it was saddled with an administration which was exceptionally ignorant and irresponsible? After all, all socialist countries where there is a command system seem to have been gasping for breath since the mid-1960s. Difficulties with exports mount, and growth rates in the national income and real wages have declined. Symptoms of stagnation, regression even, are in evidence. Not one of these countries, however, has attempted to solve its problems in such a dramatic way, or with such desperate determination. Neither did any of them become the setting for such a severe economic collapse and political crisis. So why Poland in particular? It is this question which we now want to address. Our suggested answer forms also the core of this essay.

Apart from the systemic factors, common to all East European countries and the USSR, clearly one must examine a country's specific social and national make-up for their influence on how a command system functions. It is worth looking at how the civic and cultural traditions and the standards of civilization which influence social attitudes and patterns of behaviour were shaped by the different historical experiences of the communist-ruled countries. What are of interest are those factors which elude attempts at closer definition, and often arouse legitimate doubts and reservations, but which make up an important reflection of the real concept of the national character as a phenomenon of social reality.

Looking at the question from this point of view, one could suggest that the communist-ruled countries in Europe fall into two spheres of culture and civilization with clearly defined differences. For lack of a better definition, one can divide them into the *Prussian* and the *Byzantine*. Naturally, this is not an attempt to endow complicated phenomena with precise definitions. It is more an attempt to use certain symbols to promote associations that will, as far as possible, be free from value judgements and enable the actual differences in the attitudes and behaviour of various national groupings to be registered. It is worth considering the way in which the attachment to these two different zones has influenced the functioning of the system under discussion in the various socialist countries.

The command system, with its economy centrally controlled through a hierarchical organized administrative apparatus, developed out of the 'Byzantine' zone of cultural and civilizational traditions, and it found its backing in the patterns of social behaviour which emerged from them. These traditions formed the pillar on which the Soviet model of central economic administration rested, with its basis in strictly hierarchical structures and the unquestioning obedience of subordinates.

An historically conditioned propensity to subordination is not the only prerequisite for an efficient centrally-managed economy. There must also be precision in the issuing and carrying out of directives, a high level of internal co-ordination, and, above all, a disciplined, well-organized and knowledgeable apparatus for economic management which can rely on the inherent willingness of subordinates to co-operate and efficiently implement the directives filtering through the successive levels of the hierarchy from top to bottom. The Byzantine tradition did not have and has not bequeathed any such institutions, abilities or predispositions to the Soviet system, and this had a disastrous effect on the economic efficiency of the latter from the very start, and particularly so in agriculture, where concepts of discipline, quality and productivity schedules differed from industry in that working patterns were not dictated by machines to the same extent as in industrial production.

For many years, the Soviet command system relied on the easily accessible economic resources at its disposal. Rapid, though costly, economic growth was facilitated by massive reserves of labour, drawn mainly from agriculture, and by great reserves of all kinds of mineral resources which were relatively easy to mine. But by the second half of the 1970s, the Soviet economy had begun to run into trouble. Stripped of its protective coating of easily accessible reserves to finance its programme of extensive growth, the command system found itself in an impasse. This, among other factors, created in the USSR the situation which, in the mid-1980s, gave birth to the idea of 'perestroika', a reform programme intended to exploit better the key resource, namely the creative potential of the Soviet people.

Following on from this, let us now examine how the foreign command system fared when it was imposed on the soil of the cultural traditions and civilizations of countries like East Germany and Czechoslovakia. Prussian and also Czech civilizations, which had a similar economic status, passed down to socialism a spirit of obedience and subordination. The Prussian tradition in particular passed on the cult of the bureaucratic, centralized state. All of this combined to provide the perfect support for the newly transplanted command system in these countries. In this respect, the conditions which had been created for it were not unlike those which were to be found in its original home – the Soviet Union.

But this is where the analogy ends. Prussian and Czech civilisations also left a spirit of order and punctuality, an inherent willingness to co-operate, the habit of doing every job properly, precision and thoroughness in the issuing and carrying out of orders. It passed on all the characteristics which together define the phenomenon known in Europe as 'the genius of German organization'. What was also significant was the fact that in these two countries the historical process had allowed many more generations to pass through the filters of urban industrial civilization than in Russia, which was not drawn into the orbit of industrial development until later. Therefore, in contrast to Russia, the command system could be supported there by *both* of the necessary pillars that history had bestowed upon it – one being *obedience*, and the other, good *organization*.

Loyal and efficient execution of orders ensures a reasonably efficient co-ordination of the operations of various economic units, but it cannot guarantee fast growth to an economy which lacks substantial reserves of raw materials and human labour. What is needed is rapid technological progress, high-quality products and a healthy level of exports. All this can come only from enterprise and initiative, which the command system is not in a position to produce, even in a society with Prussian civilization and cultural traditions.

This too is why evaluations of the economic efficiency of both countries will vary depending on the context. In Czechoslovakia, and particularly in East Germany, the soil of historical tradition on to which the Soviet system of administration was transplanted turned out to be particularly fertile. This helped to limit the system's inherent inefficiency from the start. It is therefore no accident that this system functions better in these two countries (and in the Baltic Soviet republics) than in the heart of Russia where it originated, and makes those countries' living conditions significantly more tolerable.

The question takes on a different aspect when one compares Czechoslovakia or East Germany with the market economies of their capitalist counterparts. During the inter-war years, living standards in Bohemia and Moravia were on a par with European countries such as France, and indeed were higher than those of neighbouring Austria. During the last forty years, both France and Austria have left Czechoslovakia far behind. The gap between living standards in east and west German societies is also growing.

The incompatibility of system and culture in Poland

Poland has been omitted from this division of the socialist bloc countries into two cultural categories because it does not belong to either. Situated on the eastern edges of the Latin world, Poland developed its own civic and cultural traditions, even though it drew extensively from western European civilisation. The Polish Republic's parliamentary system before the partitions and its liberal institutions were in clear conflict with both the Byzantine tradition and the Prussian. The struggle for national identity against the partitioning powers of Russia and Prussia (from the time of the partitions until 1918) spread over 150 years of Polish history.[1]

The Polish national tradition provided a particularly unreceptive soil for the Soviet-type economic administration. This tradition had nothing of the Byzantine and Prussian predisposition to submission and compliance, fear and blind obedience to a hierarchical and bureaucratized state authority. But the set of characteristics which make up the Prussian spirit of organization, co-operation, precision and discipline was also missing, whilst economic underdevelopment which, in contrast to western Europe, was rapidly affecting Polish territories from as early as the seventeenth century, made it difficult for models created by urban industrial civilisation to be spread more widely. Both of the pillars, namely the tradition of obedience and that of organization, on which the command system might have rested, were therefore missing, and this fact augured the system's total failure from the start.

However, in the Polish national character there were certain features which provided substitute pillars on which the command system rested in the early post-war years. Historical experience had given Poles a ready tendency to assume heroic attitudes. The suggestive programme of rapid reconstruction and industrialization inspired the people and gained the support of practically the entire population in a poor and backward country which had been cruelly devastated by war and humiliated by occupation. Hence, in the first decade after the war, a subordination to directives issued from above sprang from a selfless patriotism and replaced with good result a historically determined spirit of obedience. The nation's fortunes had also left the Poles with a talent for organization and co-operation under the most critical and extraordinary conditions in the name of causes which were clear and unambiguous, and which had widespread and willing acceptance. This ability has often been demonstrated in recent history. The situation facing Poland in the years immediately after the war and the aims of the economic programme formulated by the authorities fitted this perfectly. Therefore this specifically Polish ability for improvisation and endurance in unusual and difficult situations acted as a successful substitute for the common organizational sense, habit of loyal co-operation and solid work which had been instilled in the Czechs and particularly in the Germans by long-established traditions.

Other factors which attenuated to some extent the inefficiency of the command system in the first fifteen years after the war were the rich reserves of labour and significant reserves of certain raw materials, particularly coal, which at that time were relatively cheap to exploit. These material factors which facilitated rapid economic growth and which were supported by a strong patriotic motivation meant that in the first fifteen years after the war, the command system was not less successful in Poland than in the other socialist countries, or in such economically comparable European capitalist countries as Spain, Greece and Portugal.

Heroic attitudes, however, are short-lived. The pattern of Polish ordinary day-to-day behaviour which had been shaped by the historical traditions of the country was soon found to be different from the one the system required. In other words, this system was exceptionally unsuited to drawing out the best in the Polish national character. Thus the fact that radical reform of the system was not carried out in time inevitably affected the economy's performance. By the 1960s, the command system was already yielding significantly worse economic results in Poland than in the other socialist countries. The state of the economy inevitably influenced the mood of society, and under the specific conditions in Poland it led to an even stronger sense of social discontent than the statistical data of the time might have suggested.

The demonstration effect of pre-war Poland's islands of prosperity and of the post/war capitalist West

It is a well-known fact that people do not view their own situation solely on the basis of their own private and collective resources of income and consumption. They also have consumer aspirations which have developed according to patterns influenced by history, and the confrontation of those aspirations with reality which has an impact on how they assess their individual situations, which in turn determines the social climate. As the wounds of war began to heal, a whole series of factors began to push the consumer aspirations of society steadily upwards. By the late 1940s, the capitalist world was entering a phase of exceptionally rapid economic growth. The influx of goods, and family and tourist visits from the highly industrialized countries of Western Europe and the USA, presented Polish society with some very attractive models of consumption. The shift in favour of the consumption patterns flowing in from the West was natural. The reception they had was further aided by the extensive links between the native population and what was by the standards of eastern Europe an exceptionally numerous population of Polish origin spread over the USA and western Europe, as well as by the openness and mobility of Polish society resulting from the relatively liberal cultural and travel policies pursued by the communist authorities after October 1956.

Another influence which played a significant role in creating high consumer aspirations at this time was the line taken by government propaganda, which declared the absolute superiority of the new social order, shown above all by its capacity to ensure a high standard of living for working people.

Among the other factors which determined consumer aspirations, particularly significant, we think, were the memories of consumption patterns before the war, which in the 1960s were still fresh in people's minds. This may seem strange in the light of the fact that Poland between the First and Second World Wars was a poor and economically backward country. Although this is true, there were vast differences in the living conditions of particular social and professional groups, as well as of the populations in the various economic regions.[2] This fact had important and far-reaching social consequences for the future which merit closer examination. What has been written about Poland's most recent socio-economic history does not seem to have taken this sufficiently into account. In the sea of poverty and backwardness which characterized Poland between the wars, there were economically developed 'pockets' where professional qualifications, workmanship and remuneration were more or less on a par with European standards of the time.

As the attached statistics demonstrate,[3] in the 1930s Poland was the only country in Europe which combined a relatively low national income and export per capita with Western European pay levels for skilled workers, employment legislation and social security.[4] And it was not only the skilled worker in modern industry who was paid as much in real terms as his counterpart in Germany or France. Doctors, lawyers and engineers were also highly paid, as were post office and railway workers and municipal functionaries, as long as they were in employment (during that time unemployed people lived in poverty in Western Europe, too). Moreover, the groups encompassed within these 'pockets' had in Poland an even easier access to a more comfortable lifestyle since widespread poverty made labour-intensive services, such as domestic work, cheap and readily available.[5] A farmer with an average standard of living from the Wielkopolska region or the Pomorski region in the rural pockets of prosperity did not differ drastically from either the German or the French farmer in terms of his living standards or conditions. The same applies to certain categories of skilled artisans, particularly the localized ones, in the more highly developed and prosperous regions in the country.

However, the overwhelming majority of the country's population, particularly in rural areas, simply vegetated, sometimes altogether outside the market. Very few of the rural unemployed migrated to towns, which were not even in a position to offer proper employment to their permanent inhabitants. Poland was therefore the setting for a potentially explosive social mix created by high consumer aspirations co-existing with the reality of low standards of living. Neither ingredient in the 'mix' came into contact with the other, however, because they were shared out amongst various social groupings. The massive differences in the living conditions of various population groups corresponded to the differentiation in their consumer aspirations.

The changes in the socio-economic order which took place after 1945 led to an obvious drop in the living standards of those Poles who had previously enjoyed developed 'European' conditions. Although in comparison to what had been meted out to them during the war and the occupation, their standard of living had improved rapidly, they never actually regained the material position they had enjoyed before the war. The dramatic increase in employment throughout the entire economy was accompanied by an equally dramatic process of levelling and equalizing the living standards of all those in employment. For the millions of the previously unemployed and partially employed people who migrated to industry from the overpopulated countryside, this was an undoubted improvement in their material standards and quality of life. However, whilst it was an improvement for a peasant with little or no land, it was clearly a regression for the technical intelligentsia and for certain categories of skilled workers.

But what significance does the sense of disillusionment and regression tormenting a relatively small number of people have when compared with the sense of progress and satisfaction which must have been felt by the vast mass of people who were moved from their overpopulated villages into urban areas and industry, and whose conditions of employment and cultural and material prospects had in fact significantly improved? A philosopher on the side of the new social order might be forgiven for the elementary error of falling victim to the logic of numbers inherent in the formulation of such a question. For it was to the very representatives of 'modern European' standards, with their secure place in society, their professional status and their high degree of social authority that the significant role of the opinion-maker fell. They had retained their ambitious consumer aspirations and their former professional class status, but they were not in a position to maintain their former standards of living.

The patterns of consumption which originated in these socio-professional groups and the sense of a deep discrepancy between the expected and the actual state of affairs therefore spread to the whole of society, particularly in urban society. The fact that the expected state of affairs was felt by them to be attainable, since after all it was not something which was based on tales from distant times and far-off countries, but something which had been experienced first-hand and was known to have been possible here in Poland, laced this discrepancy with a particular bitterness. The newcomers who poured in from outside formed their evaluation of the material situation under the influence of these groups and, as newcomers often do, they tended to exaggerate their criticisms rather than minimize them. After a time, the most dissatisfied elements often turned out to be those who had experienced the greatest social and economic promotion. And so the widespread nature of genuine social advance for millions of people led to a situation where the justified economic frustrations of a relatively small section of society ceased to be a socially marginal phenomenon. They became widespread, powerful, duplicated a hundred times over, and this way an explosive and specifically Polish concoction began to emerge from the state of relative immobility in which it had lain in pre-war society.

From the point of view of the increase of real average wage rates, Poland found itself on the bottom of the table in Europe between 1960 and 1970, lagging in this respect behind both socialist and capitalist countries. But it was largely on the basis of real wages that the older working class, technical intelligentsia, etc., judged the economic system and policies and passed their judgement on to the whole of the working community. Any other form of improvement in living standards either failed to be perceived, or was linked with a growing burden in people's everyday lives, for instance in the case of growth in family incomes through female employment. As a result, even instances where the system could justify its existence with fairly substantial, statistically measurable achievements – such as the growth in overall consumption resulting from greatly increased employment, and the improvement in living standards achieved by an increase in national per capita consumption because of changes in the population's social and professional structure – failed to win the expected social approval. It all amounted to nothing more than a 'statistical truth' increasingly at odds with the truth instilled in people's perceptions.

Under these conditions, it was inevitable that the collision of society's consumer aspirations with reality would result in a particularly deep and widespread dissatisfaction. However, the dissatisfaction which characterized the social climate in Poland was only one important link in the chain of circumstances which hold the answer to the question: Why Poland in particular? It is time to examine the other links.

The inefficiency of the system had a negative effect on consumer standards and living conditions everywhere in Eastern Europe, and did not give any particular reason for satisfaction anywhere. This could not be perceived by a Czech observing the rising living standards of neighbouring Austria, or by an East German for whom the living standards of West Germans constituted an adequate framework of reference. Neither was it perceived by the Russian, who was cut off from the outside world by his system, but who was also sceptical and reflective by nature. For him, the relentless propaganda about constant economic advance inevitably seemed increasingly suspect. Nowhere, however, did the lesser or greater discrepancies between consumer aspirations and actual living standards lead to a mass adoption of attitudes of social dissent, since in some countries the Byzantine tradition, and in others the Prussian, had conditioned social attitudes in the spirit of obedience and submission, resulting in resignation and the adjustment of aspirations to what was attainable. The Soviet system in particular was able to exploit these characteristics to the full, maintaining social peace in the country despite its difficult living conditions. It is significant that this social peace was also maintained in post-Stalinist times when the repressiveness of the system was significantly eased: Tocqueville's principle did not hold true there. The long tradition of submission exerted its influence.

In Poland, however, the universal dissatisfaction led to a state of growing social tension and the widespread adoption of certain attitudes and desires, the scale and intensity of which went even beyond the particularly wide gap between consumer aspirations and the extent to which they could be fulfilled. This particular reaction was again determined by a different historical heritage. The other countries have taken from their past a hallowed concept of the authority of the state and its organs which was so typical of the Prussian and particularly the Byzantine traditions, and this bred a climate of resignation and obedient submission. On the contrary, Poland inherited from its past a spirit of opposition and revolt. It grew out of the liberal political institutions and the traditions and customs of the First Republic which preceded the partitioning of Poland. It was further consolidated and stimulated by a long tradition of struggle for independence and national identity waged against the foreign partitioning powers. The system therefore lacked in this country the specific social shock absorbers for its economic inadequacies which history had bestowed on countries with other civic and cultural traditions, in the form of a social readiness to patiently tolerate stagnating living standards.[6]

The factors of limited democracy and sovereignty

The economic demands of the working class were undoubtedly intensified by a sense of being barred politically from any real participation in the country's public affairs, a feeling which was shared by the whole of society and was popularly linked with the limited sovereignty of the state. Similar convictions were probably common in all the smaller socialist countries to a greater or lesser extent but, in Poland, memories of the splendid past, coloured and maybe exaggerated by a natural need for compensation, were still alive in the national consciousness and sustained the particularly bitter feeling of dissonance. If a Russian citizen was feeling the strain of his economic situation, his mood was undoubtedly lightened by the thought of his country's political status, whilst the thought of Poland's political position only served to increase the Polish people's bitterness. The experience of standing in a queue for scarce commodities is quite different depending on whether one queues in the knowledge that one is the ruler of half the world or whether one queues in the knowledge of being not only an economic but also a political pariah.

The authorities were initially unable to grasp the social, psychological and economic foundations of the workers' claims. In their view, any source of mass social unrest had been buried once and for all along with the old order of the social relations of private ownership: the fact that the new reality had not removed conflict-ridden tensions, but had only changed their source, somehow escaped them or failed to be recognised as a rational explanation. That too is why they tended to explain the discrepancies between their own vision of the world and the new order of social relations – which they had themselves created without understanding the roots of the conflicts which were tearing it apart – in terms of reality being distorted by the demons of counter-revolution as personified by the representatives of the former property-owning classes, the agents of foreign intelligence services, etc. Clearly, they followed in the footsteps of Cervantes' famous hero. . .

The workers in turn did not have any authentic representation for the articulation of their economic demands. Other ways to assimilate such demands within the new socio-economic order in Poland were also lacking. Transplanting the redistribution model of the trade union movement in capitalist countries to a socialist economy and a socialist society would not have had the desired effects. Only a programme of radical reform of the whole system, formulated in the language and from the perspective of the state, would have created the core of what was needed. How and when were the workers to formulate such a programme, however, if the appropriate organs of the state authority were not able to do this? The only means left to workers who wanted to articulate their economic demands was strike action and taking to the streets. The only means available to the authorities were those of repression.

As a result there was unrest, the scale of which exceeded anything that took place in Poland before the war. The first revolt broke out in Poznań in June 1956. After a few years of liberalization, following the events of October 1956, a further wave of increasing social tension resulted in a great eruption on the coast in December 1970 which was crushed with force by the police and the army. The dates and locations of both of these events are not incidental. The workers at the Cegielski plant in Poznań were working in the heart of 'modern' pre-war Poland and had been the greatest losers after the war. They also had the most difficulty in adapting to the new rules of the game under the conditions of the command system, which often contradicted their own professional code. In addition, the Baltic ports had 'a window on to the world' from which the growing gap in earnings between the countries of Western Europe and Poland could easily be seen.

Poznań 1956 was only the first warning signal. The events of 1970 in the Baltic ports shook the existing order to its very foundations. It was clear that any further revolt on this scale would have untold consequences. It was under these conditions that power has shifted into the hands of those who would be responsible for the economic policies of the 1970s. The historical circumstances determining the further course of events were thus already in place.

Conclusion

To summarize, the malfunctioning of the command system, with its politically conditioned inertia and inability to change, is what constituted the systemic determinant for the Polish economic crisis and gave it its general non-national characteristics. On the other hand, the fact that a defiant working class came out effectively against this system and exerted pressure on the authorities created a dramatic need somehow to find the extraordinary resources needed to improve the situation. This defiance and pressure gave the crisis its specifically Polish features. Thus the severe economic collapse of the 1980s was caused by a combination of national and systemic factors: the powerful social pressure and institutional blockade created by the existing socio-economic system. It was no longer possible to do things in the old way and there was neither the will nor the ability to do things differently. Such a combination could only end in a bloodbath or madness in economic policy. In the early 1970s it led to the latter, with well-known consequences, and in the early 1980s it led to the imposition of the 'state of war'.

Notes

1 It has been our intention not to attempt any valuation of Poland's civic or national traditions. Independently, however, of what our assessment might be (Polish historiographers have approached this question from very different points of view), these traditions are nevertheless clearly different from the traditions of the countries which border Poland. It is only this fact which interests us here. It merits closer examination and the drawing of appropriate conclusions, since it plays an important part in shaping the social reality of the country.
2 The gap between the actual living conditions of various socio-professional groups within the population and its accompanying civilisation and cultural standards were a feature of all European societies, but some historians have drawn attention to the fact that in Poland this difference was particularly great. For example, Henryk Zielinski writes that during the Second Republic (1918–39) 'for a variety of historical reasons, this difference was significantly greater than anywhere else to the east of the river Elbe, that is, in regions which are historically comparable in terms of their social, economic and political development' (*Historia Polski 1914–1939*, Warsaw: Ossolineum, 1983,

282). Within this context, the fact that the difference in living conditions within the working class was incomparably greater in Poland than in the countries of Western and Central Europe is particularly significant. Ludwik Landau highlighted this fact in his contention that the range of pay between skilled and unskilled workers in the larger towns (he compares Warsaw with Berlin and Prague amongst others) and that of average rates of pay between large industrial centres and rural areas was significantly greater in Poland (L Landau (1957) 'Pay Levels in Poland and Economic Development', *Selected Writings*, Warsaw: PWN, 239, 251). Landau was the author of pioneering works concerned with economics and social politics and researched into the economic structure of the national income of various countries, some of his results being published in the inter-war period with Michal Kalecki.

There was probably a greater difference in the living conditions of various groups of population in countries such as Rumania and the other Balkan states than in western and central Europe. Poland, however, differed from these countries in that the population groups whose level of civilization and standard of living were significantly different from average conditions in the country were relatively much greater (see note 3). This is related partly to Poland's greater degree of industrialization as compared with the other agricultural European countries (according to Landau, the level of industrial production per capita between the wars was twice as high in Poland as that in Rumania and the other Balkan countries, see op. cit., 410), and particularly to the much more developed state and municipal sectors of the economy, where Polish workers' earnings were relatively high. Amongst the smaller European countries which are now socialist, only Hungary was presumably comparable with Poland.

3 In respect of national income per capita, Poland surpassed only Portugal and the Balkan countries in Europe, whilst in respect of export per capita, it came last in 1937 and second last in 1929 in Europe. This fact is confirmed by all known statistics, differing only as to the quantitive extent of the distance between Poland and the other countries, which is not relevant here. It is, however, significant that at the same time the real earnings of the more highly skilled industrial workers in Poland were more or less the same as the rates of pay in the highly developed countries of continental Europe. The table below demonstrates this specifically Polish phenomenon.

Table 6.1 Comparison of national income per capita of eight countries

	National income per capita (1929)	Exports per capita 1929	Exports per capita 1937	Real earnings of skilled workers[1] 1930
Poland	100	100	100	100
Germany	289 (308)	496	525	111
France	300 (251)	470	345	86
Spain	123	173	121	72
Hungary	126 (126)	208	288	—
Rumania	100 (73)	96	120[2]	—
Bulgaria	74[3]	136	144	—
Yugoslavia	74[3]	100	142	66

1 This category of pay was much nearer average pay levels in highly developed European countries than in Poland.
2 1936.
3 The Balkan states have been taken as an average here.

The information about national income in the table above is taken from Landau's estimates (op. cit., 414–15) in which he used a category closely related to gross national income. Some results of other estimates for 1929 are given in parentheses from Kostrowicka, J., Landau, Z. and Tomaszewski, H. (1975) *Polish Economic History of the Nineteenth and Twentieth Centuries*, Warsaw: KiW, 364, based on Western European sources. (Similar results can be found in other publications, e.g. Clark, C. (1957) *Conditions of Economic Progress*, London: Macmillan, 188–9.) The export figures have been taken from the *Statistical Yearbook of the League of Nations* (1938), Geneva, 224–5.

The figures relating to real levels of pay are based on the results of surveys conducted by the International Labour Office in January 1930 which Landau obtained (op. cit., 249–350) from source materials published in 'Comparaison des salaires réels dans quelques villes' (1930) *Revue Internationale du Travail*, vol.XXI, nr.4, 582, and vol.XXII, nr.4, 1930, 565. The surveys concentrated mainly on highly skilled and better-paid workers from chosen branches of industry, and information was collected on the basis of individual pay (per hour, per day, etc.) from a few of the larger towns in each of the countries compared, in Poland from Warsaw, Łódź and Katowice. It should be noted that the estimates of real earnings were based almost exclusively on the costs of food.

The relation between the figures in the Table did not change much during the period of the economic crisis. It is significant that in accordance with the known estimates the number of the groups surveyed representatively included about 15 per cent – 25 per cent of workers outside agriculture in Poland in the early 1930s. The high levels of their pay cannot therefore be seen as being of marginal social significance. The numbers in these groups were, however, not large enough to have any substantial influence on average wages. This is why 'average pay levels strayed away from the levels in western Europe, if worse paid categories and smaller towns are taken into consideration, and this made the living conditions totally incomparable' (Landau, op. cit., 252).

All in all, the statistics in the Table above seem to characterize the Polish phenomenon of relatively high pay levels for highly skilled workers in a poor European country. The survey does not demonstrate a similar phenomenon in other relatively poor countries like Spain or Yugoslavia. There are many indications that this phenomenon did not exist in the Balkan states, although there is insufficient statistical proof to back this view. It seems that in this respect only Hungary may have been similar to Poland.

4 This is a widely held opinion among experts.

5 Domestic service accounted for 50 per cent of the female labour force outside agriculture in Poland (*Maly Rocznik Statystyczny* (1939), GUS, 260).

6 In Poland, the command system was affected not only by history but also by nature. The natural absorbers of the system's inefficiency such as favourable natural conditions which would allow reasonable results (a kind of 'God's bounties') to be achieved at low cost, despite the economy's low efficiency and low competitiveness of its products on the world market, were lacking there. Despite the myth about Poland's great natural resources which continues to be widespread and to distort national consciousness, Poland belongs to a small number of countries which have the worst and most difficult climatic and soil conditions in Europe. It does not possess significant areas of fertile soil situated

in good climatic conditions and on land that can be worked mechanically with ease, as in Hungary, Bulgaria, Rumania and Czechoslovakia. The Institute of Soil Science and Forecasting in Sofia has estimated that if the bioclimatic potential of the Leningrad region of the USSR is 100, it is 143 in Bulgaria, 139 in Hungary, 126 in Rumania, 118 in Czechoslovakia, 113 in the GDR and only 103 in Poland. Reserves of Polish coal and copper are extracted with great difficulty at sharply increasing marginal costs of extraction.

Appendix

Poland's position with respect to net national income per capita (GDR = 100) has been as follows:

Table 6.2 Comparison of net national income per capita of five countries

	1960[1]	1968[1]	1980[2]	1985[3]
GDR	100	100	100–100	100–100
Czechoslovakia	93	100	91–94	78–80
Hungary	66	71	75–85	61–74
Poland	66	71	63–66	46–48
Bulgaria	60	71	66–68	62–64

1 Zienkowski, L. (1971) 'Ways of calculating national income', Warsaw: PWE, 268.
2 Havlik, P. (1983) 'Comparison of real products between East and West 1970–1983', Wiener Institut fur Internationale Wirtschaftsvergleichungen, nr.115, 35, 37). The author uses two methods to calculate the exchange between national currency and US dollars which give similar results.
3 The authors' own calculation.

Translated by Monika Bobinski.

7

The Polish intelligentsia in a crisis-ridden society

Maria Hirszowicz

Reading University

Anyone who deals with the stratification and political culture of communist societies invariably comes across the problem of the political attitudes of the intelligentsia. This term was used to denote a separate, culturally homogeneous, stratum of people in Eastern Europe and in Tsarist Russia in the nineteenth and early twentieth centuries, but has evolved into a more universal sociological concept of a certain theoretical importance.

It is widely accepted that the intelligentsia as a separate stratum did not and could not have emerged in the West, where the educated strata were from the start fragmented by serving different classes and institutions. In conditions of a rapidly developing economy, growth of the state administration, emergence of political parties and the expansion of public and private services, educated people were to be found everywhere, wherever general knowledge and specialized training were necessary: their status was determined primarily by the prestige of the professions they pursued and the positions which they occupied in the political and social structures.

In Russia and in Poland the situation was completely different: the practical applications of education were limited by the backwardness of social and economic life, while at the same time the advance of progress and the desire for social change manifested themselves primarily in the realms of culture, ideology, and social and political thought. The cultural heritage of the Enlightenment, the belief in progress, the budding movements of the working masses, and the national aspirations reflected themselves in the East in the new mood of educated elites, who resented their marginal position and aspired to the function of spiritual leadership. In partitioned Poland the importance of the national problem enhanced the leadership functions of the educated stratum: the Polish intelligentsia became the major force in preserving national traditions, developing national identity and cultivating the idea of national independence.

Seen from the perspective of the nineteenth and early twentieth centuries, the East European intelligentsia as a separate stratum appears to be a purely historical phenomenon: in independent Poland between 1919–39, it became more and more fragmented and stratified in line with the processes which had previously occurred in western societies, while in communist Russia it had been replaced by the new Soviet intelligentsia which was closely controlled and subservient to the Party state. One would have expected that in Poland under communist rule a similar process would take place. And, indeed, the development of communist Poland between 1945 and 1980 brought about the rise of a 'new intelligentsia', which was closely linked to the establishment, serving the authorities as administrators, managers, professionals, teachers and doctors. There were reasons to believe that the new intelligentsia was on the way to merging with the Party state bureaucracy in a process which could be described as the bureaucratization of the intelligentsia and the professionalization of the bureaucracy.[1] The period of Gierek's rule in the 1970s was the peak of this tendency. De-ideologisation of the Communist Party, accelerated modernization of the economy, wide contacts with the Western world, economic benefits generously allocated in the early 1970s to some groups of professionals (particularly those belonging to the technical intelligentsia), all opened opportunities to members of the educated stratum which they had never before enjoyed.

It is characteristic that in the 1970s some Hungarian sociologists, referring to the Hungarian experience, held the view that intellectuals were on the road to power. Although in Poland such a statement could hardly be justified, in view of the restrictions and deprivations suffered by many groups among the intelligentsia, a substantial majority of the Polish intelligentsia under Gierek recognized the improvement in their economic situation and professional status and displayed a high degree of optimism with regard to the future.

It was only in the late 1970s, when rising expectations clashed with the reality of the approaching economic crisis, that the voices of discontent and criticism became more numerous. The few dissidents who for years had struggled for attention amid relative indifference and isolation suddenly became the avant-garde of the disenchanted groups among the intelligentsia. During the final two or three years before Gierek's fall, the centres of political opposition mushroomed. The ethos of the old Polish intelligentsia, which seemed almost dead, appeared to revive in the atmosphere of growing restiveness in Polish society.

There were very few people in the communist establishment who expected such a change in the hearts and minds of the educated stratum in Poland. As Żółkiewski, one of the more prolific communist writers in the field of the theory of culture, wrote in the early 1960s:

> The traditional normative model of an intelligentsia as envisaged by Żeromski and Nałkowska was possible only in a society of deprived masses. The liquidation of these deprivations transforms the normative and statistical patterns of the intelligentsia and limits the specific character and distinctive nature of the traditional, extra-occupational, totality-oriented role of this intelligentsia.[2]

Żółkiewski assumed that forms of deprivation would not emerge under communist rule and subsequently did not believe that there was any role to be played by the intelligentsia on a national scale. The crisis which erupted in the late 1970s proved the opposite and led to unprecedented support for the rebellious workers from the intelligentsia.

The eruption of the Solidarity movement undoubtedly constituted a turning-point in the relationship between the Polish intelligentsia and the communist establishment. The support of the substantial majority of the Polish intelligentsia for the striking workers and their unions was enthusiastic and unqualified, and encompassed many members of the Party, who defied the official line and voiced their support for radical social and political change.

The most characteristic features of the political and cultural activism of the educated stratum in the 'Solidarity' months of 1980–1 were as follows:

1 The movement among the intelligentsia was not, as previously, confined to the intellectual elite but encompassed rank-and-file intelligentsia as well.
2 It was not led by rebellious Party members as in 1956, but by the non-Party intelligentsia.
3 It was not confined to the great cities, but spread into the medium-sized and small towns, which often became independent centres of intellectual and cultural activities.
4 The demands put forward by the members of the intelligentsia were not focused on their sectional interests, but predominantly expressed the demands and aspirations of the nation as a whole.

The activism and 'totality-oriented' approach of the Polish intelligentsia continued after the defeat of Solidarity and found its expression in the wide participation of the educated stratum in different forms of political opposition. However, the big question asked by many in the aftermath of the military coup and the ensuing 'normalization' was how long would the relentless resistance to this policy last? Would the rebellious mood of the Polish intelligentsia persist against all political odds, or would it subside and give way to a growing tendency to accommodate the establishment as had happened, albeit in different circumstances, in the 1940s, late 1950s and early 1970s?

Past experience of the normalization processes would suggest that the latter development was most likely. In a society dominated by frustration and hopelessness, political apathy and survival strategies would invariably dominate the public spirit, as had happened in Czechoslovakia after 1968 and in Hungary after 1956. The bureaucratic Party-state apparatus in such circumstances offered the only niches in which people could rebuild and plan their future. As long as they were eligible to follow administrative and professional careers, many members of the intelligentsia would invariably accommodate to the system in a trade-off of political independence for economic and social security. There are, however, many aspects of the present situation in Poland which defy such conclusions and make the full integration of the Polish intelligentsia and the Party-state apparatus more difficult than before.

The causes lie not only in the unusual political experiences of the years 1980–1 when most people felt free, and many participated in politics on a massive scale, had a sense of power vis-à-vis the state and were imbued with a sense of religious and national unity based on the heritage of Catholic, independent Poland. Such experiences cannot easily be erased and exercise an enormous influence on the generations who participate in them, but their long-lasting effects are usually modified by the realities of social, economic and political life. It is in those realities that we suggest lies the key to the understanding of the present attitudes of the Polish intelligentsia.

The four factors which seem to have a decisive influence on the relationships between the Polish intelligentsia and the communist regime are: the economic situation; the new role played by the Church; the development of the opposition movement; and the revival of dissent within the establishment. As we shall see, all these factors combined with the political crisis have moved the Polish intelligentsia to the forefront of political life.

The educated stratum in a shortage economy

The precarious economic position of the Polish intelligentsia was one of the most characteristic features of post-war Poland. Poland, it should be noted, fared much worse under the impact of accelerated industrial growth than many of her East European neighbours because of the fact that the tertiary sector in Poland was almost completely devastated during the war and the short period of reconstruction did not suffice to rebuild the schools, transport, hospitals, shops and restaurants, small workshops and servicing units. Moreover, as soon as the policy of accelerated growth of heavy industry began, the services in Poland were cut to the bone, contributing to the general decline of living standards.

The shortage economy contributed to the growing dependence of the educated stratum on the government: provisions bestowed by the state, in the form of housing, holiday homes, low-price cars, foreign trips or posts abroad, food-cards and cash bonuses, determined the quality of life of those whose positions entitled them to enjoy the benefits and favours reserved for the chosen few. Intellectuals, writers, poets, literary critics, professionals and officials were turned into clients of the all-powerful state. The system of allocations subsequently became an instrument of political and ideological control to no less a degree than the political police, conformism being rewarded by material privileges, and rebellion or non-cooperation being punished by severe financial deprivations.

Although the economic situation improved under Władysław Gomułka and had radically changed for the better (albeit for a short time) under Edward Gierek, the almost total collapse of the economy in the early 1980s led to an unprecedented impoverishment of large sections of the Polish population, including most of its intelligentsia. There is no wonder that a general feeling of hopelessness prevailed in Poland, in spite of the piecemeal improvements in economic life in the last few years.

The economic situation of the Polish intelligentsia in the 1980s is characterized by: a direct pauperisation of many members of the intelligentsia; a deterioration of the relative earnings of educated people as compared with the earnings of non-salaried workers; the growing differentiation of incomes within the educated stratum; and the importance of informal contacts and proper channels in gaining access to certain goods and services.

The differentials of income between specialists and skilled and un-skilled workers were already declining in the years 1947–80, but the deterioration in the relative earnings of the educated stratum reached an unprecedented level after 1981 when the government pursued the policy of placating the more militant groups of workers by pay rises while strictly controlling the incomes of white-collar employees. The following figures are most significant:

Table 7.1 The ratio of the average salary of employees with higher education to the average pay in the public sector[3]

Years	Relationship
1980	120.5
1981	104.4
1982	77.3
1983	89.6
1984	81.9

In 1980 the average salary of an employee with a higher education was thus 20 per cent higher than the national average; in 1984 it was 20 per cent lower and in 1986 it was *25 per cent lower*! In production, engineers earn 20 per cent less than the workers.[4]

The general discontent among the intelligentsia due to economic difficulties is increased because of the enormous income differentials within the white-collar occupations. The relationship between the maximum and the average earnings within the same occupational group in the year 1986 was 1:4.64 in manual occupations and 1:7.05 in non-manual occupations.[5] A miner thus has an average of 65,741zl per month, but there will be some who will earn 100,000zl. A bus driver averages 29,000zl but some come up to 74,000zl. Even a low-paid cleaning woman who earns an average of 13,000zl can in some cases earn 48,000zl. The system is thus sufficiently flexible to apply incentives for particularly important, unpleasant or demanding jobs, but not consistent enough to make those differentials acceptable and rational.

In non-manual occupations the average earnings of directors are 40,000zl but some reach 140,000zl. A teacher gets an average of 16,800zl, but some can earn 50,000zl. The intergroup differentials are also considerable.[6]

As far as the average incomes of the major professional groups are concerned, they are not only low in terms of comparability with the high-income groups in both the manual and non-manual jobs, but also in terms of their purchasing power. Poor supplies of everyday commodities and exorbitant prices of products regarded as luxuries (including cars, colour televisions, woollen carpets, etc.) combined with the high rate of inflation add to the misery of an average number of the intelligentsia in Poland.

Moreover, economic difficulties have led to a general decline in the quality of state-supplied services, including the health service, public transport, public sanitation, education and housing. As far as the majority of the intelligentsia are concerned, they find it increasingly difficult to maintain their acceptable minimum standard of living and quality of everyday life. Hence, the never-ending struggle against adversity and desperate attempts to increase one's earning capacity and to widen one's access to scarce goods and services.

Economic difficulties are not the only cause of discontent among the Polish educated stratum. After all, 38.4 per cent of them assessed their economic situation as good or fairly good, as compared with the 16.3 per cent of qualified workers.[7] As far as the professionals are concerned, they feel growing restrictions in carrying out their tasks according to professional standards: in a crisis economy, drastic cuts in financing professional services constitute a grim reality. Hospitals lack the necessary equipment, scientific libraries are deprived of new foreign publications and cannot afford to pay for current journals and magazines, research laboratories have to use obsolete instruments and progress in the information sciences is far from satisfactory, all of which frustrates young and ambitious individuals and generates a feeling of general gloom and hopelessness.

The mood of the young Polish intelligentsia is best reflected in the attitudes of Polish students. According to a public opinion poll the majority of students who plan their future would like, instead of working in the public sector (which they believe to be the most likely), to go abroad for long periods, work in foreign firms in Poland, or own a private workshop. Only 58 per cent of students indicate Poland as a country in which they would like to live (78 per cent in a previous study carried out in 1979).[8]

By contrast to previous periods of normalization, such dreams and plans are by no means unrealistic. Many of those who do not wish to work in the public sector and look for an alternative way of making a living have a real chance of achieving this. Two factors are most relevant in this respect: increased opportunities to leave Poland, either temporarily or permanently, and the widening role of the private sector. Some people defect while on business or tourist trips, others find employment and ask for an extension of their stay in the West, still others seek jobs via the Polish agency, Polservice. The total number of people with higher education who left Poland in the years 1983–7 amounts to 59,500, which includes 19,000 engineers and 5,500 doctors.[9] The widening role of the private sector allows many educated people to opt out of state-controlled employment and become self-employed or to take a job with a private firm (see Chapter 10).

The existence of these new patterns of stratification has been acknowledged by many Poles and is illustrated by the following public opinion poll findings:

Table 7.2   Who are the people regarded as privileged groups? (Studies carried out by the Centre of Public Opinion Research in 1984.)[10]

The owners of private industrial, trading and servicing firms	74%
Directors of large enterprises	67.7%
The apparatus of power	67.3%
Doctors with a private practice	59.1%
Owners of large farms and specialised farms	57.8%
Militiamen	55.1%
People working on contracts abroad	45.9%
Military personnel	38.6%
Priests	37.6%
Best paid workers such as miners	30.5%

The thirty years of communist rule have thus resulted, paradoxically, in the growing importance and prestige of private entrepreneurship in a country in which the intelligentsia was known for its contempt for 'trivial' industrial pursuits and business. Money-making by the members of the intelligentsia is no longer stigmatized; on the contrary the new wealthy elite has acquired a new respectability which it has never enjoyed before.

The parallel market thus lessens the dependence of the intelligentsia on the political 'paymasters' as it offers escape routes from employment in the public sector. At the same time, however, it intensifies the prevailing feelings of relative deprivation among Polish intelligentsia because it offers extra benefits to the minority who have the access to foreign currency, possess marketable skills, or simply have enough business acumen to operate successfully within the private sector.

The Church as a factor of pluralisation within Polish 'civil' society

Cardinal Jozef Glemp, Polish Primate, characterizes the evolution of the Polish intelligentsia as follows:

> Before the second world war intelligentsia adopted mostly an unfavourable, indifferent or opportunistic stance. There were also in that group some elements sympathising with communism.
>
> After the war the new generation of intelligentsia surrendered relatively easily to the marxist ideology. They joined the party without playing in it a leading part. The disappointment had to come only later. Many were protesting against the methods applied in the system. Later on the adherents of the marxist ideology joined Solidarność. Others preferred to stay apart and return only their party cards. Embittered, they regarded their life, or at least a considerable part of it, as wasted. It applied above all to the creative intelligentsia who did not know the Church or knew it simply from the old traditions. Against that background there appears a new attitude of intelligentsia towards the Church. It is expressed in the respect for its deepened spiritual life and its role in patriotic attitudes.[11]

For those members of the intelligentsia who stay aloof from the Party-dominated cultural institutions, there remains a chance of participating in the Church-sponsored forms of public life. The scope of such forms is limited and subject to many political constraints; nevertheless the government goes to considerable lengths to respect the autonomy of the Catholic Church. The Church is in fact the only recognized institution which escapes the interference and internal control of the Communist Party state. The authorities feel obliged not only to accept the existence of the Church as an independent religious institution, but also to tolerate many of the semi-secular or secular activities which are carried out under its protection.

As a result, the intelligentsia see in the Church the institution which helps them to protect their basic rights and creates the outlet for activities which are otherwise not tolerated by the establishment. The majority of the intelligentsia in Poland are therefore fully committed to the Church, both in spiritual and political terms.

Before 1977 about 54 per cent of those who had diplomas of higher education declared themselves as believers. In the 1980s, according to some estimates, about 87 per cent belonged to this category.[12] In a study reported by Edmund Wnuk Lipiński,[13] 79.7 per cent of the intelligentsia declared themselves to be believers as compared with 94 per cent of skilled workers, 96 per cent of unskilled workers and 97 per cent of farmers. When the author correlated religion with education, 72.8 per cent of those with higher education were classified as believers as compared with 96.9 of those with primary education and 87.8 per cent with secondary education. Among university students, 70 per cent declared they believed in God, and 63 per cent were practising Catholics.

The role of the Church in Poland can thus serve as an irrefutable example of the pluralization of political and cultural life in Poland. Under the sponsorship of the Church the majority of the Polish intelligentsia find not only a chance of allegiance to a faith and ideology completely opposed to communist principles, but also an outlet for social and cultural activities which go beyond purely religious issues. The Catholic press, publications, clubs and other Church-sponsored forms of cultural life offer ample opportunities for many people who do not see a place for themselves in state-sponsored institutions, and yet who do not wish to confine themselves to a private and apolitical existence.

There are at present forty clubs of the Catholic intelligentsia; some of them have branches or sections in smaller localities. The clubs carry out many functions: they organize collections, pilgrimages, educational courses, holiday camps, and open meetings at which lectures are delivered and discussions take place; they also have specialized sections which correspond to the interests of their members; there is a section dealing with family problems, an historical section, an economic section, etc.[14]

The clubs of the Catholic intelligentsia co-operate closely with the Church, but constitute autonomous institutions. The Church itself carries out many functions in which the members of the clubs of the Catholic intelligentsia, and many other intellectuals not necessarily identified with the Church, are actively involved. The most important of such activities are the so-called Weeks of Christian Culture, which take place each year in many towns. They are organized under the patronage of the local priests and consist of public lectures, meetings with writers and artists, concerts and films, etc. During the Weeks of Christian Culture several such events are organized every day so that the public has a wide choice offered to them.

In many parishes, the priests also hold regular or occasional courses, lectures and discussions, inviting well-known scholars, artists and writers to deliver speeches or papers and to participate in the discussions which follow.[15]

As we have said, all these activities create a genuine outlet for many members of the Polish intelligentsia who wish to evade the requirements and limitations imposed by the state upon cultural and intellectual activities. Yet the policy of coexistence between the Church and the state imposes considerable constraints on many of those who wish to continue their political struggle (see Chapter 4).

The political moderation of the Church alienates many radicals among the intelligentsia but attracts the support and loyalty of a substantial majority who do not believe in the success of any open confrontation with the authorities, and who see the Church as a genuine counter-force to the communist state. The net result of the forty years of communist rule is thus the commitment and loyalty of the Polish intelligentsia to the Church on a scale unparalleled in any other Catholic country.

The 'opposition' movement

The third factor which contributes to the new situation in Poland and which affects the political attitudes of the educated stratum is the significant strength of the political opposition. This opposition in Poland is not a new phenomenon. The beginning of political opposition in Poland coincided with the wave of dissident movements in the communist bloc during the period of *détente*. It is characteristic, however, that in the 1970s the Poles did not want to be labelled as dissidents: in contrast to the rest of the communist bloc, where there was one official truth and one official ideology with regard to which some intellectuals voiced their dissent, Poland had become, under Gomułka and even more so under Gierek, a society in which the Party, while paying lip-service to Communism, did not insist on ideological orthodoxy.

Poland became in that respect similar to a 'normal' police state in which the authorities were not particularly concerned with what people thought as long as they were prepared to follow the code of conduct imposed by the regime. Without insistence on ideological and cultural uniformity the concept of dissidence in the 1970s became virtually redundant; people were categorized into those who were 'well behaved' and those who by their activities challenged the established order. Those who organized protest actions, such as signing widely publicised letters, participating in public demonstrations, or distributing uncensored publications, were branded as political enemies and dealt with by the police and the courts.

A handful of intellectuals and students, some of whom played an important part in the March 1968 demonstrations, became the leaders of a new political movement. After the defeat in 1968 (which meant stiff jail sentences for some of them) and the invasion of Czechoslovakia in August 1968, most of them abandoned the hope of winning allies among the dissenters and reformers within Party ranks. If there was any chance of institutional support it was the Church which was to be relied on, argued Michnik in his study on 'The Church, the Polish Left and Dialogue'. They also redefined their role by acting not merely as intellectual rebels but as direct supporters of victimized workers, organizers of new forms of uncensored cultural activities and advocates of a programme of social movement directed against the political monopoly of the Communist Party.

At a time when the majority of the educated stratum did not envisage even the remote possibility of political resistance, the idea of self-government promoted by Jacek Kuroń and other members of KOR constituted a major shift in the development of Polish political culture. The essence of Kuroń's argument was that of the necessity of abandoning hope for a dialogue which would influence the communist rulers to change their policies, and instead building a real opposition to the existing regime. Kuroń also argued that the way to achieve changes in the Polish system, or at least to make substantial inroads into its operation, was for society to organize itself on different levels of social and political activities, irrespective of whether the authorities approved or not. His was a programme of positive action, appealing to all those who were prepared to challenge the authorities by building new social institutions and developing new forms of social co-operation.

The rise of Solidarity has been a most convincing confirmation of the effectiveness of such a political programme. Self-organization, self-management, independence of the unions from Party-state control, alliance with the Church, commitment to the fundamental national and social values, an independent press and uncensored culture were the basic principles of the Polish workers' movement in the years 1980–1. The defeat of Solidarity did not undermine the validity of those objectives; on the contrary, they seem to have become an integral part of the national consciousness in the post-Solidarity period.

To argue that the Polish intelligentsia as a whole gave unqualified support to Solidarity would, of course, be an overstatement: the educated stratum remained divided along institutional and hierarchical lines, even if many of those who officially dissociated themselves from the movement voiced their sympathy and understanding for its political platform in private. The divisions became even more conspicuous after the defeat of

Solidarity; there is no doubt, however, that those among the educated stratum who defined themselves as the political opposition have multiplied.

Why do so many people among the intelligentsia – far more than ever before – opt for various forms of open political confrontation with the establishment? There is no easy answer to this question: we are dealing with a multitude of factors which account for such a development rather than with any single cause.

There is in the first place the acute and continuing economic and social crisis. The result of this situation is the authorities' lack of credibility when it comes to coping with economic and social difficulties, and their reluctance to resort to heavy-handed methods in fighting their opponents amid general discontent. There is further a continuing and growing lack of opportunities to develop social initiatives in the areas which call for attention and require collective efforts. As the economic and political reforms did not materialize, many people experienced feelings of helplessness and powerlessness, and opposition offered them a chance of independent action. Many among those who want to influence political processes but are not prepared to do so on the terms imposed by the government, or are permanently barred from public functions because of their past political record, find thus in the opposition movement their only opportunity of participating in political life.

There is finally a new factor – the rise of political aspirations – which has survived the defeat of Solidarity. Many Poles no longer wish to endure the political restrictions which were tolerated before 1980–1, and are determined to continue their fight, or at least to support those who carry out the fight on their behalf.

The new balance of forces, the relatively liberal regime, the lack of institutional forms for carrying out independent social activities, new political perspectives and the limited scope for the institutionalization of political conflicts all combine to push the opposition intelligentsia towards developing new alternative patterns of political behaviour, and new institutions which defy an unrestrained authoritarian rule. An uncensored press, regular meetings and public discussions, unauthorized lectures and publicity campaigns are new forms of social life which were completely eliminated for many decades and yet are nowadays tolerated and accepted as a fact of political life. Publishing journals, weekly and monthly magazines, books and documents have become the major form of underground activities and the area where the opposition has enjoyed its greatest success. The impressive number of titles published during the years of military and post-military rule make Poland the country which enjoys the greatest cultural and intellectual freedom in the communist bloc.

Among the wide range of opposition activities one should mention subsidising research in sensitive areas, where official studies are banned or restricted. Another important field is the allocation of special funds for those who are victimized by the police; collecting evidence concerning important current issues; and publicising facts and data which the authorities wish to keep secret. There is at the same time constant support for the Solidarity union, collecting funds to finance some of the union's activities and supplying workers with literature, speakers and information.

Legitimism and reformism as political alternatives for the Polish intelligentsia

The state of communist ideology in Poland seems to be terminal. Even among the Party members very few people of any intellectual standing pledge their commitment to communist doctrine. The few who refer to themselves as Marxists are inclined to emphasize the differences between the original teachings of Marx and the subsequent distortions of Marx's theory in the communist movement.

A good illustration of the changes in the political attitudes of Poles in the last decade has been provided by a public opinion poll carried out among tourists and visitors to the West from eastern Europe. Only those who intended to return to their country were included. The findings of the survey indicate that Poland stands out as a country where support for the left is minimal. Interviews were conducted between June 1984 and March 1985 with a representative sample of 6,282 respondents. Only 6 per cent of the East Europeans questioned failed to assess themselves in terms of the Left-Right continuum.[16]

The policy of normalization has changed the political balance of power, but it proved unsuccessful in influencing the collective consciousness. The average educated Pole seems to speak the same language and cherish the same views about Poland, irrespective of whether he works as a university don, an army officer, a veterinary surgeon or a primary school teacher. He would certainly refer to the Russians with contempt and spite, deplore the geo-political position of Poland, express doubts about the ability of

Table 7.3 National differences in self-assessment on a left-right continuum

	Czecho-slovakia	Hungary	Poland	Rumania	Bulgaria	All except Poland
	%	%	%	%	%	%
Left	9	8	3	6	18	9
Centre	70	74	62	74	65	72
Right	21	18	35	20	17	19

Table 7.4 Evolution of political self-assessment in terms of a right-left continuum

	Poland 1977/8	1984/5
	%	%
Left	19	3
Centre	62	62
Right	19	35
No. of Cases	1,553	1,424

the government to cope with the crisis, and voice admiration for western goods and perhaps even for the achievements of western governments.

There is no doubt, however, that the centrality of the economic and social functions carried out by the communist-controlled administration poses a serious dilemma for the intelligentsia and, in particular, for the intellectual elite who have a deeply ingrained sense of social obligation and social responsibility in public affairs. The choice between a complete refusal of co-operation and some form of collaboration with the state is by no means easy, and has pros and cons which cannot be ignored.

The general mood of the Polish population does not favour, it seems, confrontation and radical policies. Moreover, people's main concern is the dire state of the economy; they are prepared to support all endeavours leading to substantial improvement in living standards in the foreseeable future.

It should also be acknowledged that the professionals who form the backbone of the Party-state apparatus are much more independent in their activities under Jaruzelski's leadership than ever before. The control of the Party over the administration has been seriously reduced; the scope of decision-making by lower-level administrators and managers has been extended, the autonomy of professional associations and research institutes has been increased, and the toleration of unorthodox views propagated at the universities and in state-sponsored publications, all the ups and downs notwithstanding, is considerable. In spite of the centralized control of economic and cultural activities, there is considerable scope for individual achievement and collective effort. The real issue at stake is, in fact, not that of participation but of the terms on which people are prepared to co-operate.

The contrast to the situation in previous decades, including the 1960s and the 1970s, lies in a much greater tolerance by the authorities towards intellectual dissent and even inner-Party criticism, a toleration which generates a legalistic and reformist trend within the Polish intelligentsia opposed to those who represent the intransigent opposition. A member of the intelligentsia is thus no longer haunted by the inevitable choice between total submission and total rebellion, but is able to find a middle ground in public life which allows him to preserve some political independence, while having room to manoeuvre, and independent political initiative.

The legalist reformist trend is represented by Party members and non-Party officials who refuse to serve as a rubber-stamp for the decisions of the leadership and try to use their positions to enforce more liberal and reformist policies, those within the Party and outside it who co-operate and participate in different organizations and associations without paying the price of total submission and, finally, those who identify openly with the opposition but try to preserve the legalistic forms of their activities.

At a time when economic and political reforms are on the agenda, all such forms of legalist dissent constitute an integral part of the search for better and more rational solutions. They mark a much higher degree of the politicisation of the Polish intelligentsia than ever before; the majority of those who participate in legalistic and reformist activities previously remained aloof from politics or were confined to the role of 'yes-men'.

The political deadlock of liberalized autocracy

Despite the positive changes outlined above, one of the greatest paradoxes of the present situation in Poland remains the discrepancy between the political awakening of considerable parts of the intelligentsia and their limited influence on political decision-making. The main dilemma faced by any member of the intelligentsia who wishes to play a part in the political process is the unenviable choice between 'resistance without participation', as promoted by some radicals, and 'participation without resistance', as often practised by the reformers.

In the first few years after the military coup, many supporters of Solidarity among the intelligentsia hoped for an early revival of the workers' rebellion. Street demonstrations took place on numerous occasions in many Polish cities, some of them involving tens of thousands of people. Yet the government was determined not to make any concessions to the outlawed union and, by developing and consolidating the security police forces against the organised underground, it tightened its grip on society.

In this new situation the main efforts of the oppositional intelligentsia understandably focused its attention on intellectual and cultural pursuits. In the realm of ideas, words and symbols, the authorities were fighting a losing battle, with the independent publications all over the country becoming a most conspicuous feature of Poland's everyday life.

In the first period which followed the defeat of Solidarity the tasks of the radical opposition were made easier by the widespread refusal of eminent artists, writers, composers and poets to co-operate with the authorities, but understandably the non-cooperation policy gradually subsided and became eroded by the influx of individuals who saw their chance of personal profit by making full use of access to the official culture.

The process of retreat from the non-cooperation policy commenced with many actors and film producers returning to their theatres, film groups and artistic sponsors. Gradually even those writers who used to present their works for publication in the underground press changed their minds, the most striking shift manifesting itself in Konwicki's decision to publish his book in an official publishing house. As he declared in an article entitled 'Nowy Świat street and its neighbourhood':

> Now I return again to my yoke. Of my own accord, I submit to the loving embrace of the noble office, which resides in Warsaw at Mysia Street [the censorship office]. Here I am already safe. Here my pen is followed by the watchful eye of my known protector, my intellectual father, my spiritual guide. How heavenly and safe I feel. At last.[17]

Konwicki's declaration is full of bitterness and irony. It reflects the dilemma of a Polish intellectual who cannot live without the public, and who is prepared to enter into the wilderness to carry out his vocation as best he can.

There is, however, an underlying layer in Konwicki's argument. He is prepared to present his book in a state-sponsored publishing house because they are nowadays allowed to publish what is offered to them by well-known rebellious writers. The writer is faced with an unexpected freedom of expression, which makes an insistence on underground publication almost pointless.

The liberalization of the cultural policy obviously undermines the impact of uncensored publications and narrows down the range of the people who saw in them an outlet for their creativity. Once cultural policy becomes liberalized, the do-it-yourself methods adopted by the underground opposition prove to be no match for the enormous machinery and resources which the authorities have at their disposal. While under the German occupation of Poland underground education and literature were the only means of national self-expression and creativity, the seminars, discussions, publications and courses promoted by the radical opposition have been but a small appendage to government-sponsored systems of education, public galleries, universities, theatrical performances, publishing houses, newspapers and the mass media. Moreover, the state-controlled institutions which specialise in cultural and intellectual activities rely on an army of fully employed specialists, while the opposition counter-culture has to rely in the first place on voluntary part-timers. Finally, there is the problem of access to the distributive media. Television, radio, daily newspapers and weekly magazines are operated under a virtual monopoly of the Party state, while the opposition has to utilise the patchy network of devoted activists and rely marginally on the hospitality and support of certain priests and parishes.

In the new situation the underground intellectual activities have to concentrate on those areas in which censorship is least tolerant, i.e., on the most sensitive political issues. Here, however, the radical opposition is faced with a growing indifference on the part of the authorities to the written word. The many years of 'the war' since August 1980 have undermined the belief of the public that words and ideas alone can change the grim reality.

One of the most interesting features of the present political system in Poland is the incongruity between the degree of freedom of the press and the effects of the publications. In a public opinion poll carried out in September 1987 by CBOS (the Centre of Public Opinion Research), on a representative sample of 583 journalists, 72.8 per cent indicated that the criticism in the official press was greater than ten years ago (i.e. in the late 1970s), but the majority (72 per cent) expressed the opinion that the effects of criticism in the press were either the same (50.3 per cent) or less (21.7 per cent) than ten years ago.[18]

For those who believe that participation in public criticism influences the decision-makers, such statements have a sobering influence. The authorities are well insulated against the effects of such criticism. As long as they can eliminate open rebellion, they can afford not to heed the voice of public opinion. At the same time public criticism helps to diffuse frustration, serves as a substitute outlet for grievances and reinforces the impression that the political leadership welcomes advice and assessment of their policies from the citizens.

The frustration of the hopes of the radical intelligentsia to exercise political influence from the outside by denouncements, accusations and articulation of collective demands is matched by the limitations imposed upon moderate reformers who opt for change from within. Many of them have learned from their bitter everyday experience that participation without political power offers little chance of influencing the decision-makers. They perceive also more and more clearly that co-option to government bodies is a poor substitute for real representation based on free elections and assignments backed by independent organizations and associations.

The last few years of the misguided economic policy are a good example of how ineffective were the warnings and arguments of the experts and consultative bodies in the face of direct pressure from the political leadership, whose main concerns were the maintenance of political stability and the avoidance of any far-reaching reforms which might affect the existing power structure, frustrate the dogmatic wing within the Communist Party, or cause damaging frictions within the ruling elite.

The moderates thus face a staggering dilemma; if they want to participate they have to do so on the terms imposed by the government, scaling down their criticism and exercising camouflage to make themselves acceptable to those in power.

In a system where criticism is muffled or disguised and open rebellion leads to elimination from political life, the distance between dissension and acquiescence, independence and servility, idealism and opportunism is easily blurred, compromises are misinterpreted and cunning manoeuvres can be regarded as a disgraceful retreat, a situation which exposes many of those who act with good intentions to public criticism.

In search of leadership

According to recent studies, approximately 25 per cent of Poles are in favour of confrontational policies; another 25 per cent support the regime. The rest constitute a volatile but potentially important centre which the communist government must cajole, or at least neutralize, in the awareness that for the first time in Polish post-war history there is an alternative political leadership in which the uncompromising and militant groups of the radical intelligentsia play an important part.

The paradox of the present situation lies, among others, in the growing dependence of the communist leadership on the members of the intelligentsia who are otherwise alienated by the system. While immediately after the war there were no more than about 100,000 people with higher education, in 1984 there were 1,600,000 such people. If we combine the last figure with that of people with full secondary and post-secondary education and incomplete higher education, we come to 6,264 million people, i.e. one out of every three persons in employment is of a general intellectual standard above the primary and vocational level, who on these grounds would qualify for the category of the intelligentsia in the nineteenth century.

Out of 1.6 million people with higher education in 1984, there were in the Communist Party only 369,000. In such a situation the claim of the Party to intellectual leadership is hardly plausible.

The Party is faced with the grim reality of the economic crisis for which they are held responsible and which they have been so far unable to solve. Although they present themselves as the vanguard of the reform movement, with promises that the new economic policy will result in a rapid increase in output and saturation of the market with consumer goods, the average Pole has little confidence in assurances of future prosperity at the expense of the present living standard, which for many has been reduced to a bare minimum.

The attempts to carry out reforms in conditions of economic imbalance and without inflicting new hardships are like squaring the circle, and the

Party is to a great extent applying crude trial-and-error methods resulting in erratic push-and-pull cycles. Gone are the days when they could claim that they were endowed with a special knowledge which allowed them to set the objectives for social development and to design the means of achieving them. Gone are the days when the superiority of Marxism-Leninism could be validated by denouncing the evils of the capitalist order. The consensus of educated Poles is the main problem which the Party leadership has to solve if it wants to overcome apathy, indifference and a lack of commitment among the hundreds of thousands of state employees in responsible jobs.

On the surface, the educated stratum in Poland favours reforms which would bring about the marketisation of the Polish economy: such reforms are supported by the Church, by the radicals and by the legalistic opposition, the opponents to the reforms consisting allegedly of frustrated bureaucrats and communist officials who see their positions threatened by economic competition and the growth of private entrepreneurship.

One should not forget, however, that the immediate effects of such reforms would be enormous price rises, which in the first place affect all those on fixed incomes, including the bulk of the educated stratum. The rank-and-file intelligentsia mostly earn their living by working for the state and depend on the policies which determine public sector spending. While managers, many well-qualified technicians and people in highly marketable professions expect their incomes to increase in line with increased demand for their services, the remainder of the intelligentsia (in common with many unqualified workers) expect a further reduction in their living standards and may opt for the continuation of state protectionism and patronage as opposed to radical change.

As consensus is so far non-existent, the ruling elite is displaying a lack of purpose and indecisiveness which is a far cry from their arrogant confidence in the past. In a crisis-ridden society there is, however, a strong demand for direction and purpose and, when those in power prove unable to respond to that need, society looks to intellectual elites to fill the ideological vacuum and to provide them with spiritual and political leadership.

Is the Polish intelligentsia able to fulfil those expectations as it has done many times previously in Poland? Is it able, in particular, to overcome the tendency towards mindless radicalism on the one hand, and toothless reformism on the other hand?

There is no doubt that in the past the domination of the conservative forces in the USSR did not leave much hope for democratic change in Poland and pushed the opposition towards the fight in favour of unobtainable objectives while depriving the reformers of the will to enforce their demands by the exercise of unyielding pressures. A new political climate in the USSR has certainly been a decisive influence on the attitudes of the Polish intelligentsia, reinforcing the trends towards 'new realism' among the political opposition and encouraging the moderates to close their ranks in the fight for reforms.

Yet the new situation has its dangers as well. The Poles are left with the choice between negotiated change and explosive confrontations which might be fuelled by the economic crisis and the high cost of social and economic reforms. One cannot forget that the state of collective consciousness in Poland has been seriously afflicted by the traumatic and frustrating experience of the early 1980s, which accounts up to now for the emotional outbursts and collective illusions. Moreover, many political groups engulfed in the historical past tend to dress in old costumes, use old vocabulary and revive old ideologies which can hardly be used as adequate guidelines in dealing with the complexities of modern economic and political life.

Conclusions

All the factors which have changed the position of the Polish intelligentsia – the economic crisis and revival of the market, the increased authority of the Church, the strength of the anti-communist radical opposition and the activisation of the reformist 'revisionism' – are, paradoxically, a product of many decades of a political regime which worked for a planned, state-owned economy, the laicisation of society and the elimination of social conflicts.

The present crisis has released new dynamic forces within the educated strata on the individual and social level, creating a situation which contrasts significantly with the complacency and apathy of the Polish intelligentsia in the past few decades. This is a development which vindicates the thesis about intelligentsia as a stratum of a particular social calling which supplies society with 'expressive leaders' in conditions when for one reason or another a revolution of consciousness is far ahead of social change.[19] In such a situation there is a sense of identity and purpose which overrides all political differences and elevates the 'freefloating' vanguard of the intelligentsia – the writers, artists, film producers, scientists and social thinkers – to the position of spiritual leaders.

The paradox of that development lies, however, in the fact that the revival of the ethos of the old intelligentsia takes place in a society in which there are new actors on the political scene. The rebellious intelligentsia faces not the amorphous masses which need to be woken up, enlightened and mobilized, but a system dominated on the one hand by the Party state, and on the other by the Church, and in which the workers, the peasants, the new enterpreneurs and the professional classes try to establish their identities. Once some basic reforms of the political structure allow the interest groups to organize themselves, articulate their claims and participate in political decision-making the functions of the 'totality-oriented' intelligentsia will wither away, leaving room for political parties, associations, trade unions and pressure groups to voice sectional demands and shape general policies on the basis of democratic electoral processes.

Notes

1 Hirszowicz, Maria (1980) *The Bureaucratic Leviathan*, Oxford: Martin Robertson, ch.5.
2 Żołkiewski, Stefan (1962) 'O polityce kulturalnej PRL w latach 1945–1948', *Kultura i Społeczeństwo*, vol. 6, no. 4, 12–13.
3 Zwolski, Jerzy (1965) 'Płace pracowników działu "Nauka i rozwój techniki" w latach siedemdziesiątych i osiemdziesiątych', *Zagadnienia Naukoznawstwa*, vol.21, no.3(83), 385.
4 Rowicki, Janusz (1986) 'Jak się żyje', *Słowo Powszechne*, 2 September.
5 Kosiński, Michał (1986) 'Zaglądanie do kieszeni', *Perspektywy*, 5 December.
6 Doliniak, Krystyna (1987) 'Płacowy ranking', *Kurier Polski*, 11 October.
7 'Z badań CBOS. Jak sie żyje?' *Rzeczypospolita*, 29–30 August 1987.
8 Rykowski, Zbigniew (1987) 'Raport o studentach', *Więź*, 5.
9 Konferencja prasowa rzecznika rządu, *Rzeczypospolita*, 24 February 1988.
10 Pardus, Jerzy (1986) 'Pojemność żołądka a szare komorki', *Rzeczywistość*, 29 June.
11 Glemp, Józef (1987) 'Droga Kościoła w Polsce Ludowej' *Pregląd Katolicki*, 24 May.
12 A note in *Sprawy i Ludzie*, 7 May 1987.
13 Lipiński, Edmund Wnuk (1987) *Nierowności i upośledzenia w świadomości Społecznej*, Warsaw: Polska Akademia Nauk, Ch. 2, 45–6.
14 Słomińska, Janina (1987) 'Apostolstwo Laikatu-wariant polski', *Więź*, 2–3.
15 Ibid.
16 Shafir, Michael (1987) 'Left and Right in eastern Europe', *Orbis, A Journal of World Affairs*, Summer.
17 Konwicki, Tadeusz (1986) *Nowy świat i okolice*, Warsaw: Czytelnik, 6.
18 Urbanowski, Henryk (1987) 'A teraz za kulisy', *Sztandar Młodych*, 10 October.
19 Gella, Alexander (ed.) (1976) *The Intelligentsia and the Intellectuals*, London: Sage.

8

The myth of the market
and the reality of reform

Lena Kolarska-Bobińska

Institute of Philosophy and Sociology, Polish Academy of Sciences, Warsaw

There are many phenomena in Polish economic life that seem strangely paradoxical and lacking in common sense. They appear less startling, however, if one takes a closer look at their causes, the social, political and economic reasons. If the factors which govern behaviour and attitudes are examined, these irrational phenomena can even be seen as rational and logical reactions on the part of individuals and organizations.

In this article, I shall concentrate on certain features of public opinion during the reforming of the economy since 1982. I will be seeking to identify general characteristics of these features as well as looking at the interests and attitudes of specific groups in Polish society. I shall seek their explanation in phenomena which are in evidence in the socialist countries, such as the dominance of politics over the economy, the welfare state, and the inefficiency of the centrally managed economy. Factors such as propaganda and individual everyday experiences are also relevant in shaping social consciousness. The influence of each of these phenomena, however, is not always unequivocal or easily foreseen. It is some of these influences that lead to the unexpected and seemingly paradoxical reactions mentioned above.

The myth of the market in a centrally planned economy

One striking feature in the surveys of public opinion which have been conducted during the last six years has been the general acceptance of the market economy.[1] In a survey about the working population's view of the economy, between 63 per cent and 82.4 per cent (depending on the category) of those questioned about what constitutes good economic practice gave the highest priority to subjecting all enterprises to the laws of the market and free competition without interference from superior organs.[2] In a survey entitled 'Desirable social and political order in the economy', conducted in 1984, 82 per cent of those questioned were in favour of 'introducing the laws of the market and free competition into the economy'.[3] In 1985, 87 per cent of respondents employed in industry were of the opinion that it was right to move towards free competition between different enterprises.[4]

The indications are, therefore, that the laws of the market and free competition elicit a very positive response. What meaning these laws have, however, may vary from respondent to respondent. The vast majority of the Polish public has never had any experience of a market economy, and therefore any conception or view of it has been shaped by factors other than direct experience. It could even be claimed that in a society which has functioned within a centrally planned economy for the past forty years, a 'market economy myth' has arisen. This has happened because the market mechanism and free competition are identified with a highly efficient economy and a high standard of living, neither of which has been achieved by the centrally planned system. It may seem paradoxical that the phrase 'market economy' has positive associations, when one takes into account that for years the propaganda has defined it as a manifestation of revisionism in its purest form, a foreign body in a healthy socialist economy. It could be argued that these positive associations are a consequence of the last few years: they have been shaped under the influence which accompanied the origin and the implementation of the reforms. However, despite the fact that the essential role of economic mechanisms is mentioned in the reform programme formulated in 1981 under the title 'Directions for economic reform', there is no unequivocal statement as to the ultimate character of the economic system. It is only said that:

> The economy will be run on the principle of central planning, with market forces being taken into account. Under the new system, market forces will be a means for determining the economic activity of any given enterprise as well as a factor which will give the activity of enterprises direction, within the aims defined by 'the central plan'.[5]

In 1982, after the introduction of martial law, the first stages of the reform based on the above-mentioned programme were announced. However, the changes which were introduced between the years 1982 and 1986 deviated from the guidelines in 'Directions for economic reform', and could not have been identified as moves towards a free market economy. An example of this deviation is the continuing widespread practice of the central allocation of raw materials and other inputs during this time. Another has been the consolidation of hierarchical management structures in many important branches of the economy. Meanwhile, the media, which mirrored the clashes between the pro- and anti-reform tendencies, totally obscured the nature of the actual reform and the ultimate economic changes to which the reform was supposed to lead. Economists and sociologists have said again and again that change is not possible if society at large is not presented with a clear aim which the reform is intended to achieve. This aim could not be properly expressed, however, on account of the aforementioned discrepancies within the power apparatus and the differing aspirations of the pro- and anti-reform lobbies. As a result, the media said in a very general way that the aim of the reforms was to improve economic efficiency and living standards, whilst at the same time creating a picture of nineteenth-century capitalism with iron discipline, unemployment, etc.

I shall discuss the consequences of the way the reforms were presented to the public later on. My intention here is merely to emphasize that the contradictory signals coming from the economy and from the media during the first half of the 1980s could not have helped the shaping of the positive associations which the idea of the market economy engendered. Without doubt, the discussion which went on in the press and on television legitimized the presence of the market and certain other 'capitalist' mechanisms within an existing system of socialism. It also had a certain indefinable influence on the growing acceptance of material differences as well as on the growth of anti-egalitarian attitudes. Nevertheless, there is a basis for suggesting that the myth of the market economy was created independently of the processes connected with the reform, several years before the latter was begun in 1982.

The awakening of powerful consumer aspirations within Polish society in the 1970s had a definite influence on the shaping of this myth. During this period, society was encouraged to believe that its aspirations could be fulfilled within the framework of a perfected system of central planning. The economic crisis and the collapse of the economy led to violent disillusionment with this type of system, and a growing belief that it was unable to satisfy society's needs and aspirations. Hopes of a better existence were redirected towards the market economy. It is relevant to note that, as a consequence of years of propaganda, the concepts of the free market and central planning exist as two mutually exclusive opposites in the public consciousness. Favouring the market economy is in a large measure the consequence of a negative attitude towards existing economic practices in Poland, and not only a positive attitude towards the idea of the market economy itself.

Lack of awareness about the connection between production and consumption within the market economy has undoubtedly influenced the shaping of the belief that the source of fulfilment for society's needs and aspirations lies in the free market. As I will demonstrate later on when discussing attitudes towards price rises, society's view of the market economy is based on extrapolations from its direct experience of certain features of the centrally planned economy. One of the most basic features of the planned economy to have been identified by many groups in society is the lack of connection between the spheres of production and consumption, between skill or output and remuneration, between income and purchasing power, and between the work done and the privileges given. It may be assumed that the myth of the free market is based solely on the perception of the level of consumption in countries in the West, without the necessary reference to the sphere of production. This is not only the result of extrapolation from features within the planned economy, but equally of the simple fact that the sphere of consumption in the West has been more accessible and familiar to Polish society than the sphere of production which, with all its social consequences, is a specific feature of the market economy.

Whatever the factors which have brought about the myth of the market mechanisms may be, faith in their superior effectiveness and in the high standards of living which they are thought to guarantee has led to a disregard for the limitations of the market, and a tendency to treat it as a universal cure for all the shortcomings of the Polish economy. This is one of the reasons why the myth has arisen in the consciousness of a number of social groups. One might think that acceptance of such a myth would make it easier to introduce economic reform in Poland. Since a large section of society is convinced that a reform of the centrally controlled system would bring little change, and perceives the need for fundamental change in the Polish economy, reforms directed towards a market economy ought to be greeted enthusiastically and enjoy wide public support. This, however, is not the case and there are many factors to explain this. They can be summed up in a general way under the following categories: first, the myth of the market economy and the reality of its consequences; second, the way in which the reforms have been introduced; third, the character of the institutions introducing the reform and how society perceives them; and fourth, the interests of various social groups.

The myth of the free market economy and the reality of its consequences

The myth of the free market means that although it is accepted as a general concept, this acceptance may decrease when it is related to concrete economic solutions and indeed to their social consequences. An example of this is that although in 1984 80 per cent of people were in favour of the laws of the market and free competition, only 59 per cent of those questioned said that they were in favour of increasing opportunities for the private sector within the economy.[6] This high percentage decreased further when respondents were asked about their attitude

163

towards the privatisation of different parts of the economy and various types of enterprises. In 1987, 59 per cent of workers and 76 per cent of directors were in favour of removing all restrictions on the setting up of small privately owned workshops; 24 per cent of workers and 25 per cent of directors were in favour of removing restrictions on the setting up of small privately owned enterprises; 11 per cent of workers and 8 per cent of directors were in favour of removing restrictions on medium-sized enterprises.[7] Does this imply that the respondents wanted a free market economy, but without private ownership? Or were they in favour of state ownership, with the economy controlled not by the central administration but by the dictates of market forces controlled by no one? This interpretation is borne out by the results of other surveys.[8]

It is, however, difficult to give an unequivocal answer to these questions since social perceptions are formed under the influence of a variety of factors. On the one hand, private ownership has always been one of the greatest taboos in the propaganda and ideology of the political system in Poland, although this taboo is now being guardedly and timidly discarded. Furthermore, a great many people find it hard to imagine any type of ownership taking precedence over state ownership in Poland. For many, the private sector has negative connotations since its level of efficiency, the quality of its products and services and the quality of customer service are low due to lack of competition. In addition, there are many beliefs about the private sector which are not necessarily justified, but which nevertheless result in negative feelings towards it, e.g., the supposedly high earnings of skilled craftsmen, the illegal way they handle their affairs, etc. The media was instrumental in encouraging these kinds of beliefs until recently, and they gained credence in a society which has been particularly sensitive to improper ways of accumulating wealth since 1980. For many people, private ownership amounts to a total loss of control over what incompetent and dishonest businessmen get up to. It is worth pointing out that support for private ownership has risen in recent years because many people perceive the possibility of improving their own material position through employment in the private sector, since the employee as well as the owner of a private enterprise earns more.

The latest round of the research project 'Poles 1988' finds a change of attitude to the private sector and private property. While in 1984 the number favouring an expansion of the private sector was 59 per cent, in 1988 it was 73 per cent of the respondents. It was also interesting to find a high acceptance of full or partial reprivatisation of selected sectors of the economy: large-scale enterprises (12 per cent for full, 32 per cent for partial), housing construction (29.5 and 38 per cent), agricultural services (31 and 38 per cent). It is yet unclear whether that increase in acceptance of the private sector will result in greater understanding in society of the market economy, competition and economic mechanisms. However, this increased acceptance may be expected to result in greater clarity and coherence of views among the supporters of the pro-market solutions.

The discrepancy between the acceptance of the general idea of 'the market economy and free competition' and the much lower acceptance of its actual consequences explains society's attitude to the issue of employment. In 1984, 81.9 per cent of respondents supported the dismissing of incompetent employees, while only 34.4 per cent were in favour of allowing unemployment to occur.[9] Unemployment was the least popular of anti-egalitarian and pro-market views.[10] This indicates that whilst it is socially acceptable to dismiss individual employees, it is not acceptable to put larger groups out of work. One might ask whether the fact that 57.2 per cent of respondents were opposed to unemployment and 53.4 per cent were in favour of a policy of full employment represents a large percentage or not. It is difficult to answer this question without conducting a comparative survey of public opinion in countries where there is registered unemployment. It would seem that unemployment is seen as a necessary social evil in capitalist ideology. Full employment, however, represents one of the principal ideological assumptions of the centrally planned economy and is seen as a fundamental achievement of the new order: it is the foundation stone of a socialist system based on social justice. From this point of view, the percentage of people in favour of unemployment and opposed to a policy of full employment would appear to be high.

However, whether we accept the 34 per cent in favour of unemployment as an expression of social acceptance of it or not, it can be assumed that there would be strong resistance to unemployment were it to stop being a purely theoretical concept. There are many people in Poland who perceive unemployment as a means of curing the economy and instilling a healthier work ethic in other people. They feel that they, however, should be protected from it.

The discrepancy in attitude towards the idea of the market economy as opposed to its consequences is not only a result of the abstract nature of the former and the reality of the latter. In my view, the source of the discrepancy may be in something deeper, namely in society's attitude towards the different functions which the state fulfils, i.e., the political and economic functions on the one hand, and the social and caring functions on the other. Under a socialist system, the state is present in all these areas to a far greater extent than is the case in any western democracy. It is committed to developing and retaining large-scale control over the political activities of its citizens and, until now, over the whole economy. It also fulfils a variety of welfare functions, through a network of institutions which were created for this purpose. In addition, the state's economic function within a centrally planned economy is subject in a large measure to political as well as social and welfare considerations. This brings about a certain basic paradox based on the one hand on society's differing attitudes to the various spheres of state involvement, and on the other hand concerning the transferring of attitudes from one sphere onto another.

Society's differing attitudes to the various areas of state involvement are based on acceptance of the state's welfare functions and rejection of its attempts to develop its control over political and economic forces. As P. Kuczyński says, 'Ambivalence in relation to the state is expressed on the one hand through demands made on it and on the other hand through opposition towards its all-embracing monopoly. In other words, the gradual change in attitudes to the state expresses itself in the view that the state ought to "insure and care about the social security of all workers and their standard of living, and at the same time not interfere in the freedom of the individual".'[11] How is this attitude towards the state reflected in attitudes towards the free market? I differ with the writer quoted above because, in my view, many people see the market and free competition as representing a way to that most highly prized human value – freedom. It represents a means of restricting the inefficient monopoly of the state in economic life, of putting an end to unearned privilege, of making work dependent on clear assessable factors, based on its value and not on arbitrary administrative decisions, of knowing that one's career will progress according to ability and not because of political affiliation, etc. Therefore, the market economy is in part accepted because it is perceived as restricting the political and economic functions of the state, whilst a lack of acceptance of the social consequences of a market system is connected with valuing the social benefits which many regard as their due.

The close connection mentioned above between all functions of the state causes attitudes to be transposed from one area into another. The desire to restrict state control in economic life on grounds of efficiency and for political reasons is accompanied by a fear of state care being withdrawn from economic life. These attitudes influence public feeling about the various proposals for economic reform. One example is the attitude to the idea of the market determining price levels, which I shall deal with more fully later. At this point, I wish only to emphasize society's paradoxical attitude to the policy of the state determining price levels. Although the state introduced the price rises which met with such strong social opposition, and was at pains to convince society of their necessity, three-quarters of respondents in 1985 were opposed to the market determining price levels and were in favour of state control over price levels.[12] In the opinion of S. Nowak, price rises in Poland were perceived as evidence that the state was not fulfilling its welfare function.[13] One hypothesis is that the growing criticism of the efficiency of state care increases the expectations by certain social groups of more welfare. Others, however, see state care as being thinly spread and ineffective. They therefore abandon the idea.

The result is that despite the fact that the state introduced price rises, it was perceived by many as protecting the standard of living of its citizens. This paradox may be a result of the above-mentioned perception of the state as a widely conceived source of social care. This idea is supported by the media which presents both state-owned and private enterprises as pushing up prices in a wilful, uncontrolled and unjustifiable manner. Many people maintain the belief that enterprises which are not subject to state control make wild profits at the cost of the consumer. On top of this, the media promotes an image of a free market where unreasonably high price levels are set in an arbitrary fashion by the producer. This idea is widespread since it is backed by common experience over many years: price levels in the planned economy were set in an arbitrary fashion in accordance with political, ideological, or social principles. They had no basis in economic principles such as the balance of payments, competition, or the laws of supply and demand. This experience effects conceptions of the market economy, with the additional feature that in this economic system there would be many more agents making arbitrary decisions about price levels. This brings us to the second reason why state control of prices is supported: it is much easier to negotiate price rises with one partner – the state – than with numerous invisible enterprises beyond one's reach. As the experience of 1971, 1976 and 1980 demonstrated, pressure on the state can bring results.

I have shown the disparity between acceptance of 'the market economy' and acceptance of some of its more important consequences. One of the reasons for this is the mythical and abstract character of the idea of the market, as opposed to its actual character in terms of how it affects people's lives. The disparity is intensified by the approach taken by the media, which, whilst emphasizing the favourable influence of market mechanisms on the economy as a whole, has at the same time pointed to the negative effects on the individual's personal situation. K.T. Teoplitz writes that in this type of propaganda, reform is associated with financial burden, price rises and belt-tightening: great emphasis is placed on putting across the message that this all stems from a sincere desire to warn society that there are hard times ahead.[14] Its aim is to strip the idea of the free market of its mythical character and explain its reality. The problem, however, is that if the positive influence of market mechanisms on people's personal situations is not emphasized and only the influence on the abstract concept of 'the economy' is underlined, the whole of this propaganda takes on the above-mentioned character of 'alarming' the public with visions of 'nineteenth-century capitalism'. The connection between what is happening in the economy and the individual's personal situation is only perceived by a small minority. It is worth emphasizing that, for many people, the myth of the market system was formed under the pressure of consumer demand, in isolation from the sphere of production and its social consequences. This strategy of stripping away the myth by emphasizing the social cost only serves to widen the divide between the positive associations which the idea of the market economy engenders and the resistance to its consequences.

If the idea of the market system has positive connotations, what is a reform which is supposed to be based on market mechanisms identified with? With the idea of 'the market' which arouses positive feelings, or with the actual consequences which often arouse opposition? I shall answer this question by looking at the influence the following factors have had on the public's attitude to the reform; the way in which the reform has been introduced; public attitudes towards the institutions bringing in the reform; and differing group interests.

The way in which reform has been introduced

It was only in 1986 when the architects of the reform drew up its 'second stage' that they clearly articulated their intention that market mechanisms were to be its basic element. From the moment the reforms were announced in 1982, until 1986, there was no clear vision of the system being proposed. As a result, the public was not in a position to associate the reform with a concrete picture of the proposed economic system, and as a result the reforms were identified with a vague idea that they would make the country better off.

The haziness and the 'hybrid' nature of the reform were accompanied by a total lack of logic in the way it was implemetned. Five years of the so-called first stage of reform (1982–6) have resulted in nothing more than minor changes in the economy which are not easily perceived by society.[15] The majority of people merely perceived the systematic introduction of substantial price rises. The mass media continued to convince the public that price rises were inescapable as the reform was being implemented. Since these increases were not, however, accompanied by any other perceptible changes, the result was that the public began to identify the reform solely with price rises, that is, with something that hit them hardest of all.

An interesting point is that the price rises have not only been perceived on an individual level by the general public but also by workers in relation to the goods produced at their factories. In answer to the question of what changes had taken place within the last year at their workplaces, 62 per cent of those employed in enterprises embraced by the reform mentioned the price increase on their own products, whilst only 11 per cent of those working in enterprises not embraced by the reform mentioned this.[16] If there was hope initially of improvement in people's material and personal situations when the reforms were first being introduced, it began to slide away as time went on. The following statistics bear this out:

Table 8.1 Evaluation of the economic situation (in percentage terms)

The economic situation	85	86	87	88
	Dec	Dec	Oct	Mar.
Good and fairly good	11.9	12.2	6.7	2.3
Neither good nor bad	34.8	26.8	18.7	15.0
Bad and very bad	46.0	58.5	73.8	81.3
Don't know	7.1	2.0	1.0	0.7

Table 8.1b Hopes for improvement in the economic situation (in percentage terms)

The economic situation	85	86	87	88
	Dec	Dec	Oct	Mar
Will improve	42.4	29.9	23.3	20.0
Will not change	27.7	32.7	25.3	24.4
Will worsen	16.4	28.2	38.8	41.5
Don't know	13.3	8.9	12.1	14.0

These statistics have been taken from a survey conducted by the government office for public opinion polls.[17]

The survey indicates that public pessimism was at its highest six years after the reform had begun, that is, when the country was embarking on the so-called second stage of reform. It is worth pointing out that the negative attitude towards price increases represents a natural protest against lowered living standards and is motivated more by lack of faith in the process of change than by a negative attitude towards change itself. In 1985, 25 per cent of the public thought that reform of the economy could never succeed, whilst 48 per cent felt that reform was being introduced too slowly.[18] Public opinion about the reforms was influenced by the way they were implemented and by people's everyday experience, not by any vision of the new face of the economy. One relevant factor which also influenced social attitudes towards the reform was the evaluation of the institution which was introducing the changes, i.e., the political system. Obviously, attitudes towards change depend to a large degree on the evaluation of the person or the institution introducing the change, and any readiness to accept change depends on an evaluation of the intentions of the people behind it.

Attitudes towards the institutions bringing in change

Since 1982, economic reform has formed the basis of the party's programme. At the same time, the general picture of the state of political consciousness in 1984 bore a striking resemblance to the picture in 1981, although the attitude of particular socio-economic groups towards the role of the Polish United Workers' Party has undergone a change.[19] Since then, there has been a perceptible shift towards support for the authorities, but it is difficult to state unequivocally how many people accept the existing power structure and how many people are opposed to it. In 1984, K. Jasiewicz stated on the basis of a survey that 25 per cent of the public supported the political leadership of the PUWP, 25 per cent were opposed to it and 50 per cent belonged to the 'centre', had no opinions or did not wish to express them.[20] However, other statistics suggest that 25 per cent opposition to the system represents too low a percentage.[21] Nevertheless, it shows that about three-quarters of the electorate are people whose confidence in and support for the authorities cannot be taken for granted: some of them do not trust in the sincerity of what the authorities say or do not know whether they should be trusted.

Lack of confidence in the statements made or in the actual institutions which issue them can be regained not by successive declarations, but by actions which prove their sincerity. In this case, however, the lack of coherence with which the reforms were implemented, the perceived contradictions between statement and fact, and the contradictory actions of the authorities only served to increase mistrust. This experience reinforced the stereotypes which had been built up over the years and maintained the population in the conviction that those in power, now as in the past, did not want to give up their influence and authority, even at enterprise level. This mistrust stems from society's perception of the interests of groups which represent the authorities, or groups which have a connection with them. Furthermore, the same authority which authored and declared its support for a reform based on the market system is associated by many with pro-egalitarian economics. It is therefore associated with certain ideological principles promulgated over many years, and not with the current programme of change: it is associated with the existing centralized system and not with market reform. Despite the media campaign and the intentions of the authorities, the PUWP has been associated paradoxically with forces that seek to maintain the status quo and resist change. In 1984, a survey showed that acceptance of the authority of the PUWP was linked to support for an egalitarian state system, whereas non-acceptance was linked with anti-egalitarian and pro-market views.[22] In other words, supporters of the PUWP were found to be in favour of a programme which the party was abandoning. Within the general context of the findings, there is also an indication that anti-egalitarian and pro-market principles were often perceived as being in opposition to the existing power structure and many respondents treated them as a form of protest against the authorities.

I have already said that the myth of the market economy materialized as a rejection of an economic system which had been operating in Poland for many years. This myth also emerged in opposition to the existing political system as an expression of protest against it. In the late 1970s and in 1980, Polish society expressed dissatisfaction with the existing power structure by appealing to egalitarian arguments. The demand for equality was in fact a demand for the privileges of those in power to be dismantled. After 1981, that is after the preceding administration had been brought to account, the means for expressing social dissatisfaction changed. For some, they took the form of favouring the market as an institution which was ideologically contrary to the prevailing political system in Poland. Forming a vision of a better economic system on the basis of opposition to the existing political system is not a phenomenon that is exclusive to the Polish experience. In Great Britain, 'radical attitudes towards the economic order tend to go with radical attitudes towards the political order. . . People who tend to have conflict models of management/worker relations and who disapprove of the existing distribution of income and wealth are the most cynical about politicians and the least trusting of government'.[23] Because the British government is Conservative, a negative attitude towards it is associated with greater egalitarianism. Since the political system in Poland is identified with egalitarian principles, a negative attitude towards it is expressed amongst other things by greater anti-egalitarianism. It should be emphasized, however, that this was only one of many reasons for the growth of anti-egalitarian attitudes. Other reasons such as the identification of the market with wealth or the growth of publications which propagated anti-egalitarian principles have already been discussed in this chapter.

It may seem paradoxical that the function of protest which the market economy began to fulfil came into being at the very time when the reforms were being announced by the authorities (at the beginning of 1982). It should, however, be remembered that the reforms were first announced towards the end of 1981, under pressure from Solidarity at a time when it had a legal existence. Furthermore, the principles underlying the first stage of reform did not have a clear market character, which made the definition of the market as an opposition concept easier.

The situation has changed somewhat since the middle of 1987, when the authorities decided to favour a pro-market reform more decisively. The PUWP began to include in its programme non-egalitarian slogans and to popularize them in the mass media. The January 1988 survey still confirmed the old rule that the PUWP is supported (rejected) above all by individuals with egalitarian (non-egalitarian) preferences.[24] However, the rule was weaker than four years earlier, as the PUWP began to be identified also with non-egalitarian slogans.

It needs stressing that the survey quoted above was done before the government of Mr Rakowski came to power. That government declared itself even more clearly in favour of a non-egalitarian and pro-market reform. While it is too early to predict any substantial change of long-standing attitudes, it is safe to say that, if public confidence in the political system is not increased, the situation will remain much the same: the Party will go on trying to introduce an economic system which will enable it to retain its authority, and the reforms will be seen as merely tokenistic. Therefore, any attempt to introduce reforms must be accompanied by moves which would substantially increase the influence of various groups in the decision-making process. Distrust of a system derives largely from a lack of a sense of control over it.

This interpretation is borne out by the results of the referendum which took place in Poland on 29 November 1987. 68 per cent of the electorate took part, and 44 per cent of these were in favour of swift economic reform without regard for the cost to society. Among the reasons for such meagre support for the government's proposals, it is worth mentioning the fear of the high price rises announced by the government. The only definite and immediate change was to be the introduction of price increases. The rest of the changes which were to take place were not defined and were difficult for the average citizen to picture. Because of this, the reforms were identified yet again with price rises and not with some hazy future benefit. In addition, it can be assumed that some people who supported the government's proposals for change did not take part in the referendum because of their lack of trust in the architects of these changes. Those who did participate in the referendum were groups which for various reasons support the existing political system or wish to co-operate with it. These groups consist mainly of pensioners, agricultural workers, unskilled workers, certain sections in the administrative apparatus, and some skilled workers. Surveys indicate that these groups contain the most supporters of the egalitarian system and the welfare policies of the state. Some members of these groups were against a swift change to a market economy. Others voted in favour of it as an expression of support for the authorities rather than for the market programme. Undoubtedly there were those who supported the programme of rapid economic change because they saw it as an opportunity for furthering their individual and group interests.

Differing group attitudes and interests

How, in the light of the above-mentioned considerations, do group interests manifest themselves in relation to the future shaping of the Polish economy? One striking fact is that the market economy is supported by groups which might be expected to oppose it. During the period 1981–4, there was a socially widespread increase in anti-egalitarian attitudes, in the form of acceptance of economic differences between individuals, unemployment, private sector activity and market principles.[25] However, the greatest reversal has taken place among skilled workers. In 1980 and 1981, the views of skilled and unskilled workers were similar. These groups formed the bedrock of support for egalitarian attitudes. By 1984, skilled workers were more aligned in their attitudes with the anti-egalitarian stance of the specialists and technicians than with unskilled workers. This does not mean that skilled workers can be classified as confirmed anti-egalitarians, since this group represents a variety of views. It is fair to say, however, that there has been a significant change in their attitudes. For example, 35 per cent of skilled workers and 15 per cent of unskilled workers in 1984 saw unemployment as an acceptable phenomenon. The change in the attitudes of skilled workers suggests that they were not afraid of the negative consequences of the market economy and that they thought that workers like them would not be affected. They felt secure in their employment, a fact borne out by other studies.[26] Skilled workers represented a group whose earnings had increased most sharply in the previous few years. They therefore expected their situation to remain unchanged or possibly improve with a change of economic system. In 1981, 82 per cent of skilled workers were in favour of an upper limit on the income of the highest earning groups; in 1984, it was 54 per cent.

The situation changed somewhat in 1988, which saw an end to the growth in support for inegalitarian values, support which had been rising since 1981. There are various reasons for this, the most important being the strong effects of the economic crisis and inflation which depressed the living standards of many. The slowing down of the trend towards inegalitarianism as well as a slight increase in support for policies aimed at full employment reflect the feeling of high uncertainty which is being experienced by some social groups. This feeling was strengthened by fears of major price rises. The survey was conducted in January 1988 on the eve of the first wave of price increases. This slowing of the trend was particularly in evidence among skilled workers who, as a consequence, increased their support for the policy of full employment. (The policy of increasing inegalitarianism was supported, in 1988, by 30 per cent of the skilled and 16 per cent of the unskilled workers.) This may suggest that skilled workers were hit by the crisis more strongly than others. The slowing of the trend, however, does not alter my thesis that fundamental changes are taking place in the modes of thought and action of many people.

The growth of support for anti-egalitarian and market principles can also be perceived among people who say they belong to Solidarity. In 1980, the members of Solidarity were somewhat more pro-egalitarian than the members of the 'old trade unions'. By 1984, they had become somewhat more anti-egalitarian. This fact put Solidarity activists in an interesting position. As trade union activists, they should have been supporting a programme of labour rights, whereas the laws of the market could only lead to their restriction. Much has been written in Poland about the fact that the reform should have been accompanied by a diminishing of the protective functions of individual enterprises and the state. For example, the right to employment was to be conditional on the demands of the new economic system. It could be assumed that laws which defended workers would be weakened, and new ones would be introduced to make it easier for enterprises to dismiss incompetent employees. Furthermore, it was expected that there would be unemployment among those working in enterprises which went bankrupt; that there would be decreased universalism and increased selectivity of benefits, increased repayment of social benefits, the replacement of benefits by less costly equivalents, etc.

In the face of such changes, Solidarity as a trade union should have been speaking out against market reform. This was not the case, however. Obviously, the market reform was perceived as a means of eroding the influence of the political authority rather than as a factor which would lead to the erosion of labour rights. It should be emphasized, however, that this way of thinking emerged when the controversy over the introduction of the reforms was at its height. It can be assumed that if market reforms were introduced, a split would emerge amongst the supporters of Solidarity in the form of a right-wing element (in favour of the market economy) and a left-wing element (defending labour rights). In that event, their beliefs and the way they defined themselves would be influenced by their attitudes towards basic social issues rather than their views on the political leadership in the country.

The official trade unions found themselves in a different, though no less complicated situation. They operated in co-operation with the government and were perceived as doing so by their members and by the general public. In 1984, many more members of the official 'new' trade unions than non-members supported the view that the role of the Party in governing the country should be strengthened.[27] On the other hand, the unions' entire programme was directed towards the defence of labour rights and the defence of the living standards of their members. This programme was the basis for their existence, but it also placed it in opposition to the government programme of reform and proposed price rises. The spokesman for the government gave trade union opposition as one of the reasons for the unexpectedly low support for the programme of change in the referendum.

The greatest divisions regarding the introduction of reform have occurred within the power apparatus itself. The reforms which became their own party's programme forced them into a change of ideology, a rethinking of the basic principles of socialism. The reforms also represented a direct threat to their interests. This basic conflict would emerge if Party members were really the principal force introducing and supporting the reforms. Surveys show, however, that although in 1984 (in comparison with 1980) the popularity of the egalitarian option decreased among members of the PUWP, this was more a reflection of processes taking place in the whole of society than of a concrete political direction being followed by members of the Party itself. Evidence of this was that PUWP members perceived economic issues in much the same way as the rest of society, although they had different views on the role that the Party should have in the governing of the country. Therefore members of the PUWP could not be said to represent a particular group which is supporting a programme of change: indeed, many of them perceived reform as a process which limited the influence of the Party on public life. At the same time, there was a hardening of political preference among the Party members who opted for an egalitarian system and the strengthening of the role of the PUWP in the governing of the country. This group (about 35 per cent of Party members) had the clearest and most definite preferences. Defending an unreformed system which guaranteed certain authority and privileges, this group based its stand on ideological principles as well as on lobbies by groups whose interests might have been undermined by the reforms. It also had support from sections in society whose primary concern was the defence of basic standards of living, for whom reform merely meant price increases.

It is interesting to note that, in 1988, Communist Party members were decidedly more inegalitarian than the rest of society. Over the past two years the Polish United Workers' Party has begun to introduce inegalitarian themes into its ideology. It is difficult to say whether the growth of support for these new policies represents more an ideological lip service or a perception that market mechanisms present a real chance for improving both the functioning of the economy and their own material position. It may also be the case that party members now openly admit to having views which before they kept to themselves. After all, over 20 per cent of the party membership hold a higher education diploma of one sort or another and thus could be expected to support inegalitarian values. Whatever the reasons for this change, the fact that many members of the Party support unemployment and a widening of differences in living standards reveals an interesting aspect of this organization, one which deserves separate analysis. It is in any case clear that above all the issue has divided the Party between those who want to joint the private sector themselves and those who feel committed to the standard ideological principles.

In the light of these considerations, the question is whether a coherent introduction of reform will change the political views of various groups. Will the supporters of the market economy support the political leadership if it turns out that the leadership is actually carrying out its programme and is therefore acting in their interests? It would seem that political change in the country is also needed if this section of society is to change its views. Although it is a good thing in itself from the point of view of this particular group, economic reform is also supposed to be a road to democratic freedoms and not a substitute for them. The situation for social groups such as people without educational qualifications, unskilled workers, agricultural workers, workers from small industrial enterprises and the elderly is rather different. Will the introduction of reforms which are not in their interests cause them to withdraw their support for the authorities? It is not possible to say for sure. Although public attitudes towards the political system are closely linked with their attitude to the welfare state, this is not the only determinant of political attitudes. Other determining factors may be the greater respect for authoritarianism found amongst older people, the rural population and people who have few educational qualifications. The greater the respect for authoritarianism, the less need people feel for more democracy.[28]

Conclusion

I have analysed the myth of the market economy and society's attitude to the reforms. This particular discrepancy does not embrace the difference between the reform's intentions and its implementation, since social conceptions of the market and free competition are connected neither with the verbal nor the actual process of reform. This might seem incomprehensible if it were assumed that the Polish reforms are market in character. However, as of 1988, neither the intentions of the reforms nor indeed their implementation has had such a character. Moreover, during both the period when the second stage of reform was being introduced and during the referendum, the general public did not have a clear idea of the character and consequences of the changes. As K. T. Teoplitz says, when the public was turning out to vote, it did not know 'what kind of Poland there would be two or three years after the introduction of radical reform. An economy divided into three sectors? What kind of social structure? How would it be administrated economically, socially and politically?'[29]

Any vision of reform and any attitude towards it came mainly from observation and everyday experience. Opinions on what reform was intended to achieve were not clarified but made even more confused by the media which issued a number of conflicting pictures. Other influences on society's view of the market and free competition include psychological mechanisms in the perception process as well as the values and interests of differing social groups, their aspirations and political affiliations, the available information, personal experience and finally propaganda. The number of different factors covering such a variety of areas and making themselves felt in so many directions is the reason for the series of paradoxes emerging in people's consciousness and attitudes. These seeming paradoxes are wide-ranging and affect many aspects of public opinion about the economy. The interconnecting nature of ideological, political, economic and social phenomena in Poland has played an important role in developing and strengthening public opinion. In this sense, public opinion both reflects and transforms actual features within the system. Lack of decisiveness in the implementation of reform; haziness about what will actually happen; propaganda which gives different signals; and the disparity between what is said and what is done, have added to a deepening of the contradictions within the public mind. These contradictions, reinforced by the experiences of the last few years, make the idea of the free market economy even more difficult to implement.

Notes

1 An opinion poll conducted in 1981 showed that 20 per cent of respondents were in favour of 'reinforcing central planning in the running of the economy' whilst 51 per cent were opposed to it (22 per cent had no opinion): Kolarska, L. and Rychard, A. (1982) 'Political order and economic order', in W. Adamski (ed.), *The Poles 1981: Perception of Crisis and Conflict*, Warsaw: Institute of Philosophy and Sociology, Polish Academy of Sciences (in Polish).

2 Sterniczuk, H. (1984) 'Management of the economy: instability of the power relations', in *The Economy in the Eyes of the Employees*, Warsaw: Institute of Philosophy and Sociology, Polish Academy of Sciences.

3 Kolarska-Bobińska, L. (1986) 'Desirable social and political order in the economy', in K. Jasiewicz *et al.* (eds), *The Poles 1984: Dynamics of Conflict and Consensus*, Warsaw: Warsaw University (in Polish).

4 Morawski, W., and Kozek, W. (1986) 'Polish society on the problems of reform and the economy', in W. Morawski (ed.), *Economy and the Society: Values and Interests of Industrial Workers*, Warsaw: Institute of Sociology, Warsaw University.

5 *Directions for Economic Reform* (1981), Warsaw: Polish government (in Polish).

6 Kolarska-Bobińska, *op. cit.*

7 CBOS (1987).

8 In answer to the question of what form of ownership should predominate in Poland, 21 per cent of workers said that there should be state ownership centrally controlled by the state; 43 per cent said that there should be state ownership controlled by workers' councils; and 11 per cent said that there should be private ownership (Morawski, *op. cit.*, 1986). On the other hand, in answer to another question, one-third of workers were willing to accept private ownership in medium-sized enterprises and in foreign trade (Kuczyński,

1986, see note 11). These results are not contradictory since the first question related to a 'predominant' form of ownership and the second to its general existence.

9 Kolarska-Bobińska, *op. cit.*
10 Ibid.
11 Kuczyński, P. (1986) 'Political consciousness of the workers; between modernization and normalization', in Morawski (ed.), *op. cit.*
12 Morawski and Kozek, *op. cit.*
13 Nowak, S. (1984) 'Attitudes, values and aspirations of the Polish society: evidence for a fare-cost', in S. Nowak (ed.), *Polish Society of the Time of Crisis*, Warsaw: Warsaw University.
14 Teoplitz, K. T. (1987) 'A view from a satellite', *Politglas*, 12 December.
15 The following table depicts the views of society in 1985 on the reforms introduced so far.

Table 8.2

About the reform	Agree	Disagree	Don't know
Economic reform will never succeed here	25%	39%	36%
To date, there has been no perceptible change as a result of the reforms	52%	32%	16%
The reform itself is a good thing but not the way it has been implemented	61%	12%	27%
The reform has been brought in too slowly	48%	22%	29%

Morawski and Kozek, *op. cit.*

16 Morawski and Kozek, *op. cit.*
17 CBOS (1987, 1988).
18 Morawski and Kozek, *op. cit.*
19 Rychard, A. (1986) 'Political views: attitudes towards the rules and institutions of the civil society', in Jasiewicz *et al.*, *op. cit.*
20 Jasiewicz *et al.*, *op. cit.*
21 Rychard, *op. cit.*
22 Kolarska-Bobińska, L., and Rychard, A. (1986) 'Relationships between politics and economics in the social consciousness', in Jasiewicz *et al.*, *op. cit.* I refer to a general tendency in the answers of the respondents, rather than a percentage analysis.
23 Heath, A., and Topf, R. (1987), 'Political culture', paper presented to the Polish–British Conference on Social Responses to Economic Difficulties, Oxford.

24 *The Poles 1988*, Warsaw: Warsaw University.
25 Kolarska-Bobińska, *op. cit.*
26 Kuczyński, *op. cit.*
27 Rychard, *op. cit.*
28 Koralewicz-Zebik, J. (1986) 'Authoritarianism in the Polish society of 1984', in Jasiewicz *et al., op. cit.*
29 Teoplitz, *op. cit.*

Translated by Monika Bobiński.

9

Poland's economic dilemma: 'de-articulation' or 'ownership reform'

Jadwiga Staniszkis

Warsaw University

To use a term borrowed from Karl Polanyi,[1] the 1980s may be described as a decade of 'great transformation' within Poland. The qualitatively new social and political facts which have marked this period are primarily the following:

(i) The formation of a means for independent collective activity in August 1980, in the form of the trade union Solidarity. Despite its delegalization in December 1981 the union has continued to exist, especially within the collective consciousness. The ideas and motivations which led to its creation fulfil the role of a new ideology which is influencing the social and political conflicts in Poland.

(ii) The striking revelation, with the introduction of martial law in December 1981, of the previously well-camouflaged authoritarian nature of the state and its true centre.[2] The nature of the state as revealed by this event is also clearly in conflict with the ideological formula of the Party's 'leading role'. The result is that the Party apparatus has since been, and continues to be, unsure of its status.

(iii) New developments in Polish-Soviet relations since 1982, which have meant that the Polish government has lost some control of certain important resources on its own territory.

(iv) The entry of the socialist mode of production into a phase of 'de articulation',[3] whereby socialist production relies on supplementary economic structures.

These new facts, and the resulting dilemmas and paradoxes, are closely interlinked: decisions relating to one area tend to determine freedom of manoeuvre in another. There is in addition a clear link between the dilemmas facing Poland – and the rest of Eastern Europe – and the situation in the USSR: this relationship is, I believe, far more complex than its coverage in the West would imply.[4]

What economic reform?

The ruling groups in eastern Europe are at present faced with a choice between two variants of economic reform: the first based on the institutionalization of the de-articulation of the socialist mode of production, and the second based on introducing substantial property ownership changes within this socialist mode of production. The de-articulation of the socialist mode of production in Poland, and to a lesser extent in the rest of the socialist bloc, means a situation when the state sector, in order to function reasonably well, requires an increasing support of external economic structures.

There are several types of such de-articulation. First, in order to meet the growing consumer demands originating from within the state sector, more goods in the private sector and the 'second economy' have to be produced. The second type is related to the fact that under the present circumstances the state sector can only produce at its full capacity if it has a constant supply of raw materials and energy from the USSR, partly at the price of the Soviet Union dictating Polish investment and export policy. The origins of the present production structure in Poland's state sector can be traced to decisions taken in the period 1948 55. The economic system which has been imposed on Poland and Poland's specialization within COMECON are responsible for the constant reproduction of this structure. The resulting high demand for Soviet raw materials and energy has not only forced Poland to invest in sources of energy in the USSR,[5] but has in the years 1982–6 also led to a trade deficit in relations with the Soviet Union. The Soviet Union, in turn, has used its position of key supplier as a lever for imposing further integration of the two economies through long-term, direct agreements between selected enterprises. These agreements represent a means of instituting in Poland the type of export structure favoured by the USSR. Thus this particular expression of the de-articulation of the state sector is related to the sector's low efficiency, the diversion of capital from that sector into obligatory domestic and Soviet projects, and the limitation of the state's property rights in cases where direct links between enterprises have led to the USSR acquiring some of these rights.

However, I should like to emphasize that this vicious circle of self-reproducing dependence is also Poland's means of maintaining social equilibrium, because it allows a greater utilization of the economy's resources in their present structure. For the same reason, any significantly different form of participation in the international division of labour is now unrealistic. Furthermore, any revision of this economic structure would not only be a socially sensitive issue (however beneficial in the long term), but would also require further expenditure to pay for modernization and to alleviate the social costs of such a manoeuvre. In the current crisis, such resources are not readily available. Therefore the economic and social crisis is paradoxically instrumental in perpetuating the very structure in Poland (in terms of the composition of technologies used and goods produced) that is partly responsible for the crisis.

The Polish economy's inability both to generate sufficient revenue from convertible currency exports for the purchase of foreign technology, and its lack of innovation maintain or even increase still further technical backwardness and isolation from western markets. An effect of this is the third expression of the de-articulation, since in international markets socialist Poland is losing ground to countries which were industrialized more recently but which have a different system.[6] Added to this are Poland's large and growing debts. If debtor and creditor were subject to civil law, Poland would already have lost some of its property to western banks. This may not happen. Nevertheless, debt and debt repayment is a manifestation of the way in which the socialist mode of production actually contracts rather than expands.

The fourth expression of the de-articulation phenomenon of the socialist mode of production in Poland is its decapitalization. Despite the fact that wages in the state sector account for only about 10 per cent of its costs,[7] there have recently been clear difficulties in maintaining a high rate of investment. Lack of commitment to the cost-effective regeneration of fixed assets which are state-owned goes hand in hand with enterprises treating state investments as costless. This leads to excessive resources being tied up in unfinished investment projects, whilst the fixed assets already in use become obsolete too fast. This represents a double decapitalization and, in effect, a further contraction of the state sector.

In the above situation, Jaruzelski's economic reforms may be interpreted as being based on 'institutionalizing the process of de-articulation': strengthening the 'supplementary supportive structures' outside the socialist mode of production and making no substantial changes within the mode itself. Minor adjustments are made in relation to the instruments of management within the state sector, but these adjustments do not recreate the economic interests eliminated by collectivization.[8] To summarize, strengthening of the supplementary structures to facilitate the regeneration of the state sector in its present form relies on the following: the legalization of the 'second economy';[9] the expansion of the private sector up to a defined ceiling[10] and the rationalization of its links with the state sector;[11] making use of the hard currency in the hands of the public, although the potential for these funds to function as capital is still limited;[12] an attempt to rationalize the situation of dependence on the USSR through economic integration;[13] and ensuring a modest though steady supply of foreign currency to meet the sector's basic requirements.

By tapping shallow reserves such as these, the de-articulation of the socialist mode of production yields some positive results relatively fast. It is also less costly in social terms than any fundamental structural and property ownership changes within the state sector would have been. In this respect, it appears to be more attractive for both the authorities and for society. Solidarity's last 'economic programme' does not in essence propose anything more than de-articulation.[14] However, this type of reform does not solve the problems of the functioning of the state sector, nor does it rationalize the allocation of the means of production in the state sector. Whilst it is true that some of the recent official proposals for reform[15] have in theory gone beyond the 'de-articulation' programme, it is plain that these proposals are not being implemented in practice.[16] Much, for instance, has been said about the fact that manufacturing potential is hampered by production relations in the state sector,[17] and about the need to create interests in this sector which derive from property interests and not merely from the profit motive.[18]

However, none of the proposed solutions go as far as suggesting the rational pluralization of ownership and the abandoning of the 'uniform state ownership' formula. Yet only pluralization – in the form of institutional, group and private ownership, company ownership with mixed capital and share ownership – could make the creation of a capital market and strong pro-efficiency interests possible.[19] Proposals to change the role of the state in the economy by abandoning the use of the state budget as a substitute capital market[20] and by commercializing the banking system have also been rejected. The reason for this resistance is fear on the part of the authorities that property and banking reform would make it more difficult for the economy to be used as a set of control instruments for maintaining social stability through the redistribution process. It would also be more difficult for them to fulfil their obligations towards the USSR.

As the example of Poland shows, those concerned with the ideological realm[21] are paradoxically more interested in radical property reforms in the state sector, such as the introduction of shares for the workers, than those who are directly responsible for the day-to-day running of the economy. For the latter, any renunciation of direct intervention and administrative redistribution is very difficult, particularly when there is considerable social imbalance. The former perceive workers' participation in ownership not in terms of a capital market but as a means of recreating the interests which were destroyed by collectivization. The workers – as share-owners – would be supposed to press for innovativeness and efficiency from the managers: this would give material substance for workers' self-management.

The source of these concepts lies not so much in the theories of Hayek and von Mises as in the work of R. Bahro,[22] and even in the arguments used by Lenin at the Bolsheviks' Eleventh Congress; namely that after the revolution, the workers would no longer be the 'proletariat', since the relations (the source of conflict) which had made them a 'progressive force' would have been eliminated, along with economic interests within the sphere of production. Therefore, those within the ruling group who advocate radical property changes of this type are motivated more by rationality of control (in its new meaning) than by economic rationality. Their principal concern is to direct working-class frustrations away from generalized attacks on the Party and towards confrontation with the local administration, and to refashion working-class identification, away from moral rejection of the system towards a more pragmatic articulation of the conflict. There is an analogy here with Stolypin's reforms in Russia[23] where the question of rationality of control as reformulated by the authorities themselves was also the reason for radical reforms initiated at the top.

In Hungary, however, the group currently formulating the most radical proposals for economic and political reform[24] is doing so in the name of professional standards and a theoretical vision of the social interest. As indicated above, there are no groups or classes within the socialist system which have a real economic interest in a fundamental transformation of the socialist mode of production. The interests behind the drive towards 'de-articulation' are, however, obvious. Moreover, the protests made in the name of fulfilling material needs more effectively only reproduce the redistributive role of the state and the present character of the socialist mode of production. Therefore, any mechanism for transformation within the socialist system must be decidedly different from, for instance, the mechanism accompanying the transition from feudalism to capitalism, where the dynamic for change was based on the interplay of real economic interests, one of which was in fact the fiscal interest of the absolutist state.[25]

It is characteristic that state interests also manifested themselves when the 'second economy' was legalized within the socialist economy. The evolutionary process in the West[26] led to property gradually being apportioned with legal rather than political guarantees, and to a gradual universalization of the market. This was accompanied by a progressive strengthening of civil society, which in turn constituted a social guarantee of the lasting nature of the new legal realities and the continuation of change. Under socialism, any such change has to be undertaken in the name of a 'theoretical interest',[27] and the social groups whose actual economic interests are linked with the continuation of the process of changes will come into being only when these changes will have sufficiently progressed. It is a paradox of the Poland of the 1980s that those individuals who matured during the period of revolt, and who articulated the conflict in terms of human rights, material needs and moral rejection of the system, actually hold back property reforms on account of the social cost involved in the initial stages.

Another problem within the socialist system is the question of legal guarantees, since there must be a self-limitation of power before even the first traces of a civil society can emerge. Any such self-limitation would require an abandoning by the community of the philosophy of rule which is characteristic of the 'authoritarian state'. This philosophy, still obligatory throughout eastern Europe, is based on two assumptions: first of all, that politics is above the law. In other words, all institutions and laws or law judgements can be suspended in the name of political aims as defined by the authorities themselves, and this process of suspension is neither controlled by superficial legislative considerations, nor by society. Second, it is the authorities who decide what at any given moment constitutes 'politics'. This means that there is no guarantee of perman-ence attached to any legal regulations or institution. Changing this philosophy of state and Party rule is, in my opinion, even more difficult than the pluralization of ownership of fixed and circulating assets in the state sector. The question of legal guarantees, or rather the systemic barriers which make them impossible, is being discussed openly for the first time. Hungarian economists attached to the Communist Party's Central Committee[28] simply put forward the thesis that any such guarantees could do no more than define the limits for accumulation of capital within the private sector, beyond which any further income would be fully 'socialized'.

However, there can be no real guarantees against the possibility of such limits being lowered by the state, particularly in times of economic crisis and political pressure for a more energetic administrative redistribution of resources. Control and stabilization would continue to be the state's principal interest, even if property changes were introduced (unless the principles governing recruitment to positions of authority changed and accountability of state functionaries, possibly in the form of verification through election, was also introduced). It is clear that the problem of legal guarantees and whether they can last does not lie in the letter of the law, but in the structure of interest and social forces, and the extent to which they can influence the formation of power structures. In this sense, there must be considerable political change if property changes are to last. It is not merely a question of initiating these changes (as it is possible that the ruling group itself will do this, in the name of a more modern conception of the rationality of control), but one of guaranteeing their permanence. In other words, the question is whether these changes can continue if the interests of the authorities at any given time dictate that they should be abandoned.

It would be possible, nevertheless, to give the power apparatus an interest in initiating and establishing continued property changes in the state sector, despite the social cost in the first stages of this process and the deterioration of conditions for realising rationality of control. The path of transformation formulated by Liszka and Sarkozy in Hungary springs to mind here.[29] It is based on giving the power apparatus priority status within the new system of property rights, for instance through access to information about new business opportunities, or to loans and licences. This kind of privilege is already perceptible in the de-articulation process, in the sense that certain individuals in the power apparatus and their families are occupying desirable posts within the supplementary structures. In other words, the power apparatus, particularly its middle-ranking members, would have to be won over to the idea of a change from a political to an economic middle-class status. It is difficult, however, to imagine a programme involving the 'enfranchisement of the power apparatus' being formulated in Poland, where broad political mobilization is articulated around egalitarian slogans and great sensitivity is felt towards all privileges connected with power.

To summarize, there are two key considerations in the question of property ownership reform within the state sector: that of legal guarantees, as discussed above, and that of negotiating a change in the present conditions of dependence on the USSR. Without legal guarantees, it is unlikely that there could be movement of capital between the private and the state sectors, or between economic organizations within the state sector itself. These organizations are bound to be deeply apprehensive about decreasing their organizational assets. Consequently, the command system of central allocation along with the nationalization of capital assets could be reintroduced at any time. Meeting the second condition, that of redefining present relations between Poland and other eastern bloc countries and the USSR, also seems unlikely. Because the USSR allocates roughly 25 per cent of its national income for defence and defence-related investments (the USA allocates for that purpose about 8 per cent of its GNP, which is between two and two and a half times greater),[30] any opportunity for acquiring additional resources reduces the inevitable tensions. Therefore, the policy of dependence pursued by the USSR is based on forcing east European economies to produce specified goods for its own use with a specified model of allocation in the area of investment and exports. As such, this policy represents a prime consideration in any lasting coalition concerning Soviet foreign policy between the Gorbachev camp, and the military sector and ideological apparatus. The latter perceives eastern European dependence as an additional instrument for political control, notwithstanding internal reform and the diversification of government in specific countries. In the light of this, Gorbachev may be seen as a new and more effective public relations officer. Resistance to the new policy of creating dependence is being made more difficult because of his reputation as a reformer. Even in the West, this resistance is sometimes interpreted as a sign of 'the anti-liberalism' of the ruling groups in Eastern Europe.[31] This brings us to the second dilemma currently facing the ruling elites and societies of eastern Europe, including Poland.

The costs and benefits of de-articulation versus ownership reform

The motives for choosing the de-articulation alternative become clearer in the light of the Polish experience where new forms of dependence and their connection with a particular type of economic structure have been particularly noticeable. The breakdown of Poland's credit standing in 1981 led to the collapse of the import of western inputs and consequently the immobilization of a significant part of the country's economic potential.[32] This situation led the Polish authorities to accept the USSR's offer of new patterns of co-operation in the form of processing additional raw materials in exchange for a percentage of finished products.[33] This alleviated the social cost of the loss of imports from the West to some extent, but did nothing to effect structural changes within the economy. This policy was followed by the introduction of long-term agreements between enterprises in Poland and the Soviet Union guaranteeing exports to the USSR of consumer goods in demand there, with increased pressure from the USSR to eliminate the deficit in the trade exchange with Poland. The political basis for these new links was the agreements between General Secretaries Jaruzelski and Chernienko[34] (and later with Gorbachev[35]) as well as between Prime Ministers Messner (and later Rakowski) and Ryzhkov.[36]

The qualitatively new features of these links are:

(i) Their formalization so as to prevent any future reorientation towards the West, as well as any reversals of the new forms of dependence in the event of political change in Poland.

(ii) The exploitation of the local interests of enterprises involved in long-term agreements by guaranteeing them supplies of raw materials from the USSR, priority for domestic and imported goods in short supply through co-operation agreements, and modest sums for investment. The fact that these long-term agreements are not in the social interest and often entail the partial loss of property rights is not perceived as being a 'cost' by the management of these enterprises.[37]

(iii) A clear segmentation of the economy. In Poland, the enterprises which have entered into long-term co-operative agreements are co-ordinated as a specific segment of foreign trade. On the Soviet side, they represent a particular segment in their economic planning. In Poland, this is not the case, probably so as to inhibit political control by the Sejm (Polish Parliament) over this sector, or to make it impossible for the scale and consequences of these new forms of co-operation to be perceived. Although the scale of these developments is yet limited, they have nevertheless created new problems for the Polish ruling group, since a part of the country's economic potential is now beyond its control. The tensions connected with this loss of control are reminiscent of the problems which emerged in the course of the 'peripheralization' of the Asiatic mode of production, where the local state no longer controlled all of its resources and the ruling elite underwent segmentation.[38]

The Polish economy's entry into these new forms of dependence has, on the other hand, enabled it to sustain production in the state sector and helped to satisfy society's basic needs, albeit to a lesser degree than before the crisis. In other words, this increased dependence enabled the economy to adapt quickly to the dramatic collapse of trade and credit relations with the West, without any substantial structural changes taking place in the economy. The social cost of the crisis was thus lessened, as well as the uncertainty and apprehension which would have accompanied any structural changes to the economy, involving cutting back on energy-intensive production, closing loss-making enterprises, restructuring the composition of goods produced, pluralization of forms of ownership in the state sector, commercialization of the banking system, and the intensification of links between the state sector and the private sector, giving the latter equal access to the means of production and to opportunities for expansion. Instead of this, agreements with COMECON about specialized production and with the USSR were concluded. One of the reasons for this response to the economic crisis was the military character of the ruling group in Poland. It was probably difficult to say 'no', all the more so because of the experience of the bloc-wide integrated defence sector – which had been integrated since the founding of the Polish People's Republic – and because of internal factional infighting and the need for support from Moscow. Another important factor was apparently the fear of the social cost involved in restructuring the economy.

The segmentation in the power structure which has accompanied the new forms of co-operation with the USSR has created additional tensions in the local party apparatus of the dependent country. Not only are the military leadership and the Party elite now trained outside the country, but a part of the foreign trade and planning apparatus is also directed towards groups other than the local party apparatus. Equally, part of the management cadre in enterprises belonging to the Soviet 'imperial cluster' is actually almost entirely beyond the operational reach of the local party committee to which it is nominally accountable.[39] These frustrations are exacerbated by the fact that the managers of these enterprises are organised in a separate group which is not affected by the traditional *nomenklatura* mechanism. Part of the 'civil' economy is beginning to function in the same way as the defence sector. These tendencies, and the social tensions which derive from a situation of permanent consumer shortages, may lead to a nationalist faction being openly articulated among middle-ranking members of the party apparatus. This faction could also be anti-liberal, since it would be safer for it to link its nationalism with support from opponents of Gorbachev's reforms within the Soviet Union.

I have interpreted the institutional forms of Polish-Soviet economic integration dating from 1982 as a reaction on the part of both countries to the collapse of Poland's credit-worthiness. For Poland, these new agreements constituted the only means of more fully activating its industrial potential in its present form.

From the Soviet perspective, there are perhaps three particularly important factors which have influenced their policy. The first is the need for adjustment following the fall in energy prices in world markets since 1985. This means that supplies of goods in demand are to be assured now, to a greater extent than before, by means of direct links at enterprise level and through long-term agreements. This policy may be interpreted as an expression of the Soviet Union's anticipation and acceptance of its future import problems. These direct links would also resolve the problem of control over eastern Europe because they represent another (non-military and non-political) means of exerting pressure.

For a fuller picture of the situation, it is necessary to examine the position taken by the advocates of the new forms of economic integration. In their view, there are three positive aspects in the new developments. They point first of all to the fact that the Soviets have shown themselves willing to apply cost analysis on enterprise level (see the position taken by the Institute for Research into the Socialist System under Bogomolov in 'Magyar Hirlap', 29 May 1987, entitled 'The Reform of the COMECON'). In response to this argument, it should be remembered that the basic cost of these new forms of co-operation for eastern European countries does not lie in the financial calculations of specific transactions at a micro-economic level, although obviously the introduction of a cost analysis may somewhat affect the quantity of products destined for the Soviet Union. Even if some or even most Polish enterprises were to benefit financially, the country would still have to absorb the resource cost of forced exports of the factors of production that are in short supply. Equally, the type of specialization within COMECON and the type of exchange with the USSR (including the investment expenditure involved), as well as the choice of individual Polish enterprises included in the 'imperial cluster', are decided by administrative means and with the aim of supplying the Soviet Union with what is of particular use to them. The proposals to introduce cost analysis do not affect these decisions, since in general they would be taken on a political level.

Second, the advocates of direct links find great cause for optimism in the Soviet wish that these links between enterprises should exploit local advantages. But a closer look at this argument reveals that what the Soviets have in mind is that the existing branch structure of industry in the COMECON countries should be fully exploited, whereas only an extensive restructuring of t' ɔ economy would make economic rationalization in these countries possible.

Third, the advocates of these new forms hope that the modernization and expansion of certain enterprises and branches included in the imperial cluster will also enable them to do business in western markets. This view fails to take the technological chasm between the two markets into account. There are very few areas, apart from primary products such as energy and metals, where enterprises could function in both markets. In the majority, segmentation of the economy is inevitable and in turn represents one of the fundamental barriers to reform.

All these factors will contribute to the destabilization of the situation in Poland in the coming years. It is important to remember, however, that the second option for dealing with the present crisis, i.e., the process of restructuring and extensive reform, would also have a destabilizing effect on account of the inevitable social cost which would be concentrated into a relatively short space of time. The cost of 'integration' and reorientation in the form described above is significantly greater in the long term, but it is spread out over a longer period of time. However, only by choosing the second option of radical reform can the civilizational regression of Poland, as well as of the rest of eastern Europe, be halted.

The authoritarian state versus the formula of the leading role of the Party

The power structure within socialism of the Soviet type can be characterised synthetically as the combination of two features. The first is the dual state as defined by E. Fraenkel.[40] Contrary to the common interpretation,[41] it is not based on the parallel structures of state and Party rule where the Party deals with extraordinary situations and the state with routine administration. Fraenkel's interpretation of dualism is related to the idea that the 'authoritarian state', which encompasses both Party and state structures, removes certain areas of public life from its own control and makes them subject to legal regulations. In other words, it allows the existence of a 'normative state' in some areas. The 'authoritarian state' itself constitutes the institutionalization of revolutionary rule which rejects all legal regulations, following the assumption that politics is above the law. Furthermore, the definition and scope of what is 'political' can change according to the interests of the ruling group at any given time. Therefore the periodic emergence in, for instance, the economy of pseudo-permanent institutional and legal solutions is based on the 'self-limitation' of power and as such has no guarantee of permanence.[42] There is no social control over this process.

The centre of the 'dual state' as understood in the Soviet socialist context has moved noticeably from the Communist Party as a whole to a grouping in which the Party is neither the only nor the most important element. This was apparent from the organizational methods used in the preparations for martial law in Poland.[43] Moreover, there is a clear connection between that grouping and a similar grouping in Moscow, the capital of the whole bloc. Since the intervention in Czechoslovakia, the 'internationalization' of the decision-making process has appeared to be connected with the appropriate cells in that capital becoming automatically involved as any crisis deepens.

The second specifically Soviet socialist feature in the structure of rule is based on the claim of the authority to represent historically 'essential' social interests. This claim has its roots in its 'revolutionary legitimization'. It involves on the one hand Lenin's vision of post-revolutionary society where the workers are no longer the 'proletariat' because the capitalists have been eliminated,[44] and, on the other hand, their mission of modernization. According to these pretensions, the Communist Party 'must' replace the non-existent 'proletariat'. In other words, the party represents the 'objective social interest', even when real workers oppose its policies. The state in turn is supposed to play the role of the 'collective capitalist'.

As the phenomenon of the Stalinism of the intelligentsia[45] has demonstrated, several factors in this rejection of reality (which has had great appeal for some) in favour of an abstract vision in which the authorities become a kind of 'substitute society' have not been taken into account. The first is that collectivization of property meant that the key economic interests related to material reproduction were also eliminated, since capital and resources became public property. The capital market which made economically rational allocation possible also disappeared. Under such circumstances, the state cannot in the process of modernization become the functional equivalent of a 'collective capitalist'. Second, the interest of all authority, including the party apparatus, is to reproduce itself. The 'politics above the law' formula deriving from the ideology of the 'authority as substitute society' creates opportunities for abuses of power which were unknown in earlier structures of rule. There is some resemblance in the type of legitimization which invokes a particular ontology for society, namely one which demands a new role for the state, to certain Third World regimes which are undergoing modernization and are attempting to establish a nation. The formula of 'the leading role of the party' was only fully built into the political system during its initial stages. At present, it is clear that there are tensions not only in its relation to society but within the political structure itself. The fact that the centre of the 'authoritarian state' has shifted to the military and the security apparatus (as well as the 'authoritarian' state's continuing powerful links with decision-making centres in the bloc's capital) has conspicuously limited the role of the local Party. This, as mentioned already, was evident in the preparations leading to martial law.[46] Even the concept of 'the party as arena' for the political process does not seem to reflect the real dynamic of political life.[47] The third factor is linked with the questioning of the Leninist vision of the Party state as 'substitute society' (representing 'essential historiosophical' interests) together with the emergence of Solidarity and the opposition's vision of an 'independent society'.

To summarize, the three processes referred to above are: (i) the segmentation of the power structure in Poland together with a new form of 'imperial cluster'; (ii) the military and security forces rather than the Communist Party as the centre of the authoritarian state and the former's powerful links with groupings on the imperial scale; finally, (iii) the mass questioning of the authorities' pretensions to legitimization. These processes have revealed the real character of the structures of rule and the brittleness of their legitimization. They have also questioned the need for the Party as a subject in the public arena, for the ritualization of the Party and the demobilization of its apparatus fits these new structures of rule best. This has also increased the sense of marginalization and the frustrations within the party apparatus. Alongside this too, there have been ideological problems connected with the de-articulation of the socialist mode of production, since the creation of external supplementary structures has meant a departure from the principles of egalitarianism and corruption within the ranks of power. In addition, the complex relations with the Catholic Church, which represents a certain guarantee of control and stabilization during the phase of permanent crisis, are a source of tension for the Party apparatus. There is also the difficulty of articulating the political status of the Party. One example is the surrealism of the formula of the 'Party as guarantor of legality', articulated in Poland during the discussions in 1980–1, and at present in Hungary.[48] One of the very reasons for the disorganization of the law is that it is impossible to formalize the principle of the 'leading role of the Party', rooted as it is in its pretensions to 'revolutionary' legitimization. Also, the formula of the Party as 'defender of the social interest', when it in fact constitutes the power apparatus through the mechanism of the *nomenklatura*, does not seem realistic, if for no other reason than that it is not in a position to control the mechanisms which determine living standards.[49]

Notes

1 Polanyi, K. (1944) *Great Transformation*, New York.
2 Schmitt, C. (1922) *Politische Theologie*, Munich; English edn, MIT Press, 1985.
3 The concept of the 'articulation' of the mode of production as defined by P.P. Rey in '*Articulation des modes de dépendance et des modes de production dans deux sociétés linéages*' (*Cahiers d'Études Africaines*, 1969, nr.35, 415–40). See also: Wolpe, H. (1980) *The Articulation of Modes of Production*, London: Routledge & Kegan Paul. A given mode of production is not fully articulated if the conditions whereby it is reproduced are linked with a second mode of production which entails significant costs in terms of the reproduction of labour.
4 The literature on the subject tends to represent relations between the national ruling groups in eastern Europe and Gorbachev's group in terms of the former's opposition to introducing a domestic programme of reform, or in terms of the Soviet Union subsidizing eastern Europe, a concept formulated by Vanous and Marrese in 1982 which is now outdated (even if the methodology employed by the authors for calculating the benefits and the costs is accepted). See Vanous, J. and Marrese, P. (1982) *Implicit Subsidies in Soviet Trade with Eastern Europe*, Berkeley: University of California Press.
5 The Chairman of the Polish Planning Commission, M. Gorywoda, has stated that while Poland's commitment to supply energy-intensive production to the USSR has increased by 60 per cent, the Soviet Union's commitment to supply additional raw materials and energy has increased by 30 per cent (effective until 1990). According to him, it is essential for Poland to invest in sources of energy in the USSR (costing about one billion roubles), for which the Soviets pay with additional deliveries of energy products (*Trybuna Ludu*, Warsaw, 6 February 1987).
6 Comparison of Eastern Europe with Latin America in K. Poznański's (1986) 'Competition between eastern Europe and developing countries in the western markets', *Eastern European Economies*, vol.2, Washington: Joint Economic Committee, US Congress.
7 Statistics from M. Mieszczańkowski's article in *Życie Gospodarcze*, from 5 January 1986.
8 This relates to interests in the accumulation of capital and economic reproduction (in the sense of rational reproduction from the point of view of future accumulation of capital) and regeneration of machinery and equipment. The impetus for investment within socialism does not constitute an economic

interest: it stems from organizational premises (expansion) and subjection to groups of interests.

9 One of the reasons is the better fulfilment of financial requirements by the state budget. It is interesting that the initiative for legalizing the 'second economy' in the USSR in September 1986 came from the Ministry of Finance.

10 The latest proposals in Poland (M. Nasiłowski, manuscript, also *Ekonomista*, February 1987) are concerned with increasing the non-agricultural private sector to 25 per cent of the GNP (presently at 7 per cent).

11 For instance involving the private sector (particularly *'Polonijne'* businesses which deal in hard currency) in co-operative agreements with state industry, and not, as is the case at the moment, restricting it to the production of consumer goods.

12 The state purchase of foreign currency from private individuals at current 'black market' rates was introduced in the spring of 1987: there is still opposition, however, to suggestions that this foreign currency (estimated at about $6billion – $3billion in the PKO and $3billion in private households) should function as capital in the form, for example, of private individuals buying shares or bonds or forwarding loans in hard currency to state enterprises (so as to avoid bottlenecks in co-operation which are often due to a lack of relatively small sums).

13 See interview with the vice-president of the Planning Commission, Mr Długosz, in *Życie Warszawy* (17 October 1986) and the discussion on the convertibility of the ruble in *Życie Gospodarcze* (in an article by M. Krzak, spring 1987).

14 See *Tygodnik Mazowsze* (Warsaw), nr.207–8, also *Le Figaro*, 26 June 1987, where it is proposed that the private and state sectors should have identical treatment; that the private sector should be expanded and given legal guarantees; that managerial 'dependence' on the state authorities – acknowledged as the main source of low efficiency – should be abolished; and that self-management should be strengthened and that the function of the budget should change (the administrative redistribution of resources should be limited). What is striking here is the failure to evaluate the phenomenon of forced allocation (which includes investment and export), deriving from the Polish economy's dependence on the USSR and political pressure from the latter. The author merely states that 'it is difficult to assess who benefits most from barter-type conditions of trade, in other words in the exchange of goods for goods'. There are clear echoes here of the concept of 'subsidy' which I have already criticized.

15 In Poland: Theses relating to the second stage of the reforms (*Rzeczpospolita*, April 1987); also *'Raport Komisji do spraw strucktur w gospodarce'* (*Rzeczpospolita*, May 1987); earlier: Kwiatkowski, S. (1987) *'Na ręcznym hamulcu'*, 21 March 1987. In Hungary: an exchange of views between a group of economists from the Institute of Finance and economists from the Central Committee of the Communist Party in *Kozgazdasagi Szemle*, July 1987, Budapest.

16 See press conference (July 1987) given by Deputy Prime Minister Sadowski (Radio Free Europe Daily Report), stating that even the introduction of the 'second stage of the reform' would not change the terms of the five-year plan

in which – according to L. Zienkowski's 'The debate over the division of income', GUS 1986 – about 70 per cent of investment is connected with the reproduction of an economic structure based on the preponderance of heavy industry and the production of the means of production.

17 Commission on matters relating to organizational structures in the economy, *op.cit.*

18 Hungarian party economists, Kwiatkowski, *op.cit.*

19 I have written about this in more detail in my book, *The Ontology of Socialism*, Oxford: Oxford University Press, forthcoming in 1990.

20 Party economists in *Kozgazdasagi Szemle*, *op.cit.*

21 P. Ruszkowski's paper on the subject of shares for workers, at a conference on the theory of 'real socialism', organized by the Centre of the Student Academic Movement, Kazimierz, January 1987. Also Krajewski, M. (1987) 'Will a new form of socialism emerge in Poland?', *Akademia Nauk Społecznych*, Central Committee of the United Polish Workers Party, mimeograph, September 1987.

22 Barho, R. (1976) *Alternative in Eastern Europe*, London: Pluto.

23 The purpose of these reforms, which were proposed in the aftermath of the events of 1905, was to create a middle stratum within the peasant class which would have an interest in accumulation, social stabilization and the development of a market economy. In order to achieve this, the turnover of land had to be made possible. The redefinition of the concept of the rationality of control (and their own interests) by the authorities themselves therefore became the basis for wide-ranging systemic reforms.

24 In addition to proposals for commercializing the banking system, introducing the capital market into the state sector and pluralizing ownership, the group attached to the Institute of Finance (*op.cit.*) proposes political reforms, namely the right to organize in clubs and corporations (which would also extend to delegates to the National Assembly, thus constituting a substitute for the multi-party system) as well as limiting the powers of the state in the economy (e.g., the subjection of budgetary decisions to the National Assembly).

25 See the analysis relating to the West in North, D.C., and Thomas, R.P. (1974) *The Rise of the Western World*, Cambridge: Cambridge University Press.

26 North and Thomas (*op.cit.*) indicate that the motor for the evolutionary process derived from the pressures connected with the relative scarcity of specific production factors (which change in time), and the dynamic of interests, including state interests, developed against this background. According to this conception, the technical transformations within the sphere of production (in effect, the changes in the 'forces of production') occurred only after changes in property ownership. Therefore, this theory differs from the Marxist line of argument and, of the two, is confirmed by economic history to a greater degree.

27 The theoretical interest as understood in this context is related to a better exploitation of the human and practical potential in a given system, and one which does not relate to the actual economic interests of any of the social groups. Only a change (e.g., in property rights) which creates a new configuration of interests can make this theoretical interest the actual interest

of some groups. Another possibility is that in such a deep crisis the realization of the actual interests of all groups (including the interest of the authorities in stabilization and control) will not be possible. This could lead to a redefinition of the concept of the interests of society (and the ruling elite) and the acceptance of the costs of transformation as essential costs.

28 *Kozgazdasagi Szemle*, op.cit., 668.

29 Sarkosy, J. (1982) 'Problems of social ownership', *Acta Economica* (Budapest), vol.29, 236–45, 246–56.

30 See the statement made by A. Marshall (Director of Net Assessment, Department of Defense, USA) during the seminar at the Wilson Center entitled 'Balancing economic and military factors in determining the US national interests', *Security Digest*, July 1987.

31 One example is the oversimplified perception of the policies being pursued by the Czechoslovakian authorities, who are not only opposed to Gorbachev's reforms but are also against new forms of dependence.

32 In 1982 only about 60 per cent of Poland's economic potential was being utilized.

33 The agreement concluded in January 1982, stating that in exchange for additional raw materials, Poland would supply finished consumer goods: during the first period 80 per cent of products, then 50 per cent.

34 The co-operation agreements of May 1984 reproduced an economic structure (in terms of emphasis on energy-intensive production) which had to maintain its state of dependence if it was to function at all, and this resulted in economic imbalance, civilizational regression and political consequences.

35 The developments in 1986 detailing the 1984 agreement which further increased Poland's commitment to produce for the USSR goods such as rails, pipes, wagons, heavy machinery, etc., at the price of the internal imbalance of the Polish economy.

36 The agreement made in October 1986 foresaw a Polish surplus in its trade with the USSR until the end of 1989 (which because of the growing need for Soviet sources of energy and raw materials as a result of the Gorbachev-Jaruzelski treaty of 1986 required additional exports). In 1986, Poland's exports to the USSR grew by 8.9 per cent, to the West by 0.9 per cent. At the same time the internal market imbalances grew – and the prices of consumer goods on the internal market increased. The second element in this agreement was the undertaking of direct agreements between Polish and Soviet enterprises, which was to be the way in which exports could be politically dictated (the mechanisms of foreign trade would have been ineffective). In some, negotiations leading to the Soviet side gaining rights of co-ownership were begun (with the help of credit from COMECON'S Development Bank).

37 There are now 'Directors' Clubs' in enterprises belonging to or aspiring to belong to the Imperial cluster. They are organized according to Voivodship and some 800 directors in the whole of Poland are members. The organizer and co-ordinator is Z. Szalajda, Deputy Prime Minister until Autumn 1988. See interview with a director of an enterprise belonging to the Imperial cluster in *Polityka*, 3/1550, 1987.

38 The description of this collapse in: Kayder, C. (1976) 'The dissolution of the Asiatic mode of production', in *Economy and Society*, vol.5, nr. 2, May; also –

with reference to India – Dumont, L. (1980) *Homo Hierarchus*, Chicago: University of Chicago Press, 314–36.

39 The *nomenklatura*'s new mechanism, which emphasizes the right to 'access to secrets' over party qualifications, is largely answerable to the security forces (as in the dispute over the choice of director for the Falbet factory in Warsaw in November 1986).

40 Fraenkel, F. (1941) *The Dual State*, Oxford: Oxford University Press.

41 See Rigby, T.H. (1970) 'Politics in mono-organisational society', in A. Janos, (ed.), *Authoritarian Politics*, Berkeley: University of California Press.

42 One example is the militarization of the Polish economy when martial law, suspending the labour code and all institutional forms of articulating interests in the economy, was introduced in December 1981.

43 See interview with Colonel R. Kukliński in *Kultura*, Paris, April 1987.

44 See the debate at the XIth Congress of the Bolshevik Party, Moscow. Particularly statements made by Lenin, Zinoviev and A. Szlapnikov.

45 See A. Walicki's self-analysis in *Rozmowy z Miłoszem*, 1986, London.

46 According to Kukliński, the first stage of preparations directed by the National Defence Committee (whose personnel was already different from that of August 1980 when the same Committee was formed to carry out the transfer of power) involved mainly the army (for instance, the extraordinary legal regulations were prepared there) and the security services. This was then followed in the Spring of 1981 by a systematic inclusion of the Warsaw Pact leadership.

47 See Commisso, E. (1986) 'Introduction: state structures, political processes and collective choice in COMECON states', in *International Organisations*, vol. 40, no.2 (Spring), where the concept of the 'party as arena for the political process' is applied.

48 Propositions such as these are put forward in Hungary by the Front for National Reconciliation.

49 According to the research on the mechanisms which influence differences in income (Zieńkowski, L. (1986) *Wałka o podzial dochodów*, Warsaw: Głowny Urzad Statystyczny) as much as 70 per cent of variation of incomes reveals the size (rather than the economic efficiency) of the economic organization in which an individual is employed. In other words, its competitiveness and its standing from the point of view of rationality of control/stabilization.

Translated by Monika Bobiński.

10

The decay of socialism and the growth of private enterprise in Poland[1]

Jacek Rostowski

School of Slavonic and East European Studies, University of London

Introduction

It is the contention of the present chapter that: (1) private economic activity can no longer be considered a marginal phenomenon in the Polish economy; (2) Aaslund's Law,[2] according to which private economic activity in communist countries fluctuates around a necessarily low level, no longer holds in Poland; (3) we are seeing the birth of a new economic system which consists of a complex network of co-operation and inter-penetration, but also conflict, between the still dominant socialized sector and the various forms of private economic activity which, at present, are expanding rapidly. It is this process which I call the decay of the socialist economic system in Poland. It is the purpose of this chapter to justify the statements above; explain why these events have occurred; describe the economic system which is emerging in Poland; and discuss the policy and systemic implications if current developments continue.

The main conclusions arrived at are: (1) private economic activity is likely to continue expanding in Poland; (2) the main reasons for this are: (a) the continuing economic crisis affecting the country, (b) the loss of belief in socialist ideology even among the communist elite, (c) the difficulty of devising effective 'market socialist' institutions, and (d) the growing importance in modern economies of services, maintenance and small-batch specialised manufacturing which are particularly unsuited to centralised direction; (3) with the decay of the socialist economic system, Poland is evolving in the direction of a 'mixed economy kleptocracy', in which a highly intrusive, but corrupt, bureaucracy would use bribes and co-ownership in private firms to 'tax' a large, though not necessarily predominant, private sector.

The importance of private economic activity in Poland

There are a number of ways of estimating the share of private economic activity in Poland. If we look at the number of people involved, out of an official labour force of 17.2 million some 4.9 million worked officially full-time in the private sector in 1986. If we add to this the 600,000 estimated[3] to work, both full- and part-time, in the black economy, total private sector employment accounts for nearly one-third of the labour force. Of this 3.9 million are in agriculture and some 1.6 million in the non-agricultural private sector (both registered and black).

Another way is to look at the private sector's share in national income produced (*Dochód Narodowy Wytworzony*). According to official figures this was 18.2 per cent in 1986,[4] with 10.2 per cent contributed by agriculture and 8 per cent by the registered non-agricultural private sector. These figures are considerably understated because they do not include: (1) unregistered activity by the registered private sector (both agricultural and non-agricultural); (2) activity by unregistered private entrepreneurs; (3) illegal work by Polish residents in the West. At the same time the contribution of the socialized sector to national income produced is exaggerated as a result of the tendency of enterprises to overstate production so as to be able to claim fulfilment of plans (under the traditional centrally planned system which still controls an important part of the Polish economy such as coal-mining), or so as to qualify for tax relief (in those parts of the economy which are run on the principles of the reformed economic system[5]). It is not very meaningful to estimate the contribution of the three unreported kinds of private activity to national income produced, because it would have to be assessed at the same prices as those which are used to calculate the socialized sector's contribution.

What can be done is to estimate the share of money incomes generated by private economic activity. This is done in Table 10.1 for 1986, where three estimates of this share are given. The first, based on official figures, gives a total private sector share of 24.5 per cent in national product. The second 'low' estimate makes a number of, on the whole restrictive, assumptions (see Appendix), and results in a figure of 38 per cent. The third 'high' estimate puts this share at 45.2 per cent. The private sector's true share in national income produced is probably considerably smaller than the share in personal money incomes, because in cases in which the private and socialized sectors sell similar goods, the registered private sector, far less encumbered by price controls, is likely to charge a much higher price, as one of its main functions is to provide goods which are in short supply in the state retail network. The black sector earns much of its income by what might be called a transfer payment: reselling at market-clearing prices state-produced goods which are sold at below equilibrium prices by the retail network. We should not include these payments in the black 'product', but they must be included in black income. The value of dollars earned abroad (which are included in the two estimates) is calculated at the black market rate of exchange; this rate is three to four times the official exchange rate which is used (roughly) to evaluate the contribution of workers in exporting enterprises in the socialized sector. Only in agriculture is the situation ambiguous. Farmers receive subsidies in the form of official procurement prices which are higher than the retail prices charged to consumers, and in the form of subsidised industrial inputs. From this it follows that we ought to deduct both subsidies from agriculture's product. However, there is excess demand for most food products, so it is impossible to tell what agriculture's share of national income produced would be under a free market regime.

The share in money incomes gives us some idea of the private sector's control over resources used for consumption. However, as a measure of this also, the figures presented in Table 10.1 are likely to overstate the importance of private economic activity as they ignore the administrative allocation of consumer goods, services and housing by the socialized sector to politically favoured groups (such as members of the *nomen-klatura*), and economically important ones (such as miners). Nevertheless, such access may in fact represent a surprisingly low proportion of official money incomes,[6] possibly as little as 10 per cent. More important is that collective consumption provided by the socialized sector, which accounted for 21 per cent of official money incomes in 1986, is also ignored. If we guess that the total value of the non-monetary elements in incomes is about three-tenths of official incomes, then the private sector's control over consumer resources would be under 20 per cent if we accepted official data, slightly over 30 per cent on the 'low' estimate in Table 10.1, and almost 38 per cent on the 'high' estimate.

The importance of private economic activity cannot, however, be fully gauged by looking at its share in national income or personal incomes. There are additional factors that have to be taken into account. Almost half of all net inflows (excluding interest payments) into the current account of the hard-currency balance of payments are the result of private economic activity (see Appendix). Thus in 1986 and 1987 hard currency earned abroad by individual Poles, mainly as a result of illegal work in the West, was almost equal to the hard-currency trade surplus earned by the whole of the socialized sector. Private economic activity is thus vital to Poland's ability to service its hard-currency debt. Over 55 per cent of personal savings are held in hard-currency accounts[7] (at the black market rate of exchange), and possibly three-quarters of the money supply (cash held by the population) is also held in hard currency.[8] The result is that Poland has a dual-currency economy, with the zloty definitely the inferior currency. This reduces the state's control of the economy considerably.[9] As a result of the decline in the construction of new socialized housing, over two-fifths of new housing in the country as a whole, and 28 per cent in the towns, can be classified as private.[10] Combined with purchases of existing socialized housing stock by private individuals, this means that in the 1980s the private sector's share in housing is no longer declining for the first time in the history of post-war Poland.[11]

Thus, although we cannot arrive at a fully satisfactory figure for the share of private activity in the Polish economy, whether we are looking at its share in national income, personal incomes or its importance to Poland in other ways, it is clear that it is not a margin (although it is still, clearly, a minority share), any more than the public sectors of western economies can be considered marginal. For this reason alone it deserves careful analysis. What is more, private economic activity has been expanding rapidly in the 1980s, and its role has been changing as some of the more draconian controls on the sector have been relaxed. The functioning of the sector has become somewhat more normal (by western standards), although it is still very far from achieving such a state. One example of these changes is that the relative importance of agriculture within the private sector has declined considerably (to about 30 per cent of personal money incomes on both the 'low' and 'high' estimates in Table 10.1).

The breakdown of Aaslund's Law

The usual view among western economists of the role of private economic activity in communist countries has been most ably put by Aaslund.[12] He holds that as a result of the initial assault on private economic activity that usually occurs some two to four years after communists take power, the private sector (usually, though not always, agricultural as well as non-agricultural) is reduced to a rump. However, the shortages of consumer goods which a centrally planned economy inevitably generates arouse an awareness in the leadership of the importance of the private sector in satisfying the wants of the population. During economic crises attempts at reviving the private sector often occur since gross market disequilibria pose a political threat to the rulers. Nevertheless, a backlash is highly likely long before consumer markets have approached balance. This is because, first, the disequilibria lead to exorbitant private incomes, which are unacceptable ideologically to the leadership (and often politically to the population as well); and second, state enterprises want to protect their resources (mainly skilled labour) from private competition, and call for restrictions. Consequently, private sector expansion is halted as soon as shortages are slightly alleviated. As a result of restrictions the sector remains small and incapable of meeting the demand which exists for the goods it produces. Inevitably entrepreneurs have exorbitant incomes. Due to the inability to obtain materials legally (because of restrictions imposed by the state), private entrepreneurs have to bribe suppliers in the socialized sector. The size of the private sector thus fluctuates around a low level, and its small size itself ensures that, in a situation of generalised excess demand and price and quantity controls, the sector is 'legally degenerate' in Aaslund's phrase.

In fact, in Poland since 1980 we have seen a continuous expansion of private economic activity in nearly all areas in which it has operated. The level of employment in the registered non-agricultural private sector has increased 90 per cent between 1980 and 1987, reaching 1,147,000, whereas its increase in the whole of the 1970s amounted to only 43 per cent. What is more the growth rate of employment in this sector is not tailing off (Table 10.2). Unregistered private economic activity (by both registered and unregistered persons) more or less doubled between 1977 and 1985[13] on the best estimate we have, from 5 per cent to 12 per cent of personal money incomes. The importance of the 'hard currency' has increased sharply, and continuously, during the 1980s. Whereas hard-currency savings accounted for only 15.5 per cent of total savings accounts (at the black market rate of exchange) in 1983, in late 1987 they represented 56 per cent.[14] Part of the increase must represent the emergence of dollars already held 'under the mattress', but the continued buoyancy of hard-currency deposits (see Appendix), suggests that dishoarding is only a small part of the explanation. The contribution of private transfers to the hard-currency accounts has increased each year (from $318 million in 1982 to $1,500 million in 1987).[15]

Even in those areas in which there has not been much expansion of the private sector, such as agriculture, there have often been structural changes and a reduction in the degree of state control, which have made the sector more efficient. Thus, while the number of people and the amount of land employed in private agriculture increased only 2 per cent during the whole 1980–6 period, the structure of landholding has improved, with the share of the largest farms (those above 15 hectares) increasing from 18.1 per cent of private land in 1980 to 23.8 per cent in 1986.[16] What is more important for the overall picture, the expansion of socialized agriculture, which characterized the 1970s (when the private sector lost 10 per cent of its land), has been halted (and even to some extent reversed). Thus although private agriculture is expanding far less rapidly than other forms of private activity, which is hardly surprising given the usual relative decline in the importance of agriculture as the economy grows, it is, nevertheless, partaking to some degree in the general expansion of the private sector.

In those areas in which rapid expansion has been followed by a restrictive policy aimed at limiting further growth (as has been the case with Polonia firms[17]), this has often been offset by compensatory growth elsewhere. In the case of Polonia firms, after a period of exceptionally rapid growth in employment by this sector in 1982–3, growth has steadily declined, until it was only 13 per cent in 1986 (62,000 people were employed by Polonia firms in that year). The evident, if informal, limit set by the authorities on the growth of Polonia firms has, however, been at least partially compensated by the possibility which has arisen for purely Polish private and public limited companies and mixed socialised-private companies to be established,[18] and by the new law permitting joint ventures with large capitalist firms.[19]

These changes highlight a general point. Liberalization can manifest itself in two ways. First, in the case in which new entrepreneurs can enter areas which are already open to private sector activity (which we can call 'quantitative liberalization'); or second, in a loosening of controls which forbid certain kinds of private sector activity ('functional liberalization'), and certain types of organization within the private sector ('organizational liberalization'). Both these latter kinds can be thought of as forms of 'qualitative liberalization'. Both quantitative and qualitative liberalization are likely to lead to an increase in the number of people working in the private sector and in its share in economic activity. Both have been proceeding, more or less continuously, since 1980. Aaslund's law of the cyclical development of the private sector around a very low level clearly no longer holds in Poland.

The characteristics of private economic activity in Poland

What we have in Poland is a mixed economy, with a still preponderant socialized sector. Two aspects of this system are of particular interest: the functional and organizational structure of the private sector, and the relationship of that sector with the state and with the socialized sector.

Private economic activity occurs mainly in agriculture, hard-currency earnings, services, construction, small- and medium-scale industry, and trade. In agriculture, hard-currency earnings and services the private sector contribution is very important and lies between 40 per cent and 80 per cent. According to official figures over 80 per cent of national income generated in agriculture came from the private sector. Almost half of net inflows into the hard-currency budget come from private activity (see Appendix). Officially 32 per cent of personal services were provided by the registered private sector in 1986. If we use the coefficients used in columns 2 and 3 of Table 10.1 and add our estimate of 7 per cent of registered personal services as being supplied by unregistered entrepreneurs (see Appendix), then the true figure would be between 56 per cent and 62 per cent. In industry, construction and trade the private sector's contribution probably lies between one-tenth and a quarter. In industry only 6.6 per cent of national income produced came from the private sector, and even if we multiply this by the coefficients used in

Table 10.1, we still only get a share of 15 per cent to 18 per cent, and this is likely to be very much the upper boundary.[20] In 1986 the registered private sector accounted for 18 per cent of the total workforce in construction. One can assume that there was a particularly large number of unregistered private operators in this sector. Private building firms are concerned mainly with the construction of private housing and with repairs and 'remont' of socialized sector buildings such as offices and factories. Officially private traders accounted for only 2.5 per cent of retail trade turnover, but this is an area in which black activity is known to be particularly large, and a figure of five times the official one would not seem at all unreasonable.

Within total private sector activity, the estimates in Table 10.1 suggest that agriculture accounts for about 30 per cent to 34 per cent of the personal money incomes generated in the private sector and hard-currency earnings account for 15 per cent to 20 per cent. The rest of the private sector, both registered and black, thus accounts for 45 per cent to 55 per cent of personal money incomes generated by private activity. If we use each kind of activity's share in the official turnover of the non-agricultural private sector as an indication of its relative importance within non-agricultural non-hard-currency private economic activity then we find that industrial production (excluding industrial services) accounts for 36 per cent; construction (including construction services) for 25 per cent; personal services (excluding building services) a surprisingly low 22 per cent; and trade 13 per cent. One can assume that this somewhat underestimates the real importance of personal services and trade, and overestimates the real importance of industrial production. Nevertheless, the picture which emerges is one in which the 'productive' activities of industrial production and construction are much more important than one would have expected.

Although the stress until now has been on the surprising (if largely hidden) size and rapid growth of the registered non-agricultural private sector, there is no denying the vast array of administrative, fiscal and supply restrictions under which it labours. In the first place permission to undertake private economic activity has to be obtained from the (usually local) authorities.[21] Permission may be denied if the artisan or trader concerned does not have the requisite qualifications. Since there is a fairly detailed list of formally recognized crafts and of the required formal qualifications which correspond to each of them, not only the size but also the type of activity of private entrepreneurs is severely limited. Any infraction of the conditions upon which permission was granted can lead to the total withdrawal of permission. The result is a 'fragmentation' of the private sector, in which an artisan is strictly limited to his officially approved trade. Thus, for example a shoemaker cannot use the scraps of leather he is left with to make patchwork handbags, because this is reserved to tailors. Even worse, he cannot sell the scraps, because that would mean engaging in trade in goods, for which he does not have a trader's licence. This 'fragmentation' of the private sector is clearly intentional and pervades regulations covering private economic activity. It is, for instance, reflected in the barriers to co-operation which have been set up between western joint ventures and Polonia firms. Only socialized enterprises can enter into joint-venture agreements. Clearly there is a feeling in the bureaucracy that, if entrepreneurs can be kept small and prevented from co-operating or expanding their activity into diverse fields, they can be more easily controlled. Furthermore, the more regulations there are binding the private sector, the more potential there is for officialdom to extract bribes from it.

The main problems for the private sector arising out of the tax system are its extreme progressiveness and its arbitrariness. If single, the private entrepreneur begins to pay tax at an income equivalent to 43 per cent of the average wage in the socialized sector, whereas wage-earners in the socialized sector pay no tax until they reach extremely high incomes.[22] The effect of the highly progressive structure is to limit the growth of firms and is one of the main causes of the 'dwarfism' of enterprises in the private sector. Average employment in private firms is only slightly above two persons, including the employer and his family, in spite of a much higher formal limit.[23] It is noteworthy that while, as in agriculture, the non-agricultural private sector has been condemned to dwarfism, the socialized sector suffers from the 'gigantism' of enterprises. Even more important in limiting the size of firms is the arbitrary nature of taxation. The authorities have instructed tax inspectors to use any excuse to reject tax returns as inadequate, which has allowed inspectors to estimate the taxpayers' income almost at will, and charge tax on that basis.[24] The result is that external signs of high turnover, such as high employment or investment, must be avoided. This is important because the potential for the private sector to expand, even in the absence of other government restrictions, must be limited if it maintains the present size structure of firms. In this context the fact that turnover tax rates are often higher for the private than the socialized sector, and that private sector firms cannot, in practice, obtain a rebate on the turnover tax they have paid for inputs, are comparatively minor problems.

Last, but certainly not least, there is administrative control over material supplies to the private sector. The source of materials used by private firms has to be indicated, and a receipt provided. The intention is said to be to prevent theft of materials from the state, or the preferential sale of materials to the private sector by socialized enterprises facilitated by bribes. However, since state retail shops will not issue receipts for materials bought of the kind that are acceptable to the Ministry of Finance, a whole swathe of private production has to go underground.

This particularly affects very small producers who often buy their materials in state retail shops.

The question is: if things are so bad for the Polish private sector, why are they so good? The answer is that bribery and tax evasion are practised on a massive scale, and that the authorities accept this. The host of repressive and often mutually contradictory regulations were originally intended to give the central authorities the ability to 'turn the screw', and limit the growth, or even cause the rapid decline, of the non-agricultural private sector should they so wish. In the meantime, while central policy is favourable to private sector growth, they provide the means by which the members of the bureaucracy at various levels can help themselves to part of the incomes generated in the sector. The drawbacks are that both the bureaucracy and the private entrepreneurs become extremely corrupt (what Aaslund calls 'legally degenerate'), while private sector activity is distorted into 'dwarfism'.

Since 1981 there has been an important shift by which the private sector has become less involved in the provision of goods and services to the population (its traditional role in communist countries), and far more involved in the provision of goods, and above all services, to socialized enterprises. The result is a considerable erosion of the 'ghettoisation' to which the private sector was traditionally subject. Thus the share of total sales to the population in the private sector's officially reported turnover fell from 66 per cent to 47.5 per cent between 1981 and 1985. This only applies to officially registered sales. The vast majority of unregistered sales go to the population, other private sector firms and farmers. Nonetheless, a considerable change has occured compared with Stalinist times, when the private sector was allowed neither to sell to nor buy from the socialized sector, and when it was limited to supplying the services and handicrafted goods for the population that socialized industry was clearly unsuited to provide. Exchange between the two sectors has grown as restrictions have been lifted, because socialized enterprises appreciate the flexibility of their private sector partners, while private firms find the socialized sector less demanding than individuals, and able to help obtain scarce inputs.[25]

Controls on the registered non-agricultural private sector lead to considerable black economic activity, both unreported activity by the registered sector itself (this is discussed in the Appendix and calculated in Table 10.1, where the gap between official and estimated registered non-agricultural private sector incomes implies that black activity accounts for some two-thirds of the activity of registered entrepreneurs), and activity by unregistered entrepreneurs. There is at least one convincing estimate of the overall size and growth of the black economy (Bednarski, Kokoszczyński and Stopyra, 1987[26]). The authors' most significant result is that they estimate that the zloty black economy has grown rapidly as a share of personal incomes, from 5 per cent in 1977 to 12 per cent in 1985.[27] This result suggests strongly that legal and illegal private economic activity are complements and not substitutes. Those on the liberal wing of the Party who argue that legalizing private activity will reduce the black economy seem to be wrong, whereas those who oppose the growth of the legal private sector on the grounds that it encourages the growth of the black economy (mainly by allowing registered private entrepreneurs to undertake unregistered activity) are right, at least given the current level of distortions in the Polish economy (of which the controls over private economic activity are themselves an important part).

One of the most important changes in the non-agricultural private sector has been the 'generational turnover' which has occurred as a result of the influx of younger people into the sector. Whereas only 17 per cent of private entrepreneurs were under 35 in the mid-1970s, today, in a much larger private sector, those under 35 constitute 30 per cent of entrepreneurs.[28] Equally important is the fact that many of the new young entrepreneurs have a higher education and have spent some time in the West. This has allowed them to accumulate capital by working illegally, and also to observe western techniques and, perhaps more importantly, western intensity of work.[29] The overall effect has been to make the private sector more modern, dealing in some cases with fairly sophisticated equipment (e.g. the private software firms that have sprung up in the last two years, particularly in Gdynia, or the satellite dish manufacturer in Szczecin). However, it should be noted that, because of the continued rigid control of permits by the state, much of the 'high-tech' private sector is black. Another important development is the legislation of three new forms of private commercial property since 1976. They potentially allow for the establishment of medium and even large private firms in Poland. So far the most significant of the new forms has been the 'Polonia' firm.[30] Such firms were first allowed in 1976, but it was only after the martial law period (from 1982) that they began to develop rapidly. In 1981 there were 117 such firms, but they employed only 3,478 workers. By 1986 there were 670 firms employing 61,619 persons (i.e. an average of 90 employees per firm, with the largest employing 800 people in 1988). However, the growth of Polonia firms, both in terms of numbers and employees, has been developing at a sharply declining rate. In 1986 employment grew by only 7,330, while the number of firms declined. It is clear that the authorities came to the conclusion that the rapid growth of these firms needed to be checked, at least temporarily. This is in spite of their generally accepted high level of efficiency (labour productivity is said to have been four to five times that of the socialized sector in the early 1980s[31]), the introduction into Poland of western methods of management of medium-sized enterprises which the Polonia firms have facilitated, and their contribution to the hard-currency trade balance through the production of import-substitutes. The fact that this last development has been achieved mainly with the use of Polish and second-hand western machines makes it all the more impressive.

Legislation making joint ventures with western capitalist firms legal was passed in 1986 and is in the process of being liberalized, as the original law failed to attract many western partners. One of the greatest weaknesses of the legislation has been the banning of participation of Polonia firms in joint ventures. An expression of the authorities' desire to fragment the private sector, it has prevented large western firms from taking advantage of Polonia firms' knowledge of conditions in Poland, one of the factors which, together with the existence of suppliers and service firms independent of the state, could give Poland a considerable advantage over other east European countries in the competition for joint venture capital.

This stagnation in the development of joint ventures makes the appearance since the mid-1980s of private and public limited companies (*spółki z ograniczoną odpowiedzialnością spółki akcyjne*) all the more important. By mid-1987 there were some 400 such companies registered,[32] and many more awaiting registration. Some 4,000 people worked for, or were partners in, the new companies, and employment ranged from two to seventy-five persons, while the average was ten (five times that in the non-agricultural private sector as a whole, and one-ninth that of the Polonia firms). Most of the firms are engaged in services, and particularly in software and computers, marketing, and technical and scientific consulting. A whole group of such firms, dealing in software and mainly servicing socialized sector enterprises, have established themselves in Gdynia, in what one might call Poland's 'silicon bay'. The location is due to easy access to personal computer hardware via the port, and to the skilled personnel of Gdańsk Polytechnic. Most of the owners of limited companies are relatively young (thirty to forty years) and with a university education.

A very important innovation is the recent encouragement given by the authorities to the creation of mixed socialized-private companies. The advantage to the private sector partners is above all certainty of supply, although assurance of a large and steady volume of demand is also useful. The advantage to the socialized sector (or rather to the *nomenklatura* which controls that sector) are the large directorial salaries which can be obtained. In the recently reported Elpol case[33] a newly established limited company voted monthly salaries of four times the national average, and 1 per cent of net profits, to the director, and three times the average salary to each of four other members of the board of directors. Most significant, however, was the remuneration of the average industrial wage voted to the nineteen members of the board of trustees who include a vice-premier, representatives of the Ministries of Defence and Finance, and representatives of large socialized enterprises.

Causes of the growth of private economic activity

The reasons for the breakdown of Aaslund's law can be divided into proximate and underlying factors. We shall examine the proximate factors first:

1 The current economic crisis in Poland has lasted far longer than the previous crises which also, as Aaslund observed, resulted in 'green lights' for private economic activity (1956, 1970, 1976). What is more, the leadership is conscious of the fact that the current crisis is likely to continue for a very long time.
2 The foreign debt aspect of the crisis, in particular, has forced the authorities to permit the expansion of the hard-currency economy by liberalizing foreign currency and passport regulations, and encouraging the creation of Polonia firms and joint ventures.[34]
3 In some areas, such as housing, the crisis has increased the importance of the private sector simply as a result of the decline in socialized provision and the desire of the state to improve its budgetary position by selling off assets (e.g. the sale of both state and co-operative housing to individuals).
4 The reforms of 1982, however limited in scope, and however ineffective in forcing socialized enterprises to become more efficient, have nevertheless reduced the degree of detailed control by planners over the socialized sector. This has almost ended the 'ghettoisation' of the private sector, and has allowed socialized enterprises to enter into economic relations with the private sector, particularly as customers, but also as suppliers (see p.206). This has considerably improved the conditions under which private enterprises operate.
5 What is more, one of the main sources of socialized sector pressure to restrict the private sector identified by Aaslund has disappeared, and indeed may have been reversed. Under the traditional centrally planned system socialized enterprises resisted private sector 'poaching' of their labour, since this reduced their ability to achieve their output targets (on which managerial and workers' bonuses depended). Under the post-1982 Reformed Economic System (RES) the formal 'government purchase orders', and both the formal targets, which determine bonuses, and the informal ones, which determine access to inputs and tax relief for the enterprise and promotion for managers, are usually formulated in terms of sales.[35] At the same time one of the main aims of the socialized enterprise under the RES is to increase the wages of

its workforce. The authorities have tried to prevent this through a tax on increases in the wage fund.[36] The result is that if skilled workers leave a socialized firm, set up a private business and work for their old firm as contractors, they can be paid more than previously, which keeps them working for the firm concerned, while at the same time their departure actually contributes to a reduction in the wages fund. All this is possible because the private sector itself is not subject to the wage fund tax.

6   The current leadership is far less ideological than its predecessors. It has learned from the Solidarity crisis that it has lost the support of the workers, who are hard to control, because once they have a home there are few sanctions short of prison that can be used effectively against them. Because of the generalized excess demand for labour, if sacked they are likely to be quickly hired by another enterprise. Also, because they often work in large factories it is comparatively easy for them to mobilize politically. On the other hand, the peasants, though ideologically even more opposed to the authorities than the workers, have caused much less trouble. Peasants have more to lose: if the authorities deny them inputs such as fertilizers, individual peasants can be quickly forced into bankruptcy. Also they are harder to mobilize because they work individually. Viewed in this light, the expansion of the urban private sector draws off many of the most energetic members of the intelligentsia and the working class from the socialized sector, where they can cause trouble, to private economic activity, in which they are harder to mobilize, and where they are far more easily controlled by the authorities, as they have more to lose. The degree of control of the private sector by the state bureaucracy may be declining, but it will always be sufficient to ruin individual entrepreneurs who have made themselves politically objectionable. And to some extent the growing dependence of private entrepreneurs on socialized enterprises will make up for their reduced dependence on the administration.

Turning to the underlying factors for the breakdown of Aaslund's Law, it is impossible to assign relative importance to each of these, but the following are some of those that seem to be more permanent than those emanating from the current economic and political situation in Poland:

1   Socialism as an ideology has become bankrupt in Poland. Much of the *nomenklatura* no longer believes that socialism is either just or effective. The result seems to have been to make state and Party officials much readier to espouse in practice the 'interpenetration' of the apparatus and the private sector in the form of bribe-taking, acceptance of places on boards of trustees of mixed socialised-private, and purely private, companies, and exploitation of the hard-currency

opportunities presented by the Polonia firms. It is said that each Polonia firm has a silent Security Police shareholding. In the past officialdom felt that it was best served by keeping a high level of restrictions on the private sector. It seems that it is now coming to the conclusion that it is better served by expanding the 'bribe base', even if the 'bribe rate' declines. We thus get a sort of 'kleptocratic Laffer curve', from which we can surmise that at some level of liberalization 'bribe revenues' will decline, as the degree of competition in the private sector reduces monopoly profits; the decline in restrictions also reduces the ability of officialdom to participate in them. Nevertheless, Poland seems to be far from such a situation. Also the effects of the ideological decline of socialism in Poland can be seen in public attitudes to private sector activity, which have become far less hostile,[37] although there is still a strong residual egalitarianism.

2   The importance of services has been growing in all advanced countries, and indeed, though at a slower rate, in the communist countries. The underdevelopment of services in the communist countries has been well documented.[38] Services are the activity which the socialized sector has been least efficient in supplying, and in which private economic activity has been traditionally more easily tolerated in communist countries. Thus, as the demand for services grows the costs of restricting the private sector increase. Unless restrictions are imposed, the general presumption that private economic activity should be permitted in services will of itself lead to increases in the size of private sector as demand increases. This factor is likely to operate in all communist countries (*vide* the recent relaxation of controls on private economic activity in the USSR and Czechoslovakia).

3   A ratchet effect operates. The bigger private economic activity, the more overall economic growth depends on the growth of that activity. Growth in the private sector is above all dependent on the confidence of entrepreneurs in the future. Thus any restrictive policy towards them becomes more and more costly. What is more, the situation is quite different from that in the 1940s, when the communist authorities could count on large gains in economic growth as a result of socialization and centralization. Most economists would agree that the potential benefits from such a policy have been exhausted long ago in Poland.

4   There seem to be certain synergies between the growth of various parts of the private sector, which mean that the growth of each part makes it easier for other parts to grow:

(a)   A private enterprise in a centrally administered economy can be thought of as an organism that requires a certain environment if it is to survive and/or grow. Survival requires, at the very least, the possibility of obtaining inputs and selling one's produce. The greater the effective (i.e. unavoidable) controls on this activity, the less likely is the enterprise to survive and/or grow. As a result the smaller it is likely to be, and the smaller will be the number of surviving enterprises. Thus, the more varied the private sector, and the greater the kinds of activity private enterprises can undertake, the more private economic activity can grow, because private enterprises can obtain inputs from, and find customers among, other private firms.

(b) Controls do not, of course, have to be limited to affecting purchases or sales, or the prices at which these occur. They can directly affect the size of the enterprise, or the number of enterprises that are allowed to operate. Restrictions on the number of enterprises allow quasi-rents to be obtained, which generate incomes which allow some of the restrictions to be evaded through bribery. Restrictions on the size of enterprises affect the kind of activities the private sector can profitably undertake. This is why the appearance of larger private enterprises (Polonia firms and limited companies) and mixed social-private enterprises and joint ventures is so important. It allows private economic activity to colonize new 'niches' in the economic ecosystem. Furthermore, it is possible that the appearance of large private and mixed capital firms will further increase the demand for the produce of small private firms as suppliers of inputs, as the large private firms are likely to lay more stress on promptness and quality than do socialized firms, particularly if they become involved on a significant scale in exports to world markets. A 'virtuous circle of privatization' might then come into being, with increases in the size of the private sector leading to further increases in demand for private sector goods and services.

(c) Another important synergy is that, as we have seen, the official and black private sectors are complementary, rather than competitive.

(d) The growing importance of private housing also strengthens the private sector by providing a safe investment, with low risk and low returns, for savings, and, given the massive housing shortage, it provides a strong incentive for private entrepreneurs to accumulate. Most of the returns are from the utility obtained by possessing dwelling space, but the new law on rented accommodation, which came into force in 1988, allows landlords to let premises vacated by protected tenants at market rates and without security of tenure, and allows the construction of new housing for rent under the same provisions.[39]

(e) The dollar market and the hard-currency accounts which are its outgrowth also provide low-risk investment opportunities. The dollar also provides a comparatively stable unit of account on which the private sector can base its calculations. For instance, contracts for the sale of dwellings have long been effectively denominated in dollars, making them zloty-inflation-free.[40] The hard-currency economy is also a source of investments for the private sector. In many cases the start-up capital for private enterprises was obtained through illegal work in the West.[41]

Many of the potential synergies have not yet been exploited. Thus only a very small part of all the hard currency held by the population has been invested in Polonia firm activity because of the authorities' restrictive policy towards these firms, and the high interest rates offered on hard-currency accounts by the state banks.[42]

5 Finally, if it is true, as seems to be the case, that market socialism of the Hungarian and Polish type is not an adequate solution to the economic problems facing European socialist countries,[43] and that the effectiveness of the centrally planned system has become unacceptably low to the ruling elites,[44] then the Polish authorities (and with time possibly those in other communist countries) may have little alternative but to pursue the path of 'privatization' of the economy. It has been pointed out that privatization is an easier solution for reformist communist leaderships than is reform of the socialized sector.[45] No complex institutional arrangements, incentive schemes or methods for making enterprises independent of interference by political superiors are necessary. Also, privatization has the advantage of ensuring the economic independence of enterprises without giving power to workers' councils, which might use this power for political purposes.

Conclusion: policy and systemic implications

Some of the economic benefits of privatization from the point of view of the authorities have already been mentioned in the previous section. Another which may become important in the future needs to be discussed here; the growth of the private sector can act as a cushion, absorbing some of the unemployment that will have to occur if inefficient enterprises are allowed to go bankrupt. There are two problems, however; on the one hand, if the authorities succeed in implementing a deflationary macro-economic policy, growth of the private sector itself may be inhibited (until now the private sector, like the socialized, has only known an environment of generalized excess demand); on the other hand, if the authorities fail to implement deflationary policies, persistence of the current hyper-inflation may also result in stagnation in the private sector. High and volatile inflation rates would make investment planning by private entrepreneurs extremely difficult. As the private sector became larger such investment would become an important determinant of its efficiency.

One possible solution to this problem may be the even more widespread use of hard currency in private sector transactions. Given the growing links between the private and socialized sectors, however, the use of hard currency in trade in the means of production between the two sectors (both in purchases and sales) would probably be necessary.[46] It is a paradox that the existence of parallel currencies in Poland, by cushioning consumers and the private sector from the effects of inflation, reduces to some extent the pressure on the authorities to deal with the problem. Since the government is politically weak, it may well choose the line of least resistance; allowing zloty inflation to continue accelerating even at the cost of an ever greater share of economic transactions being conducted in hard currency. Even if the government does not actually encourage such a 'dollarisation' of the economy by allowing a growth in hard-currency transactions between the private and the socialised sectors, the hard-currency sphere of the economy will expand if zloty inflation is allowed to continue accelerating, as at a flexible rate of exchange (such as the black market rate in Poland), good money drives out bad.[47]

None of the above implies that the continued growth of the private sector at current rates is inevitable, or even irreversible. Apart from anything else, as the number of people involved increases, the opportunities for obtaining rents from monopoly power will decline, so that the sector's command over resources will grow less fast than employment in it. The same effect will hold for the 'real' (zloty inflation adjusted) black market rate of the dollar, as more people travel to the West to work illegally. Nevertheless, further rapid growth of the private sector does seem the most likely outcome for the foreseeable future, if only because of the certainty of continued economic crisis in Poland. There seems to be little evidence for Bauer's view[48] that the scope for the successful development of the private sector is exhausted in Poland in the absence of further reforms of the socialized sector. Private sector employment is continuing to grow, and further liberalization of controls on the size of private enterprises and of regulations regarding hard-currency trade (both exports and imports), together with a less arbitrary tax system, can be expected to stimulate the growth of the sector considerably, particularly given the relative cheapness, by international standards, of labour in Poland. Doubtless, further relaxation of central control of the socialized sector would also help the private sector to grow, but it does not seem that, at present, the rules governing the socialized sector make further expansion of the private sector impossible.

A larger private sector does not have to mean a more efficient economy. In many cases private provision may be less efficient than social provision (the often quoted case of engineers working as taxi drivers, or the effects on socialized building of massive theft of materials and labour). Furthermore, it is in the interest of officialdom (and indeed to some extent of already established entrepreneurs) for there to be restrictions which act as barriers to entry in many areas of private economic activity in order to generate large monopolistic rents which can be 'taxed' through extortion, which results in the persistence of such barriers. On the other hand, by the same reasoning, the larger and less restricted the private sector, the smaller the proportion of it which obtains monopoly rents, and certainly the more efficient the private sector itself, if not the economy as a whole.

An intriguing aspect of the growth of private economic activity is its implications for the political economy of Poland. Winiecki has recently suggested a scenario for a 'buy-out' by society of the *nomenklatura*'s property rights over the economy.[49] The question is whether what is occurring at present, with the rapid growth of private economic activity, is a sort of buy-out of the *nomenklatura* by itself; a process in which the *nomenklatura* liberalizes restrictions on the private sector, while at the same time ensuring for its members individual property rights over some of the choicest bits of the private sector (Polonia firms and mixed socialized-private firms). On this scenario the *nomenklatura* would with time transform itself into a new capitalist bourgeoisie, owning some of the most profitable monopolies in the private sector. There have certainly been historical cases in which the first step in the creation of capitalism has been the transformation of privilege into monopoly property rights, which were subsequently abolished or limited.[50] It is as yet too early to say, but it seems likely that this is not what is occurring at present. What does seem to be happening is that part of the *nomenklatura*'s rights over the economy are being made fungible. Rather than limiting themselves to privileged access to goods from the socialised sector, members of the *nomenklatura* are also arranging to obtain cash from the private sector through bribes, seats on boards of trustees, etc. It is this process which is making the *nomenklatura* ever more tolerant of various forms of 'interpenetration' of its own membership and the private sector, while at the same time inducing it to accept the expansion of the private sector 'bribe base'.

Finally, there is the question of the extent to which the growth of private economic activity in Poland is a result of government policy, or of an inevitable process over which the authorities have little control. In the short run it resulted from a government response to acute economic crisis, which was speedily taken advantage of by the population, because the desire and the ability to engage in private activity were there. In the long run it may be a case of a contradiction between the means and the relations of production; as services and specialized small-batch manufacturing become more important in the economies of advanced capitalist countries,[51] socialist countries may be able to retain centralized control over the bulk of their economies only at an ever higher cost (the gap between their actual and potential levels of output). Some of the communist elites may be prepared to pay that price. It seems probable that, because of the crisis of faith in socialism and the interpenetration of *nomenklatura* and private sector described above, this will not be the case in Poland.

This does not, of course, mean that Poland will move towards a western-style mixed economy. It is more likely to become a 'mixed economy kleptocracy', on the lines of certain middle-level developing countries such as Mexico.[52] This would be a system in which a highly intrusive but corrupt state and Party administration (whose higher officials often have intimate links with, and even shares in, private sector firms, while lower officials simply take bribes) would co-exist with a large private sector, parts of which were a source of high monopoly profits, much of them in hard currency. As the share of private economic activity grew, it would be less a matter of the private sector being 'legally degenerate', and more one of the state becoming so.

Appendix: Sources for Table 10.1

The source for official figures for personal money incomes is the *Mały Rocznik Statystyczny, 1987*, 100-2. The official figures in column 1 do not include interest payments on dollar and zloty deposit. The only figure available is 'other incomes of the population', which is obtained by subtracting the figures for incomes of specified source from 'total money incomes'. The result for 1986 is 613.7 billion zloty, but this also includes net borrowing from the state bank, hard-currency sales in internal export shops (measured at the official exchange rate), etc., etc. To arrive at the 'low' estimate in column 2, I made the following assumptions: (1) There is no unregistered economic activity in private agriculture. (2) Real earnings used for consumption by entrepreneurs in the official non-agricultural private sector are 2.5 times their official level. This is because in the artisan sector (*rzemiosło*), which forms three-quarters of the non-agricultural private sector in terms of the number of people employed, the average wage of hired labour was officially 12,400 zlotys per month in 1985, well below average earnings in the socialized sector, which stood at 20,000 zlotys. Since people left the socialized sector to work in the private as hired employees in large numbers during 1981–5, and since the work of an artisan is generally admitted to be skilled, it is reasonable to assume that their wages were in fact higher, rather than lower, than in the socialized sector. Indeed, anecdotal evidence suggests that the real wage was 30,000 to 40,000 zlotys in 1985, or 2.5 to 3.2 times the official figure.[53] It is from this that we take the coefficients of 2.5 and 3.2 which

Table 10.1a Personal money incomes (1986) (percentage shares)

Summary Table	Official	Unofficial	
		Low	High
Socialized sector	75.5	62.0	54.8
from employment	56.5	46.4	41.0
from transfers	19.0	15.6	13.8
Private sector	24.5	38.0	45.2
agriculture	15.7	12.9	13.7
non-agricultural	8.8	14.9	20.5
black	–	2.3	4.1
hard currency	–	7.8	6.9

Table 10.1b Personal money incomes (billions of zlotys)

Detailed Table			
Wages and salaries in socialized sector	3596	3596	3596
Transfers	1210	1210	1210
Private agriculture	1000	1000	1200
Non-agricultural private sector	312	780	998
Part-time private sector work	121	121	386
Wages from employment in private sector	128	255	408
Total	6366	6962	7798
Black economy	0	180	360
Dollar earnings	0	604	604
Grand total	6367	7746	8762

Sources: see Appendix.

Table 10.2 Growth rates of employment in the official urban private sector

1974	3.8	1981	7.1
1975	2.0	1982	10.2
1976	2.6	1983	12.9
1977	4.8	1984	10.3
1978	5.8	1985	6.6
1979	6.0	1986	8.5
1980	6.7	1987	10.6

Sources: Aaslund, A. (1985) *Private Enterprise in Eastern Europe*, London: Macmillan, 231, and *Polish Statistical Yearbooks* for 1982–7.

we apply in columns 2 and 3. A similar figure of 3.5 times average earnings in the socialized sector is given in W. Herer and W. Sadowski, (1987).[54] (3) Earnings from part-time employment in the private sector are assumed to be as officially recorded. (4) Wages from employment in the official non-agricultural private sector are assumed to be twice those in the socialized sector.[55] (5) Earnings per person working in the black economy (i.e. by unregistered entrepreneurs) are estimated to be equal to the average wage in the socialized sector – this is because all we have is an estimate of the number of people employed black economy[56] without any indication as to whether this refers to full- or part-time activity. This is about the same figure we arrive at by an alternative procedure; it is estimated that about 6 per cent of personal services in the towns and 12.5 per cent in the countryside are supplied by unregistered entrepreneurs;[57] since the provision of services is notoriously bad in the countryside, we may guess that this is equivalent to some 7.5 per cent of officially supplied services for the country as a whole. The total value of personal services supplied to the population by the socialized sector and our estimate of the value supplied by the private sector (using the coefficient of 3.2) is 2,025 billion zlotys, of which 7.5 per cent is 152 billion zlotys. (6) Hard-currency earnings are estimated at 80 per cent of private transfers registered in the hard-currency balance of payments, translated into zlotys at the black market rate of exchange (zl.800 = $1 in 1986).

This last position is the most questionable. Transfers include the following: (a) inflows into hard-currency accounts; (b) hard-currency sales by internal export shops; (c) overseas pensions. Overseas pensions are paid into the Polish banking system in hard currency, but are paid out to recipients in zlotys. They account for 20 per cent of personal transfers (personal communication from the National Bank of Poland). But there are problems with using the remaining 80 per cent of personal transfers as a proxy for the hard-currency earnings of the population. In the first place, hard-currency sales by the internal export shops are included, but hard-currency imports by the shops go into total hard-currency imports, so that earnings from this source are gross. Although we do have figures for the value of hard-currency sales to the population of imported goods,[58] we do not know the mark-up of the internal export network, and therefore the total cost in hard, and in some proportion soft, currency of these goods. This does not reduce the value of using transfers as a measure of the population's hard-currency earnings, but it does reduce the usefulness of this figure as a measure of the contribution to Poland's hard-currency balance of payments of private economic activity by the population.

A more serious problem is that part of the increase in hard-currency accounts may be the drawing down of hard-currency cash holdings which were accumulated over many years, as a result of the high interest rates paid by the banks in Poland and growing confidence in the security of deposits. Indeed, it is not impossible that the net increase in hard-currency deposits is less than total net hard-currency earnings by the Polish population. Second, there may be an element of double counting here. Estimates of the real earnings of private entrepreneurs and of those involved in the black market may already involve a hard-currency element (e.g. earnings from the sale of zlotys on the black market to foreigners who then buy Polish goods, or the sale of private sector produce to foreigners for hard currency). Against this can be set the fact that total net inflows have continued at a very high level for three years (1985 – $764 million, 1986 – $945 million, 1987 – $1,500 million), that they have been rising continuously since 1981, and that they seem to be reasonably well correlated with the number of Polish tourists going to the West, which suggests that much of the money is the result of illegal employment abroad.

The 'high' estimate is based on the following assumptions: (1) There is an extra 20 per cent of private agricultural activity which remains unreported. (2) The earnings of the non-agricultural private sector and of part-time private sector work are assumed to be 3.2 times their official value, as are wages from employment in the non-agricultural private sector. (3) Earnings by unregistered entrepreneurs are assumed to be twice average earnings in the socialized sector. This allows about half the earnings of unregistered entrepreneurs to come from the provision of services, and the other half to come from illicit trade (so-called speculation). All other assumptions are as for the 'low' estimate.

An independent way of arriving at the share of private activity in personal money incomes is to start with the official figures in column 1 in Table 10.1 and add (1) the 12 per cent of official personal incomes which is the estimate of total zloty black economic activity for 1985 arrived at by Bednarski *et al.* (see note 13); and (2) the zl.604 billion which is our estimate of the value of private hard-currency earnings at the black market rate of exchange. The result is an overall share for private activity of 37.9 per cent, which is very close to the 'low' estimate in column 2.

Notes

1 I would like to thank Paul Auerbach, George Hadjimatheou, Peter Wiles, Stanisław Gomułka, Alan Smith and a referee for very useful comments on an earlier draft of this paper. The present version appeared also in *Soviet Studies*, March 1988. The permission to reprint it in this volume is gratefully acknowledged.
2 Aaslund, A. (1985) *Private Enterprise in Eastern Europe*, London: Macmillan.
3 Estimate by the Ministry of Internal Trade and Services reported in

Rajkiewicz, A. (1987) '*Państwo biednieje bardziej niz jego obywatele*', *Życie Gospodarcze*, 34.

4 All data are based on official data in *Polish Statistical Yearbooks* unless otherwise stated.

5 Gomułka, S. and Rostowski, J. (1985) 'The Polish Reformed Economic System: 1982–83', *Soviet Studies*.

6 Winiecki, J. ('Buying out Property Rights to the Economy from the Ruling Stratum', mimeograph, 1987) estimates the values of the privileges which the *nomenklatura* benefits from at 0.68 per cent of the total official personal incomes of the population. Even if we quadruple this figure to compensate for the fact that Winiecki does not include benefits from priority access to housing for *nomenklatura* members and their children in his calculations, we are still left with less than 2.75 per cent of official personal incomes. The true (market-clearing) value of goods sold in special miners' shops is worth at most 2.36 per cent of official personal incomes (Rusek, B. (1988) '*Sobotnie Pieniądze*', *Polityka*, 8).

7 Żukrowska, B. (1988) '*Oddam milion w dobre ręce*', *Polityka*, 2.

8 (a) The estimate, made by the Central Customs Office (*Główny Urząd Cel*), is reported in Jurkiewicz, Z. (1987) *Gazeta Pomorska*, 18, 12. I am grateful to G. Kolankiewicz for bringing this report to my attention. (b) At the end of 1986 total savings, on deposit and current accounts, stood at zl.2,091 billion, while cash holdings were zl.1,173 billion. During 1987 the former increased by zl.399 billion and the latter by zl.128 billion (*Główny Urząd Statystyczny* in *Zycie Gospodarcze*, 5, 1988). Current accounts are such a small part of money supply that they are included in savings in official statistics.

9 The ability to use zloty price increases in the state retail network to reduce aggregate demand, or as an inflation tax on savings, becomes limited. There is also the possibility of perverse wealth effects on aggregate demand when zloty prices are increased, as some people will feel (zloty) wealthier as the black market value of the hard currency they own increases.

10 Formally, of the 10.8 million dwellings in Poland at the end of 1986, 5.8 million were in the socialized sector and 5 million were privately owned. These figures are, however, deceptive. In the first place, private housing is the predominant form of ownership in the countryside, where out of 3.87 million dwellings 3.19 million are privately owned. In the towns, on the other hand, only 1.8 million dwellings out of 6.97 million are classified as being in the private sector. However, part of the dwellings classified as private have in fact been under the almost complete control of the state, which had the right to quarter who it wished in these dwellings and set the rent (these come under the so-called Public Housing Administration – *Publiczna Gospodarka Lokalowa*). There are some 550,000 dwellings in the towns in this category (estimate by the *Instytut Gospodarki Przestrzennej i Komunalnej*, communicated personally to the author). On the other hand, about 20 per cent of co-operatively built dwellings were either initially built to be supplied to those who were prepared to buy them outright, or have been bought by tenants since construction (estimate by the *Rada Mieszkaniowa*, communicated personally to the author – these are the so-called '*spółdzielcze-własnościowe*' dwellings). This amounts to half a million dwellings which are effectively (though not formally) privately owned, although there are some restrictions on

individuals' rights to sell such dwellings. Since co-operative housing is mainly concentrated in the towns we can say that about 1.8 million dwellings, or 25 per cent, are effectively in private hands in the towns.

Even more important, new private housing has been expanding at the expense of new socialized housing. Since 1980, when 161,000 socialized sector dwellings were completed, output has declined continuously, reaching 128,000 in 1986, while private housing completions have remained constant at about 57,500. If we add to this the rising share of new co-operative dwellings sold to private individuals (it now stands at about 20 per cent), then the total individually owned share of new housing is about 40 per cent for the country as a whole, and 28 per cent for the towns (almost all the 'owned co-operative' housing is in the towns). Indeed if we look at the area of new construction for the country as a whole, private housing's share (excluding 'owned co-operative') reached 45 per cent in 1986.

11 In the country as a whole the share of private housing in the number of dwellings has stabilized in the mid-1980s. In the towns it is only private housing's share in the area of dwellings which has stabilized.

12 A. Aaslund, *op.cit.*.

13 Bednarski, M., Kokoszczyński R. and Stopyra J. (1987) *'Drugi obieg w Polsce w latach* 1977–85', *Wektory Gospodarki*, 8. Using published information on the size of the money stock, (Zg), sales of goods and services by the socialised sector, (Fn), legal sales by the private sector (urban and agricultural = On), and a version of the Cambridge equation

$$Zg.R = Fn + On + Gn \qquad (1)$$

Bednarski *et al.* can solve for Gn, the turnover in the black economy if they have a figure for the velocity of circulation (R) of the money stock. This they approximate by:

$$R = \frac{365}{\dfrac{Ro + Rb}{2}} \qquad (2)$$

where Ro is the number of days' supply that inventories held by the retail trade sector are worth, and Rb is the average number of days that a unit of currency stays outside the tills of the National Bank of Poland. Apart from various other methods for measuring the change in the size of the black economy which were based on the *assumption* of a strong correlation between the legal and black private sectors, the authors used the method described in this note for both 1977 and 1985. It is to these results that we refer.

14 B. Żukrowska, *op.cit.*.

15 *Bank i Kredyt*, 9, 1986, and *International Financial Statistics*, September 1988, International Monetary Fund.

16 Okuniewski, J. and Mazurkiewicz, E. (1987) *'Stanowisko Rady Gospodarki Żywnościowej'*, *Życie Gospodarcze*, 32.

17 Officially the 'Small productive enterprise belongs to foreign capital'.

18 *'Spółki z orgraniczoną odpowiedzialnoscią'*, *'spółki akcyjne'* and *'spółki mieszane'*, Kowalska, M. (1987) *'Powiedzialy jaskółki'*, *Zycie Gospodarcze*, 25. This was made possible by the 1982 law on handicrafts and the 1983 law on private trade.

19 Burzyński, A. (1986) 'A foreign investor's guide to the law of 23 April 1986 on companies with foreign capital participation', Information and Legal Aid Centre, Polish Chamber of Foreign Trade, Warsaw, 1986.
20 There is some overlap here, because a part of 'personal services' are also 'industrial services' which are part of industry.
21 Jakubek, M. and Skubisz, R. (1987) *Formy prawne prywatnej działalności gospodarczej*, mimeo. This forms the basis of much of what is reported in this section.
22 Kudła, W. (1987) *'Polityka fiskalna wobec prywatnego sektora pozarolniczego'*, mimeo.
23 The employment limit in handicrafts (*'rzemioslo'*) has been fifteen employees excluding: pensioners, apprentices, specialists (e.g. cashiers) and members of the owner's family in 'licensed' enterprises. In the smaller 'registered' enterprises the limit for general employees has been five.
24 Kudła, W. *op.cit.*.
25 Kowalska, M. (1987) *'Prywaciarze . . .'*, Życie Gospodarcze, 10.
26 See note 13.
27 See note 13.
28 Baczyński, J. (1987) *'Ani Lek ani trucizna'*, Polityka, 37.
29 Kowalska, M. *'Prywaciarze . . .' op.cit.*.
30 Reported in A. Aaslund, *op.cit.*, 116.
31 Plesinski, K. (1987) *'Pod znakiem spółek'*, Życie Gospodarcze, 26.
32 Kowalska, M. *'Powiedzialy jaskolki . . .', op.cit.*.
33 *'Kilka Pytan'*, Życie Gospodarcze, 1, 1988. Elpol is untypical to the extent that all of the shareholders are socialized enterprises or ministries.
34 The most important liberalization of foreign currency regulations has been the introduction of 'N' accounts in 1984, which allow people to deposit hard currency (whose legal provenance they cannot demonstrate) to be interest-free for one year, after which they can be transferred to 'A' accounts which are interest-bearing. Together with the high interest rates paid (in hard currency) on 'A' accounts by the National Bank this has resulted in the amount of money on hard-currency accounts increasing eightfold in four years to $2.5 billion. These interest rates have been exceptionally high by international standards. In late 1987 the National Bank was paying 11 per cent on three-year deposits, coming down to 5 per cent on current accounts (C. Bobinski, *Financial Times*, 26 October 1987). Not only is this income tax-free (an astonishing situation for unearned income of dubious origin in a communist country), but the same rate was paid on all currencies, so that a holder of Deutschemarks would get some four times as much as he would in West Germany (arbitraging between currencies is discouraged by a charge of 4 per cent on transfers between currencies). The contrast with the return on savings held in zlotys, on which real interest rates have been negative throughout the 1980s, could not be greater. Assuming a rate of inflation in West Germany of 1 per cent per annum, and a negative interest rate of about −11 per cent for 1983–7 (based on figures for 1983–6 in *Poland: Reform, Adjustment and Growth*, World Bank, Washington DC, 1987, 172, and a rate of interest of 11 per cent and a rate of inflation of 27 per cent for 1987), the gap between the return on the two types of savings has been about 19 per cent (assuming an

average return of 9 per cent, the rate on one-year deposits, on hard-currency accounts).

35 S. Gomułka and J. Rostowski, *op.cit.*.
36 *Podatek od Funduszu Aktwizacji Zawodowej*, renamed in 1987 *Podatek od Ponadnormatywnych Podwyżek Płac* (see S. Gomułka and J. Rostowski, *op.cit.*).
37 Dorn, L. (1987) '*Świadomościowe wymiary własności prywatnej*', mimeo, and Poprzeczko, J. (1987) '*Panstwowe czy nasze*', *Polityka*, 4.
38 Winiecki, J. (1986) 'Are Soviet-type Economies Entering an Era of Long-term Decline?', *Soviet Studies*.
39 Prawo Lokalowe, *Dziennik Ustaw*, 21, 1987, poz.124.
40 This has been done through the expedient of denominating contracts in 'hard-currency vouchers' (*bony dewizowe*), which has been legal since the mid-1970s.
41 Kowalska, M. '*Powiedziały jaskółki*', *op.cit.*.
42 See note 34.
43 Kornai, J. (1986) 'The Hungarian Reform Process: Visions, Hopes and Reality', *Journal of Economic Literature*.
44 Winiecki, J. (1986) 'Soviet-type Economies: Considerations for the Future', *Soviet Studies*, October 1986.
45 Bauer, T. (1988) 'Economic Reforms within vs. beyond the State Sector', paper presented at the *Conference on Alternative Models of Socialist Economic Systems*, Gyoer, Hungary, March 1988.
46 The principle is already accepted as far as sales to the private sector are concerned. Private farmers and entrepreneurs can buy machinery in hard-currency shops. Such a system could not, of course, be expanded on a large scale, unless it were accepted that the socialized sector could also buy from the private for hard currency.
47 Hayek, F.A. (1975) *The Denationalisation of Money*, Institute of Economic Affairs, London.
48 T. Bauer, *op.cit.*.
49 J. Winiecki, 'Buying out . . .', *op.cit.*.
50 Hill, C. (1962) *The Century of Revolution: 1603–1714*, 30–40 on grants of monopolies by the Court and opposition to this and 131–8 *passim* on the restriction of monopolies after the fall of the monarchy in England, London.
51 Dyker, D. (1985) *The Future of the Soviet Planning System*, 75, and Winiecki, J. (1987) *Economic Prospects East and West*, 81–5, Cambridge.
52 Wiles, P.J.D. (1977) *Economic Institutions Compared*, 451. Wiles points out that mixed economies are best suited to kleptocracy and, significantly, that Communism was not a kleptocracy in 1977 because it retained its ideological drive. As we have seen this is no longer true in Poland, London.
53 Kowalska, M. '*Prywaciarze* . . .', *op.cit.*
54 Herer, W. and Sadowski, W. (1987) *Życie Gospodarcze*, 38.
55 World Bank Report on Poland, 1987, 127.
56 Estimate by the Ministry of Internal Trade reported by Rajkiewicz, A. (1987) *Życie Gospodarcze*, 34.
57 Grad, M. (1987) *Życie Gospodarcze*, 8.
58 *Rocznik Statystyczny* (1987), 392.

Part III

Social attitudes and everyday life

11

Contradictions in the subconscious of the Poles

Mira Marody

Warsaw University

The results of sociological research usually focus on descriptions of social consciousness. In this chapter I would like to depart from this pattern and deal with what we might call the shape of Polish society's subconsciousness. To put it more exactly, my interest will be not so much in the opinions and views directly expressed by respondents in our studies, as in the underlying attitudes towards the social reality, of which they are not necessarily aware, but which do influence their actions within that reality. These attitudes have become fairly manifest in recent sociological studies and public opinion polls, even though they were not, for the most part, the original object of these studies. Consequently, conclusions concerning their existence can only be of an indirect character, and research results constituting the starting-point for their inference have to be used as circumstantial rather than hard evidence.[1]

These initial reservations notwithstanding, any attempt to pinpoint the factors which define the shape of Polish society's actions[2] in the mid-1980s must begin with the realm of consciousness, with at least a brief description of the system of social values and needs which arc seen as the crucial variables determining the goals of human endeavour.

Without engaging in the disputes surrounding these concepts in social sciences, we shall use the term 'social values' to refer to the desirable states of social reality linked to the image of a 'good society' and the term 'needs' to refer to the desired states of the individual condition which are linked to the image of a 'decent life'.

The numerous studies of the system of basic social values recognized by Polish society indicate that it has remained considerably stable for some time. It includes equal opportunities, freedom of speech, democracy seen as the genuine influence of all citizens on the way the state is governed, justice, truth, respect for man's dignity and prosperity of the society (or economic efficiency perceived as a condition for such prosperity). As regards the changes in this system in recent years, they consist mainly in the increased resolve with which the respondents choose certain values. In other words, the image of the 'good society' – especially as perceived by young people – is more clearly defined, and, by the same token, less susceptible to modification by persuasion. The sphere of values has become an area of little dispute.

As for individual needs, one can describe two more general groups revealed by studies of various types. The first is related to material needs. Satisfying them is supposed to ensure a 'decent' standard of living, though the level is different in different social groups. However, it seems possible to point out three basic conditions which determine the 'normal' level of what is desired:

1 wages which make it possible relatively easily to satisfy basic everyday needs (food, clothes, etc.) as well as to acquire in the foreseeable future durable consumer goods, such as refrigerators, washing machines, TV sets, etc., provided one saves for them;
2 the availability of goods and services;
3 a flat of one's own.

These three conditions constitute a threshold in social consciousness – below it lies what we might call an area of deprivation and above it is the area of free consumer choice.

The second group is made up of needs which endow life with an existential dimension; satisfying these needs determines 'psychological well-being' in the lives of individuals. The most frequently cited were:

1 dignity – seen first of all as the respect the respondents expect from others, both in direct contacts between people and in more impersonal relations of the 'authorities-society' type;
2 freedom of speech – perceived primarily as the individuals' need to express their opinions and views free of a sense of anxiety. This is manifested in, among other things, the attachment of high importance to truth seen as a social value;
3 autonomy – a need manifest first of all in the negative assessment of those actions by the authorities, which, in the opinion of the respondents, are an attempt to manipulate people and influence the attitudes of society;
4 the need for a meaning to life, both in everyday life and in its 'metaphysical' dimension. In the 'everyday' dimension, this is manifest as a desire to have social life efficiently organized, actions mutually adjusted and serving to accomplish certain goals and things used purposefully – in short, a desire to see life match common sense. In the 'metaphysical' dimension, it is expressed in the desire to have faith

in something or somebody, a faith which endows the life of an individual with purposefulness and a *supra-personal* meaning.

Although needs are here divided into material and existential, the two groups should be regarded in conjunction as, in social opinion, it is the satisfying of both that determines a 'decent' standard of living.

The link between the sphere of values and that of needs calls for a short commentary. Social values may be 'autotelic' in character, meaning that the 'good society' they outline is regarded as a desirable and valuable goal in itself. It seems, however, that more characteristic of Polish society is the situation in which these values are regarded as instrumental to satisfying individuals' needs, both material and existential. In the social consciousness, the values we have outlined define the shape of that type of society, whose existence is the necessary condition for fully satisfying individual needs. (Indeed, this is precisely what makes that society 'good'.)

This system of values and needs determines the general direction of aspirations of Polish society. However, actual actions undertaken by people are always conducted in some concrete situation and their shape is determined not only by what people *want* but also by what they deem as *beneficial*, *reasonable* or *feasible* in a given situation. Among the situation-related determinants one can distinguish those which last as long as some specific arrangements (and we shall not deal with them in the present paper), as well as ones which set the conditions for activity over longer periods of time. Their durability and recurrence lead to the emergence of certain automatisms in the sphere of the individual algorithms of activity and the consolidation of more general behavioural attitudes, which, by influencing the course of behaviour, modify the goals of human action. This assumption is soundly based on learning theory, in which rewarded actions are reinforced and gradually displace punishable or ineffective responses from the repertoire of individual behaviour.

It seems justifiable to assume that the most lasting components among situation-related factors include the shape of the political and economic system which has provided the general framework for the activity of Polish society in the past forty years. Recurrence of experience connected with the rules of functioning of the system perceived in everyday life has inevitably led to the emergence of specific behavioural attitudes which have become manifest both in sociological research and in concrete actions. If we view the empirical data amassed in recent years from this standpoint, we can – in my opinion – detect the existence of seven such system-determined attitudes.

First comes the attitude towards employment in the state-run sector of the economy. This can be described as a total *devaluation of work* in its role as a factor which determines the prosperity of families and individuals. The devaluation of work in the state-run sector of the economy has, in my view, an even broader impact and encompasses deprivation not only of material needs but also existential ones; sociological studies in Poland have, however, focused chiefly on the relationship between work and prosperity.

The second attitude stems from the compulsive need for a sense of social security, with security – let us add – defined as the absence of threats, rather than the presence of prospects for meeting one's needs. Clear preference is given to the model of a welfare state seen in opposition to a state in which everyone is alone responsible for his individual prosperity. 'Welfare' in this case seems to boil down merely to an assurance of survival, but such an assurance is available to everyone, while in the 'individualistic' model everyone is assumed to be threatened with dropping out of the game altogether. Hence we can speak of a striving for *'social insurance'*, rather than for social security.

These two behavioural attitudes are clearly linked at the system level: while the striving for social insurance has taken shape largely as a result of the authorities' emphasis on the dangers to which individuals in states with a different (capitalist) socio-political system are exposed, the devaluation of work in the state-run sector of the economy is the price this system pays for the elimination or weakening of these dangers.

The attitude of *'learned helplessness'* results from what Narojek refers to as 'the nationalization of the initiative of action in collective life'[3] and is manifested in a reluctance, or a downright inability, to act independently in public life, as well as in saddling the authorities with the responsibility for one's own performance in this respect. This learned helplessness is accompanied by an attitude which may be described as the *shortening of the temporal perspective* of undertaken and planned actions, which is manifest first of all in focusing on current problems and adopting temporary solutions without considering their long-term effects. The emergence of this attitude may be linked to the instability of the institutional and normative order, which for the past forty years has been the testing-ground for the changing concepts of adjusting the social order to the premises of the system, and the requirements posed by current developments.

Two further attitudes are connected to the sphere of inter-personal relations. One is *envious egalitarianism*[4], which seems to govern attitudes towards other people. This attitude is buttressed by the principle of social equality seen as an end, rather than the starting-point for an individual career in life. Generally speaking, it finds expression in actions which block other people's opportunities to distinguish themselves, no matter whether what is involved is the implementation of an invention or the distribution of bonuses among workers in a factory department. Some authors perceive the sources of this peculiar form of egalitarianism in the continued impact of gentry values on the Polish society. It seems, however, that the rules governing the functioning of the present political and economic system have been far from unimportant in the consolidation of this attitude.

The attitude of envious egalitarianism finds a peculiar supplement in the attitude of mind which puts a premium on *mediocrity* and determines the manner in which one presents oneself to others. The statement by a respondent that he 'would like to be an average university-educated member of the intelligentsia' may sound a bit odd, but indicates a wider trend to put benefits derived from social mimicry above rewards granted to those who distinguish themselves from the crowd.

The last behavioural attitude, the origin of which can be seen in system-related factors determining the situation in which one acts, is *collectivistic selfishness*. I use this term in reference to the pretence manifest in the expectations of representatives of all social groups that the state should offer special privileges to them merely because of their membership of this group, that is, by virtue solely of the fact that they are old-age pensioners, young people, women, war veterans, scientists, miners, and so on. This attitude may be regarded as a generalized outcome of the principle of distinguishing people not according to their individual merits, but in keeping with their group membership, which has been applied since the beginning of the present political and economic system.

All these system-determined attitudes seem to have some general features in common. First, they are attitudes which govern the functioning of individuals in their public role; they are attitudes displayed at the 'macro' level. They are, in addition, conducive to the depersonalization of individuals and encourage a perception of human communities as aggregates founded on mechanical rather than organic principles. Further, they show a distinctly defensive character, since they are conducive to the formulation of 'negative' goals of activity such as 'not to suffer losses', 'not to expose oneself to danger', 'not to provoke undesirable effects', 'not to let others succeed' and so on. Actions of this sort are usually accompanied by fear. Indeed, anxiety underlines all the behavioural attitudes we have mentioned. Finally, these attitudes stabilize the political and economic system: their starting-point is an approval of the system-defined situation, rather than a striving to change it.

Consequently, these attitudes can be regarded as the outcome of the peculiar adjustment of Polish society to the existing political and economic system. This adjustment consists in the fact that in drawing up tactics for long-term strategies of activity, knowledge of the everyday rules of the system is taken into consideration. However, the recognition of the realities of the system – for this is how this sort of adjustment should be described – seems to have certain, fairly important limits. For some time, results of sociological research have revealed a widespread conviction that the political and economic system in our country is maladjusted to the needs and values of society. However, this conviction is not accompanied by any important changes in the system of values and needs described earlier in this paper, even though one would expect such changes from a 'realistically' thinking society. Quite the contrary, we cannot observe a flourishing of different methods of handling social reality thus defined. The individual algorithms of activity – imposed by the subjectively perceived maladjustment of the system to society's needs – have also led to the emergence of some more general behavioural attitudes. These can be traced in the results of sociological research and in concrete actions. Paradoxically, the most characteristic feature of these attitudes is that they seem to stand in direct contradiction to the system-related attitudes.

Thus, the devaluation of work in the state-run sector of the economy is accompanied by the emphatic *appreciation of work done on one's own account* which is seen as a means of improving one's financial standing. The attitude which seeks social insurance coexists with a *readiness to take risks* evident in the attempts to improve one's situation through actions involving a considerable amount of uncertainty. A notorious example is ventures euphemistically referred to as 'foreign-travel-for-profit' (i.e. buying goods abroad for sale in Poland). The attitude of learned helplessness exists side by side with a stressing of the importance of *resourcefulness* and of using one's own *initiative* as means to achieve individual prosperity. In turn, the shortening of the temporal perspective for actions undertaken or planned is accompanied by an *extension of the temporal perspective* in the life of individuals which finds its expression in the fact that 'Polish parents shift their hopes for their own future on to their offspring very early on in their lives (considering their biological age and the stage in family life) and cease to appear as the subject of their own aspirations'.[5]

The attitude of envious egalitarianism coexists with what one might refer to as a striving to *become a hero by proxy*. By this I mean the practice of increasing one's self-esteem through identification with individuals or communities which, thanks to their own accomplishments, have outgrown the social 'standard.' The essence of this phenomenon is perhaps best conveyed by the popular phrase 'the Polish Pope'. It should be stressed, though, that the identification may be founded on either ethnic or ideological bonds, while the person who epitomises success does not necessarily have to be that prominent. Getting a boost for one's ego from the fact that the Polish King Jan Sobieski defeated the Turks in the battle of Vienna or that Mr X delivered a particularly sharp anti-government speech has consequences which go beyond the sphere of one's personal likes and dislikes, as the circle of 'share-holders' usually strives to expand the scope of their hero's merits. In the case of the great men of the past, this attitude leads to presenting the hero's accomplishments in larger-than-life or mythic proportions, while contemporaries (especially those we know in person) usually become addressees of exaggerated concrete expectations. Attempts to meet these expectations cause events to occur which might have never taken place if it had not been for the attendants' striving to become heroes by proxy.

Another attitude at the 'macro' level, the striving for mediocrity, has its counterpart in aspirations for *self-fulfilment*, in the desire to develop all of one's capacities, formulated as a major goal in life. Finally, collectivistic selfishness comes together with an attitude which might be called *individualised altruism*, and which consists in diametrical alteration of response to the behaviour of other people once we stop perceiving them in terms of their general group membership, and start seeing them as persons displaying concrete traits. Such changes of behaviour are frequent in situations in which we turn from members of the general class of petitioners into individuals, who are addressed by their first name or even 'that charming guy with that nice smile who always tells such funny stories'.

These attitudes, too, share some more general traits. First of all, they govern the functioning of individuals in their private-life roles and thus belong to the 'micro' level. In addition, they are conducive to the individualization of persons and introduce an element of privateness into public life. Then, they are development-oriented, in the sense that the actions deriving from them spring from the hope of success, ambitions, and curiosity as well as from greed and that they are accompanied by self-confidence. Finally, these attitudes are conducive to changes in the political and economic system because they are founded on a desire to overhaul the system-outlined situation, so as to make it better adjusted to the system of values and needs voiced by individuals. Because of this indirect link with the properties of the system, these attitudes could also be regarded as determined by the system; however, given the nature of their impact, one should rather see them as a separate class of compensatory attitudes. In sum, one can distinguish seven pairs of behavioural attitudes:

1	devaluation of work in the state-run sector	vs. appreciation of work done on one's own account
2	social insurance	vs. readiness to take risks
3	learned helplessness	vs. resourcefulness, initiative
4	shortened temporal perspective	vs. extended temporal perspective
5	envious egalitarianism	vs. striving to become a hero by proxy

233

6   striving for mediocrity   vs. self-fulfilment, individualization
7   collectivistic   vs. individualized altruism
    selfishness

As has been argued in this paper, a set of values and needs determines the most general directions of any society's strivings, while the course of concrete actions is modified by situation-generated behavioural attitudes. Establishing the existence of a set of *contradictory* attitudes strips the above statement of its seemingly obvious content, especially when we assume – which is justifiable for a number of reasons – that the pairs of contradictory habits are held not by the society at large but by individual people. For next to the question of what the behavioural consequences of *individual* attitudes are (a question to be asked if one attributes the attitudes to separate individuals), there arises the question of the consequences of their *coexistence* in the actions of the same individuals. This question is linked with the more general consequences of the persistence of those conditions which have determined the situation which led to the emergence of the attitudes.

Of course, one possible answer to this question is that we are dealing here with a permanent and peculiar state of social schizophrenia, with people constantly torn between antagonistic strivings and habits. However, this answer seems unsatisfactory for at least two reasons. First, though contradictory in their content, the pairs of behavioural attitudes do not actually seem to give rise to any special mental conflicts; a fact which is only comprehensible if we consider the fact that each of the mutually contradicting habits is activated in different situations or, to put it more accurately, within the framework of different roles played by an individual. In this respect, we can even talk about a complete axiological separation of the functioning of individuals in their public and private roles. Second, the answer is unsatisfactory because it draws our attention to individuals, while sociologists are interested rather in the consequences of the interaction of individual attitudes for the functioning of the entire society, for the shape of social life.

It seems possible to posit two essential consequences of the fact that the behavioural attitudes discernible in the Polish society give rise to two sets of contradictory habits. The first might be described as the progressive 'irreformability' of the society. I have in mind here the failure – particularly manifest in recent years – of all endeavours devised to provoke changes in social behaviour in the one sphere, making use of 'educational efforts' which refer to attitudes characteristic of the other sphere. Attempts to make use of the tendencies to adjustment present at the 'macro' level, in order to alter behaviour at the 'micro' level, seem to stand as little chance of success as attempts to utilize the development-oriented tendencies at the 'micro' level to change the activity of individuals in their public roles. In other words, calls for the alteration of individual values and needs so that they are better adjusted to the present capacities of the system seem to be as ineffective as appeals to invest one's own resourcefulness, initiative or pro-social attitudes in the public domain, in order to increase its capacities. In either case, the situation-generated attitudes, belonging to the given level of social life, start functioning as peculiar defensive mechanisms against attempts to alter behaviour not preceded by a perceptible alteration of the actual situation.

At this point, it seems worthwhile to stress that, to a large extent, these habits are not controlled by the consciousness of the people involved. Developed in response to the recurrent specific conditions of activity, they function as automatisms and are not transformed into verbalized cultural standards. The subconscious character of this set of attitudes seems to be evidenced by results of sociological studies in which beliefs of the type: 'if everyone does his job well, we will come out of the crisis' as well as beliefs of the type: 'how is the state supposed to give, when it has got nowhere to take from', i.e., beliefs supporting the attempts to 'reform society' enjoy equal popularity, even though at the same time they are quite unrelated to the realities of social actions. This makes the problem of steering the actions of society both easier and more difficult. It is easier, as in order to change people's behaviour, it would suffice *just* to change the situation-related determinants; there is no need to undertake a long crusade to overhaul the national character or its cultural values. It is more difficult, because change requires an alteration of the situation-generated determinants – attempts to transform the social consciousness will not suffice.

The other essential consequence of the coexistence of opposing attitudes seems to be a mounting social *anomie* with its behavioural consequences. The axiological separation of public and private roles is not actually identifiable with the division into the private and public domains in life. On the contrary, recent years have seen the two spheres of social life intermingling at an accelerating pace. Just as acting in a public role may be intended to further some strictly private interest, so, too, private roles are frequently assumed *pro bono publico*. Similarly, a situation defined as private does not automatically involve giving up a public role, while public situations are frequently accompanied by attempts to endow them with private character. Together with the blending of the private and public dimensions of life, the behavioural attitudes accompanying particular types of roles also intermingle. Thus, the attitude of collectivistic selfishness seems to have ever more frequent application in family life, when children demand all sorts of concessions from their parents, arguing that 'other children have them' and paying no heed to the financial standing of their family. Similarly, the 'hero-by-proxy' attitude is employed in public life, even though its origins lie in individuals' need to boost their egos.

Significantly, it is not particularly easy to pinpoint any unequivocal rules which govern the choice of these attitudes. Instead, one gets the impression that, since people 'no longer know what is feasible and what is not, what is just and what is unjust; what revindications and hopes are valid and which go too far',[6] they are attempting to acquire this knowledge by trial and error. The effects have been, at best, modest, as the application by a large segment of the society of this method to acquire that knowledge has led to a mounting disarray in the normative base of social life and, consequently, to constant oscillation between the beliefs that everything is feasible and that nothing can be done.

Notes

1 For a more detailed discussion of these results see Marody, M. (1986) *Warunki trwania i zmiany ładu społecznego w relacji do stanu świadomości społecznej* (Conditions for stability and change in the social order in relation to the state of social consciousness), Warsaw: Institute of Sociology, Warsaw University. The publication comes with a detailed bibliography. See also Koralewicz, Y., Białecki, I. and Watson, M. (eds.), (1987), *Crisis and Transition: Polish Society in the 1980s*, Leamington Spa: Bero.

2 I use the term 'society' to describe tendencies predominant in results of sociological studies which by no means indicates that they refer to all citizens in this country. For a more detailed discussion of social differentiation of values and opinion in Polish society see M. Marody, *op.cit.*

3 See Narojek, W. (1986) *Perspektywy pluralizmu w upaństwowionym społeczeństwie'* (The perspectives for pluralism in a nationalised society), Warsaw (an unpublished paper).

4 The term was suggested to me by S. Nowak.

5 Tarkowska, E. (1985) '*Zróżnicownanie stylów życia w Polsce: pokolenie i płeć'*, (The differentiation of styles of life in Poland: generation and gender) in *Kultura i Społeczeństwo*, no.2, 71.

6 Durkheim, E. (1964) '*Typy samobójstw'*, (Types of suicide) in J. Szacki, *Durkheim*, Warsaw, 187.

12

The ties that bind in Polish society

Janine Wedel

University of Maryland

As I boarded the plane at Amsterdam's international airport on a crisp morning in January of 1982, I felt I was stepping into another world. I would not be able to call family or friends in the United States or even get letters from them quickly, or at all. Martial law had been imposed in Poland only a month earlier, and my plane was bound for Warsaw. I was on my own.

I arrived in Poland not only with eleven suitcases of supplies and a bundle of messages but also with the mental 'baggage' of western press reports – of starvation, imminent civil war or Soviet invasion, and political prisoners being shipped off to Soviet camps. Many Poles in the United States were nearly hysterical at the motherland's troubles. Some anticipated a bloodbath.

Yet in Poland the general mood was no more than stern stoicism. Unaware of the exaggerated western press coverage, Polish friends I made were surprised at the alarmed messages they received from friends and family abroad. The situation was ominous all right, but not in the ways portrayed in the West. Everything seemed uncertain, but civil war had not broken out – at least not yet. As one friend put it, 'Martial law was relatively bloodless. People only lost their last hope'.

I travelled to martial-law Poland expecting to find heroes fighting a totalitarian regime. During a long stay, I was exposed to curfews, phone and mail restrictions, police identification checks and the internment of friends. Yet I also encountered a society in which the state and its rules are treated less as oppressors to be brought down than as obstacles to be overcome.

Poles face a rigid bureaucracy, woefully inefficient distribution of consumer goods, political instability, and omnipresent government restrictions. Poland is a 'controlled' communist country, yet the authorities' attempts to direct society are only partially successful. For

237

every publicly administered system, there is a web of informal responses, sometimes hidden, sometimes more visible. Poland cannot be understood either in terms of its own official theory of itself or in terms of western models.

Meat and gasoline are rationed, goods such as toilet paper are scarce and urbanites wait ten to twenty years for apartments. Yet almost everyone can get what he needs to get by. Connecting with and often overshadowing the official economy, elaborate, non-public networks distribute and often produce goods and services. Such networks gather and pass on information through a grapevine critical to privately organized economic and political activity.

Poles view the state as intrusive and repressively impersonal. Yet success in dealing with the formal bureaucracy and economy depends on the ability to personalize and impart an informal quality to one's relationships. Official structures must be penetrated by warmth, familiarity and face-to-face dealings. Almost every manifestation of official power is deemed morally bankrupt and repressively impersonal. Moral credibility is won within social circles by mutual aid; the individual's security rests on the family and social networks extending from it.

I came to Poland for the first time before anyone could have imagined the emergence of Solidarity. Friendship and discussion running through my thirteen years of visiting the country have gradually given me access to the interior of Polish life. I encountered a cross-section of the nation, from the intelligentsia and clergy to military and police officials to housewives and laborers. I lived with Polish families and sang and travelled with a Polish country music group.

60 per cent of the Polish people are urban, and my main contacts were with residents of the larger cities of Warsaw, Kraków, Toruń, Gdańsk, Szczecin and such smaller, but still substantial, towns as Żyrardów, Oświęcim and Bielsko-Biała. Many of my observations concern large cities, although I also have friends in small towns and rural communities.

Unlike resident Poles, foreigners have privileged entrée to nearly all groups and levels of society. Almost everyone I met socially, and even some people I met in official settings, took me in with the eager hospitality reserved for those from abroad, especially westerners. I came to be on *ty*, or familiar, terms with individuals from widely different social backgrounds – peasants, cloakroom attendants, bureaucrats and high officials. I was on *ty* terms with many students, as well as with professors, who have a much higher social standing – a degree of collegiality that is rare, if not almost impossible, for Poles.

Yet my acceptance into any particular *środowisko*, or social circle, was only partial. Foreigners may move within and among these circles, but in a fundamental sense they are not involved. They come from another world. Whether admired for their prosperity or humored for their naiveté, they are outsiders.

Most westerners (especially political scientists and economists) conducting research on contemporary Poland set out to ask those they study intimate, yet somehow abstract, questions about their lives and work. I sought instead to participate and watch wherever possible without interrogating, observing people I knew as they coped with the economic and political turmoil of the times.

I sought to delineate the omnipresent but by no means always articulate separation between the public and the private in action, belief and assent, and loyalty and compliance throughout the Polish world.

Poles often conceal their true convictions and activities as a result of living through continually hard and uncertain, and sometimes fearful, times. Poles have instilled in themselves a caution about speaking out, which dignifies itself in a formal aura of reserve. The Communist Party and the Roman Catholic Church officially disapprove membership in one another; [until 1989] the state actively penalizes such 'anti-government' organizations as Solidarity, but some Party members quietly practise the Catholic faith or contribute funds to the underground opposition. I found it difficult to determine people's real political affiliations, connections, and loyalties, and the relationship between the three, which often differed greatly from the impression people sought to give in conversation. Because I was well-acquainted with Pani S. and her family, I was aware of her active role in the Communist Party, even as I heard her disavow any such affiliation to a foreign correspondent.

In formal interviews, Poles are masters at tailoring answers to meet their listener's anticipations or implicit wishes. Naturally officials are inclined to present the country's economic and political situation in a positive light – at least in their offices. Less official individuals are more apt to champion Solidarity and recite the injustices of martial law. But neither officials nor others will tell you how they can, on the private market, buy refrigerator-freezers for 180,000 zloty, colored television sets for 310,000 zloty, or Fiats (manufactured under licence in Poland) for 3 million zloty when the average monthly salary is about 30,000 zloty.[1] Such information is simply not appropriate to the way most Poles present themselves to foreigners. Other Poles are in a better position to guess how this is possible but would never ask.

Poles are masters of poised nuance, employing Aesopian idioms in the marketplace, on the street corner and over the telephone. Euphemisms need not always be obscure or unintelligible. I once listened to a woman as she illegally changed dollars at the black market price over a tapped telephone: 'Would you like some green material? There's lots of this green material, you could sew a dress with it.' Almost everyone in Poland knows what 'green' stands for. Euphemisms maintain appearances even

239

when underlying meanings are discernible. Public displays mask the informal organization behind them, for to reveal it would challenge the entire public facade. And it is in almost no one's interest to unmask 'public life.'

A keen ability to operate very consciously but equally inexplicitly within the contradictions of society is the key to getting along. Although skilled at mediating between the varying constraints and expectations of public and private life, and sometimes even openly proud of it, Poles acknowledge the emotional cost. Some Polish sociologists have argued that it issues in deleterious 'social schizophrenia'.[2]

The sociologists of post-war Poland describe an 'atomized' society, its mediating institutions destroyed by war and imposed revolution. Family survives in harsh dichotomy to the state; a monstrously overgrown public sphere weighs heavily on the private; reality gives the lie to 'officiality'; and the everyday mocks state and Party invocations of idealism and sacrifice. People collide with rigid institutions. The eminent sociologist Stefan Nowak evoked this vision in a single dictum: 'The lowest level is the family, and perhaps the social circle. The highest is the nation . . . and in the middle is a social vacuum.'[3]

This depiction of Polish society as absolutist from the top and passive from below arises from the elementary recognition of the coarseness and insensitivity of the ruling elite to those it governs. Humanizing go-between entities taken for granted in the West – voluntary, electoral, religious or philanthropic – here do not adequately cushion or distribute centralized power.

'Social vacuum' actually implies 'public monopoly'; the recent history of Poland is unusually characterized by an unqualified refusal to allow assertive citizens to congregate against the state. The Nazi conquest of 1939 and the Soviet 'liberation' of 1945 shared one crucial factor – an intense hostility to, and suspicion of, any but the most necessary gatherings. Institutionally, Poland was beheaded. By 1947 meetings of virtually any group of the educated class or intelligentsia had been broken up, not because of their interests but because of their membership. Parish vestries were not dissolved – that would have been too provocative – but were under steady surveillance. The 'social vacuum' was not one of western hedonistic expansion of innumerable individual choices, but of state enmity toward unauthorized groupings. The generation that arose after the 'revolution' of 1945–8 aspired to fulfill common interests, not to pursue ideological conflict. The oppression of the post-war authorities was not directed against free choice itself but was simply an illiberal reaction against any potentially rival gathering. With the dissolution of autonomous groups came a general suffocation of argument, specialization and initiative. Political decisions crippled innumerable social possibilities.

But the vision of 'social vacuum' suffers from a seemingly willed refusal to acknowledge the web of less-than-formal relationships which carries on the tradition of adjustment deriving from times long before the present system was forced into place. The 'social vacuum' *does* aptly convey the fact that Poles have been prevented from forming open, independent organizations. However, Polish society has long been structured around a complex system of informal relations, in such forms as 'social circles', horizontal linkage networks and patron–client connections, all carried on in one sense outside authorized institutions, such as the state economy and bureaucracy, but also pervading them and connecting them with the community. Although not explicitly institutional, the relationships are regularized and have clear patterns. And understanding these patterns is the key to understanding not only Polish society today, but also how it is likely to respond to coming changes. An officially impersonal government is offset by a supremely personalized network of tiny contracts, legitimated by individual, nonreplicable friendships, rituals and common interests.

The highly visible impositions from above are frequently stabilized and kept going by millions of lateral interlocks of families and *środowiska* or 'social circles' – circles of friends, colleagues and acquaintances brought together by family background, common experience or formal organization and loyal to a certain set of highly conscious values. Social circles – whether formed through resistance activities to Nazis or to martial law, whether established as drinking clubs that have expanded into industrial brokerages or high-school cliques that have endured to cut deals as factory managers – are crucially important in an environment of uncertainty and indeterminacy. They shield, reinforce, inform, and supply their members, whom they help cope with the vagaries of the system.

The social circle and the relationships extending from it are the mechanisms of social organization that underlie and permit 'informal' economic activities – those private exchanges of information, goods, services and privileges that arise in response to state regulation. Unofficial activities involve not only an informal trade of goods and services, but also a second bureaucracy of expedition within the state administration. An underlying society may exist where everything is supposed to be legalized and incapable of operating without the state's authority – perhaps, indeed, its stimulus. To its critics, of course, the system loses more than it gains by seeking official support. In such a world, it is a paradox of self-respect that many of the country's most vital institutions are publicly insubstantial. Internal discipline and pride in membership mean much more than state permission.

Assumptions that loyalty is local and private, that irrational or official instructions are to be sabotaged if group members are threatened, serve as passive–aggressive limitations on the system. A policeman ordered to arrest a friend is disgraced if he doesn't warn the friend first. The policeman can go after a stranger, but it is probably disgraceful to show zeal rather than cynicism in putting on the handcuffs. If the state vaguely wants something, no one is responsible: no one ordered this arrest, no one arrested this person; no one owned this object, no one bought it, no one sold it.

Środowiska possess a double authority: they induce the intense loyalty of a shared ordeal through demands similar to those of elite military units or medical schools. Personal differences, however severe, do not cancel lifelong fellowship earned through common endurance. Social circles differ from social networks in that a social network distributes strength, while a social circle builds it up. Within a circle obligations are intense, for the circle serves to bind its members one to another and to authenticate them to the outside world. It provides verifiable reputation and the internally stabilizing qualities of mutuality and continuity to reinforce its members against the vulnerable and disorderly outer world. These qualities further induced the confidence, self-discipline, freedom of expression, exchange of information or valuable privileges, and goodwill that bypassed or substituted for the overburdened state's procedures long before such opportunities became the means to develop a rival model of power and authority nationwide.

Few people are so socially impoverished as to have only one *środowisko*: people belong to several unconnected or loosely connected circles, although one tends to be most intense. Part of each circle's power is that it affords any member access to equally legitimate and equally powerful groupings – an armature of interlocking circles, which in extremity can be called upon for assistance to otherwise unrelated members. Participants explicitly offer and expect unequivocal commitment and dependability, functions of the fragmentation and contingency of life outside.

To personalize a relationship in a bureaucratized, scarcity-ridden society is not just to lubricate it, but also possibly to transform it into a channel for any of a hundred kinds of special, coveted access. Such exchanges are extra-official but far from random or gratuitous. Participants seek to sustain continuity in these one-on-one transactions, and, however secretive, quasi-legal or indeed illegal, they set out to clothe them in the legitimacy of the society-wide ethnics that govern such behavior. Among the parties to an exchange, the transactions may be flexible, wide-ranging and regulated with sophistication. As often as possible a successor to a job will carry on the informal relationship that his predecessor established with consumers. But such a relationship is difficult to transfer, unless it is to someone in a clearly defined niche.

Individuals can call on bureaucratic contacts on behalf of family and friends, but for a collectivity to arrange things as a group would immediately set off angry, perhaps insuperable questions of trustworthiness, problems of visibility, and the possibility of demands becoming too large for the individual facilitator. Membership in a given social circle, such as that of a Communist Party apparatus, may well confer priceless advantages on each member in finalizing transactions, but such advantages cannot be pooled.

Each transaction is likely to be determined by one's group context, but its execution is a one-on-one, face-to-face procedure. It is a public secret that certain Party cliques and core groups of bureaucrats have long-term understandings with one other in which favors are exchanged. But these understandings must be settled one at a time, not with impersonal wholesale efficiency. And only for a few of the Polish people is this system a complete alternative: for most it may be a way of life, but it is one that at best can only modify the pressing inefficiencies of the system. The large profiteers are few indeed.

The rules of networks are binding through the sheer value of trust and knowledge that public pressure will support groups when they cannot appeal to law. Their strength lies not in their standing apart from public power and resources, but in their fruitful and essential interpenetration of these forces.

The exchange system

In an informal economy of privately exchanged goods, services, benefits, privileges and information, almost everyone has something to exchange or sell – a relief package from abroad, a stolen desk, 'contacts'. The informal economy extends beyond moonlighting and illegal dealing in hard currency, gasoline and vodka, encompassing private arrangements between state managers that enable their factories to function. Illegally obtained goods are exchanged for commodities or favors attained across the entire spectrum of legal, quasi-legal or extra-legal means.

The informal economy is extensive and pervasive. Polish households spent almost 30 per cent of their income on food produced outside the state market in 1982 – according to a study conducted by economists of the Polish Academy of Sciences. The level of consumption during that year exceeded personal income by upwards of 37 per cent.[4] According to more recent estimates, 10 to 13 per cent of Polish personal income is derived from illegal transactions.[5]

People supplement their income, for instance, through profits made 'on the side' at state jobs. A car mechanic in a state garage may spend some of his official working hours fulfilling private orders for fees double his official daily earnings. People are willing to pay the mechanic more because he is likely to do the job better and quicker, and with otherwise unavailable spare parts 'arranged' through the private market for a private customer. Shoemakers and tailors use the materials and tools provided by their state jobs to make goods for private sale. Doctors and dentists use state facilities and equipment to render services during or after office hours as part of exchange relationships. In such cases, the illicit income may be far greater than wages or other rewards the enterprise can offer. As a result, workers treat their jobs often as a basis for qualifying for social insurance benefits and, often, as sources of orders and free materials. People speak of 'being employed' at state jobs, but few speak of 'working' at them.

Poland is a two-currency country, and many goods and services are more easily available for dollars. Although black-market trade in dollars was, until spring, 1989, illegal, it was tacitly encouraged by the relevant public authorities, as an indirect source of the state's hard currency coffers by way of, for example, state-operated Pewex stores that sell scarce, usually imported, goods for dollars. At Pewex, customers gaze almost reverently at Swiss chocolates, French perfume, German wine, Viennese coffee, Bic razor blades, Toni hair rinse, Marlboro cigarettes, Polish vodka, and Japanese televisions, stereos and tape recorders – all displayed on inaccessible counters. Poles get dollars from relatives in the West, from work abroad or from selling Polish currency, the *zloty*, at about one-sixth the official exchange rate. Sources in the Ministry of Finance estimate that Poles have \$4–6 billion 'under their pillows'.[6]

Poles with considerable hard currency or a hand in legal, small-scale private enterprises[7] can live very well indeed, with luxury apartments, country homes, foreign cars and wardrobes and even novel electronic gadgets – all amidst acute shortages. But most Poles' standard of living is modest. A young physician lives with her parents, grandmother and brother's family in a cramped three-room apartment, plus kitchen and bath.[8]

A rigid system of news control makes reliable information on the availability of goods and services and on the real workings of bureaucracies virtually unavailable from official organs and sources. So the pursuit of scarce resources and effective response to government action starts by word of mouth. The few institutional sources of information are considered tainted. There is no Polish equivalent of *Consumer Reports*. An owner who responds to friends' inquiries about how well his refrigerator works is not competing with a trusted institution that disseminates systematically compiled information. Poles have much more confidence in a single refrigerator owner than in an institution.

Grapevine information has market value, and access to it enhances one's reputation for acumen, since getting information is neither direct nor simple. A person who must solve a bureaucratic problem but does not know an appropriately placed bureaucrat asks friends in his social circles for help. If friends have no such direct contacts either, they will in turn try to find the right brokers in their own networks. People collect information for future reference, remembering who can help them to get what. Most successful people are not only well-placed in information networks, functioning as telephone exchanges, but also as data banks.

Women are considered to be particularly adept at 'arranging'. The prevalence of women in diplomatic, interactive positions in economic institutions makes it easy for them to trade goods and services they have access to at work.[9] Grażyna, aged 26, ostensibly puts in eight hours a day in a factory. Her colleagues cover for her while she does her shopping during work hours, and Grażyna reciprocates. She exchanges the batteries 'lifted' from her factory for rawhide leather, which she makes into handbags on an old model Singer sewing machine in the evenings to sell on the black market. Many other women take up similar extra activities to help make ends meet as the cost of living steepens. Women spend an average of three hours per day, almost as much as their husbands, on unofficial jobs.[10] The informal system of exchange is personalized, highly sophisticated and silently acknowledged. It is so much a part of Polish life that an entire vocabulary has evolved for it. Its characteristic phrase, *załatwić sprawę*, literally 'to arrange a matter' might better be translated as 'to finagle' or 'to wangle'.

The meaning of *załatwić* can be best understood by examining an all-purpose, legal, private agency set up in Warsaw several years ago. For a price, the agency will *załatwić* almost anything – from shopping or buying train tickets to caring for sick people or following the husbands of jealous wives. It specializes in 'arranging matters' in the bureaucracy. The bureau's advertisement reads: 'We will help with every problem; we will *załatwić* every matter. Nothing is impossible for us.'

Widely used terms, such as *załatwić*, conveniently obscure the distinction of legality and illegality. A baby-sitting exchange can be lawfully arranged, but to arrange for black-market meat or gasoline is on the books unlawful. It is implicit in the term that some things must be brought about in ways that circumvent institutionally approved processes, but explicit violation of law is not so implied. If I tell someone I must be on my way to *załatwić* a matter, I need not be more specific. Numerous euphemisms obfuscate the legality of an activity. In addition, certain word usages cover individual initiative and communicate passivity. Practically no one will say that he offered a tip as an incentive to get a good or service. Instead he says, 'I got an apartment'. One simply 'receives' things passively.

Exchanges among friends, neighbors and colleagues are not simple barter transactions. They entail a system of obligations, often ongoing. An exact equivalence of favors almost never can be achieved because people purposely overpay to establish credit for the future. After arranging a church wedding for an army officer's daughter in such a way that the officer's career would not be jeopardized, Mrs F. felt self-satisfied, even downright smug. She knew she could turn to the well-connected officer for a reciprocal favor even ten years later. The more one uses connections, the more one incurs obligations to friends and acquaintances, intensifying and extending one's relationships both horizontally – to those to whom one is obliged and those who in turn are obliged to one – and vertically, into the future.

If one does not have connections already in place to facilitate some necessary 'arrangement', contacts often can be cultivated through etiquette. In order to *załatwić* within the bureaucracy or economy, it is necessary to be in a private relationship with the bureaucrat or clerk acting in his official role. Poles observe unspoken rules and procedures when initiating a relationship involving official business with a stranger in his private capacity. If I want the nice leather boots that a shoe store manager is keeping hidden for private exchange, it would only offend the manager and provoke her mistrust if I strode into the store and declared, 'I'm sure you could use some coffee. How about those leather boots?' By the same token, when I first ask for the boots I must not take the answer 'They're not available' at face value. We both must show goodwill and enter into an agreement with the caution, subtlety and sensitivity appropriate for each step.

At first, we nod and smile and talk in whispers so as not to arouse the suspicion of other customers when they are present. I know our relationship has progressed on the day that the manager invites me into her back room for vodka and sandwiches or tea and apples. I address her in the personalized form, Pani Basia (Mrs Barbara), and bring her flowers on her name day (St Barbara's Day). From now on, I will be able to get goods in her store at the official price, but to maintain her goodwill, I may occasionally tip Pani Basia with a present. To *załatwić* something requires discretion and persistence.

If a scarce item is worth a lot of money, it is acceptable to give cash, but only with the greatest care. The money, it must be emphasized, is itself 'nothing' and has nothing in common with a bribe: it is unrelated to any transfer of goods or services. Terming the money a gesture of thanks protects the giver from any implication of bribery and provides the person being offered it the opportunity to turn it down. The elaborate promenade of *załatwić* enables people to sound one another out and proceed subtly to arrange their way through life.

Wherever people find it necessary to skirt the system, the boundary between legality becomes quite naturally blurred. One lawyer pointed out, 'Most Poles don't even know what the differences are, much less care or think about them. Not even lawyers can tell you.' People weigh moral and pragmatic concerns but generally not considerations of legality, which often are regarded as merely technical. What is legal is often not considered moral; what is illegal often has complete moral standing.

Laws against 'corruption' and black market dealings are strict and criminal penalties are harsh, but the system's real rules are selectively applied.[11] For most people, 'speculation' and 'corruption' – excesses of the informal economy – are social evils. Even so, almost everyone is involved in it on a small scale and considers his own activity 'normal' and acceptable. Although many engage in 'half-legal' activities, people conceal such activities because they are vulnerable. A case could be made against them at any time, and few Poles would come away clean from close investigation. A breach of the etiquette of *załatwić*, whether in content or method, can result in embarrassment or even prosecution.

Not everyone is able to *załatwić* everything. Who is able to get what depends somewhat on class membership (intelligentsia, worker or peasant), family connections, and personal achievement and skill. Communist Party membership can help in acquiring contacts and privileges.

Most scarcities are dealt with through the system of 'arrangement'. But for such goods as major household appliances, an alternative to this system has sprung up. People form 'queue committees'.

For Jarek, a 30-year-old bachelor, buying a refrigerator meant three months of showing up at a state store for daily roll calls and standing 'guard duty' every third day during that time. Jarek found out about the queue committee through friends. He went to the store one day and put his name on a list maintained by the person first in line at the time. Jarek was number 440 when he signed up.

Although refrigerators only arrived on an average of once every two weeks, eighteen members of the queue committee could be found in front of the store at any hour every day. On his assigned days, Jarek spent three hours standing with others of the group, representing the hundreds of would-be customers whose names were on the committee's roster. After three months of waiting, Jarek carried a half-size refrigerator to an apartment inherited from his great aunt. His place on the queue committee was filled by another hopeful.

Poles form queue committees for the goods – refrigerators, kitchen ranges, bathtubs, furniture, television sets, tape recorders, washing and sewing machines – that are worth investing considerable time and resources for. In recent years people seeking Italian and West German visas have formed queue committees outside the embassies in Warsaw. Although the makeup of the committee changes as individuals obtain coveted commodities and depart, the committees endure, their ranks constantly renewed.

People use the committees because they provide a relatively secure way of sooner or later obtaining one's objective. For many Poles, queue committees are more effective in a given situation than the usual informal exchanges, which depend entirely on individual initiative and complexly arranged contacts.

The existence of a queue committee, a kind of informal bureaucracy, reduces the ability of insiders to divert scarce items into private exchanges – the store clerk who saves a kitchen range for a cousin or takes a 'tip' from a customer, or the truck driver who lifts goods from a shipment. Once on the committee, it is in Jarek's interest to restrict insiders and their friends from getting refrigerators using connections, and he is reinforced by the hundreds on line. Participants in the line committee have a collective interest: to get the desired commodity according to their turn and to reduce, if not prevent, outside competition. So queue committees are a reaction against the system of informal exchange and actually do sometimes provide an effective alternative to it. But contacts are still the best insurance in Poland: social networks, family-based and extending outward into *środowiska*, power the informal exchange system continuously, and do not have to be reconstituted for each new deal. Social distance determines the degree and priority of exchange obligations; commitments to family and close friends differ from obligations between patrons and clients or reciprocity among neighbors or acquaintances. The closer the relationship, the easier the exchange negotiation becomes since more steps of etiquette can be bypassed.

Families assume mutual help – that family members will do favors for each other and receive only a thankyou and respect in return. No matter what other obligation she has, Jola, an assistant professor at the university, is always on hand to babysit for her sister's child. Malgosia obtains chicken, pork, milk, eggs, and other farm produce from her country cousins. In turn, she supplies them with batteries, light bulbs, and spare parts necessary for farm equipment, and helps them to arrange difficult bureaucratic matters. If the cousin of a physician were ill, family members would be offended if he did not use his connections to obtain a needed hospital bed. Close friends often become 'just like in the family', accepting obligations to help each other as do family members. Whether or not they care for such interdependence, relatives cannot afford to disown one another – political affiliations and views notwithstanding.

Although exchanges within the inner circle of the family and close friends are implicit, reciprocity is demanded outside these circles. Other types of relationships within one's *środowiska* are crucial in exchange. A 60-year-old professor of mathematics, Mrs Janina, meets frequently for nameday celebrations and vodka toasts with her colleagues from the wartime resistance. The former comrades are involved in diverse careers and life pursuits, but they work to maintain their circle, and not only for the sake of pleasant get-togethers. Mrs Janina arranged a coat for the granddaughter of her colleagues through her cousin who works in a state coat store. In return the colleague, a schoolteacher, tutored Pani Janina's grandson in English.

During times of economic and political hardship, people mobilize existing relationships, make them fulfill many functions, and also create new networks for the exchange of favors. One friend summed up the situation: 'Five years without connections would be the biggest punishment in Poland.'

Grievances and remedies

As imbedded as Poland's informal system of exchanges has become, it has not gone unchallenged. There are strong indications that Poles do not fully approve of the necessity to develop fixing networks in order to survive. As one Pole put it: 'The Polish system sets people up to feel insecure and to keep them guessing. To expect the worst and to finagle for the best is all one can do.'

The runaround is endemic to Polish life: there is no official word, only nonanswers. People feel controlled by the whim and fancy of whoever happens to be in control in a given situation, be it a shop manager, a bureaucrat or a shoe-store clerk. There are few protective controls and guidelines, even for those who operate within the system. If I manage to strike a private deal, I feel successful. Poles feel humiliated by the necessity of buddying up to clerks and bureaucrats in order to get what they feel should be available through upright transactions.

This humiliation arises from and is endlessly renewed by the fundamental uncertainty built into a system in which control is distributed from the top down – from the knowledge that anything can happen and that there are no guaranteed ways of affecting the outcome.

Ewa, having 'arranged' a carpet for her studio apartment, had mixed feelings about how she had done it. 'I feel uneasy about it; it is against my dignity. I have a habit of doing bad things, and I am ashamed of myself,' she conceded. But in the next breath, she justified the deal: 'Ninety-nine per cent of the carpets made in Poland go for export. If I didn't *załatwić* a carpet through contacts, I wouldn't be able to get one for five years. I realize that the situation put me to it.' Happy to manipulate a system that has humiliated her all her life, Ewa feels a kind of revengeful pride.

Private arrangements are vital, yet people have some compunction about using them to fix daily problems. Ewa takes pride in being *sprytna* – ingenious or clever in making a deal. But getting by in such a way is not morally affirmed, for while Poles feel powerful when they are *sprytny*, they also lose some self-respect. If one goes a little too far – and one can at any moment – dignity is compromised and lasting guilt is awakened. People admire a *sprytny* individual but do not necessarily respect him. Purely instrumental relationships are looked down on.

249

The official system extols honesty as a virtue yet, in practice, encourages dishonesty. One hears such remarks as: 'I'm breaking rules I haven't accepted. I consider myself an honest person, and that which I do is simply life.' The humiliating need to riddle life with extensive, time-consuming private arrangements merely to acquire the goods and services that people feel ought to be easily obtainable is tension-producing and makes for stress and self-contempt.

Załatwić arouses in Poles inextricably mixed ambivalence of pride and shame. Shame is born of the exhaustion and frustration produced by complete dependence on the whim and fancy of people in their official roles and on what one sometimes has to do to meet their terms. Pride is born of the pleasure in success at some difficult task. Both dejection (impotence and frustration) and elation (a deviant sense of success) equally typify Poles' reactions to this everyday world of intrigue and managing tasks.

Although western perceptions of eastern Europe tend to emphasize people's overt fear of the state and its apparatus, it is day-to-day humiliation that makes socialization effective. The state need not resort to overt mistreatment. Humiliation, which stems from the anger and frustration of constantly wounded pride, is one of the features of many contacts with formal organs of the Polish state.

When Solidarity emerged as a legal organization in September 1980, it denounced the idea that people must *załatwić* in order to get what they need. The independent trade union movement opposed the unadmitted, fragmented networks that had developed and espoused replacing them with public, observable ones. It fought 'corruption' and promoted an atmosphere of openness and accountability. Solidarity argued, for example, for the institution of a rationing system, so that resources could be distributed more equitably, rather than on the basis of connections.

Solidarity propagated an ideology of 'help each other' and in its rhetoric encouraged people to think beyond the interests of their families and *środowiska*. The organization offered help in solving problems with the state bureaucracy and provided some legal and material assistance; it encouraged relationships beyond the *środowisko* and broke down class barriers. Solidarity's open atmosphere created the conditions for an explosion of neighborhood and local self-government activities.

The declaration of martial law in 1981 forced a return to previous relationships – bound by family and *środowisko* – and a retreat to reliance on strategies of survival based on *środowiska*. People could no longer depend on Solidarity, now formally proscribed, for formal assistance or recourse. Solidarity went underground, to become itself a tangle of loosely organized, clandestine networks in which activity could be organized and recourse sought only through informal means.

Problem-solving networks such as underground organizations and church-based groups, which operate independently of state structures, might partially compensate for the lack of formal mediating institutions in Polish society. It is hoped that the Church and organizations such as Solidarity can compensate for the lack of vertical and horizontal aggregation in the society. But Solidarity, which was never as unified and co-ordinated a movement as it seemed from outside, has been further broken up by martial law. Although Solidarity remains an important political force, Poland's opposition organizations are fragmented.

On the other hand, the Church's historic capacity to challenge the rulers of Poland – to shelter significant systems of independent activity – has contributed to a contemporary assessment of the role of the Church as a potential force for social and political change in Poland. While this assessment emphasizes religious faith, norms, and authority, it is also based on a consideration of organizational questions. It assumes that church-based ties constitute a cohesive system of social relationships that extend into areas of Polish life otherwise fragmented. It is true that some parishes sponsor cultural activities and provide social and political forums where people can meet. During martial law the Church's 'community' activities provided a setting in which Poles could vent frustration and organize protests. The Church organized an extensive system of aid to internees and their families. Within the relatively protected confines of its premises, the Church sponsored programs by actors and exhibits by artists, often veiled protests against government actions. These events could not have been put on elsewhere without much greater risk or to much smaller audiences.

However, except in the few parishes noted for their political activism, such church organizations foster only a limited increase in social linkages among churchgoers. Urban parishes generally do not sponsor activities that draw people together socially. Inter-family relationships within urban parishes are limited; churchgoers there told me they rarely meet their fellow parishioners. Church officials I interviewed indicated that they were concerned about the 'lack of integrating structure' between family units, in town and country alike. One church official admitted, 'We have too little experience in community life ourselves.'

If relationships within the Church are in fact characterized by the same kind of fragmentation evident in state structures and elsewhere, what is the Church doing to counter such troubling influences? In recent years it has taken some isolated measures to develop an infrastructure for formal groups. Church leaders have consciously attempted to develop inter-family ties among parishioners – networks intended to cross over family and social circles and to generate mutual dependencies among otherwise unconnected people.

Since the 1970s the Church has attempted to organize small

communities in urban parishes, especially among youth. I attended such meetings, which reminded me of American evangelical Protestant services, complete with testimonials about personal faith experiences. Participants introduced guests, who also added their voices. To guitar accompaniment, people sang American evangelical songs translated into Polish.

The movement toward community has grown in the 1980s. In 1983 and 1984, clergy and lay leaders in some urban parishes began to initiate the formation of 'ties' among their parishioners. Groups met informally and often exchanged goods and favors. There is a move under way in Warsaw to organize parents in particular parishes for regular devotional meetings and co-operation in child care. For example, four previously un-acquainted young couples were introduced to each other by their parish priest to form a support group which discussed such issues as Catholic childrearing, and went on to work out extensive mutual child care arrangements. The women began to co-ordinate time spent waiting in line. Frequent get-togethers usually ended with the couples swapping vital information on where to obtain scarce goods.

These initiatives are church officials' attempts to mitigate the widely felt 'atomization' of society. The project is still experimental and, given the antagonism of Church and state, one church worker told me, 'It's better to simply take action and not to talk about it.'

In an order such as Poland's where citizens' ability to combine against the state was until 1989 severely limited, symbolic activity within and as part of one's circle becomes all-important. Poles have developed ways of fighting back that help to preserve self-esteem and sanity. Many keep alive the long-standing tradition of idealism, self-sacrifice and devotion to public ends, grounded in centuries of foreign occupation and struggle for national independence. Poles establish moral credibility by upholding their culture's enduring values of dignity and honor.

In 1980–1, Solidarity contested this system of humiliation all across Poland, crying for a restoration of respect for human dignity. Solidarity's platform included statements such as these: 'Our birth was a protest against wrongs, humiliation and injustice . . . It is our wish that the principle of man's dignity permeate everything about our union and serve as the foundation upon which relations in the new society are built.' The Church's rhetoric affirmed Solidarity's challenge. Pope John Paul II's homilies during his 1983 visit to Poland under martial law stressed the fundamental dignity of humanity. With its slogan, 'to regain dignity', Solidarity brought humiliation into public consciousness and generated open discussion. Solidarity challenged the humiliation imbedded in state structures that makes socialization and control within those structures effective.

The long emphasis on 'honor' in Polish culture makes showing honorable behavior during economic and political turmoil all-important. For honor, people have sacrificed their personal freedom, financial interests and even their lives.

In the early weeks of martial law, when several thousand people were interned or arrested, a Solidarity activist purposely appeared at the apartment of one of the movement's leaders who, it was reasonable to assume, had been taken away. The activist went as a matter of honor, knowing full well that police were likely to be waiting for whomever might turn up. He was immediately taken into custody. 'I was rather conscious I might pay the price,' he told me. Indeed, the demonstration of honorable behavior was more important than its content or the consequences of the protest action.

Underground activists displayed their loyalty to the opposition through mutual help. One activist explained the importance of 'solidarity':

It's necessary to help others and to be with others. If someone fails to help, this destroys the community, not mainly because it leaves people without resources – coffee, chocolate and cigarettes[12] are of little importance. The minimum one must do is to be with people, which involves not saying 'I'm afraid – I can't talk with you now because you're suspected.' If I neglect someone who is close to me just because he is in political trouble, then the system is victorious. What would happen if everyone were afraid of helping each other – what would happen to Polish society?

A man with a British girlfriend was interned during martial law. The girlfriend suspected that his family's apartment was under police surveillance and was afraid to visit. However, she did send letters and gifts to the family through mutual friends. When the man was released several months later, he was angry and reluctant even to speak to her. The boyfriend told her harshly:

My best friend Jacek could have avoided my family's apartment because he was afraid of being associated with me. He could have said, 'My wife is pregnant. I can't afford to go to an apartment under observation now because it might create problems not only for me, but also for my wife and child.' But instead he came to the apartment every day to see if there was anything he could help my mother with. You must understand that in this situation all actions are of great significance – how you behave, how you conduct yourself, who you visit, who you don't visit – these are all very important actions.

People take risks that demonstrate dignity, honor and loyalty and thereby show others where they stand. Such displays of personal valor are often the only recourse and source of empowerment. A personal fight against 'social schizophrenia' is all that one can make. Insistence on moral integrity is the individual's response to the guilt and humiliation generated by life in People's Poland.

Poles do not put much faith in the notion that life deals out justice. The efforts of many do not result in tangible rewards, and people do not believe that they deserve what they get or get what they deserve. Life's unpredictabilities breed cynicism and despair in some, while others turn to faith and mysticism.

Ninety-two per cent of the Polish people are at least baptismally Catholic, and many responded to martial law with an increase in religious devotion. The Church wields considerable authority. During the Pope's historic visit in June 1983, police officials ordered crowds congregating outside his private quarters to disperse. But their commands were ignored, and they were forced to turn the matter over to church officials. A priest stood before the crowd and uttered one sentence: 'We request that the crowd please disperse.' The people disbanded without protest.

Poles of all social groups have become more deeply involved in religion in the 1980s. The Church has sponsored activities that offer forums for protest and independent political expression. But the turn to religion goes beyond the Church's authority and status as the only institution capable of challenging the state. Even some intellectuals, heretofore self-proclaimed atheists, have experienced religious conversions.

For many Poles the Church is a refuge; it provides personal solace in times of political upheaval and economic hardship. As one friend put it, 'The Church is the only place where I feel safe.'

But to some the Church is like the state: yet another source of shame. Poles look to the Church for spiritual guidance and renewal and as a refuge in difficult times, but they are selective in their adherence to its teachings. Many discrepancies are to be found between church policies in Poland and the practices and positions of many Catholics in the West. The Polish Church speaks against divorce, yet official statistics show how common it is; it preaches against the abuse of alcohol, yet Poles are among the world's leading consumers of vodka, and alcoholism is rampant; the Church denounces premarital sex and abortion, yet its own documents and officials make clear that both are common.

In recent years the Church has carried out aggressive campaigns against abortion and birth control. Even so, in a country in which birth control devices are difficult to obtain and in which thousands of young people live in cramped quarters with no immediate hope of obtaining their own apartments, many women have abortions out of economic necessity. Many indeed speak of having had several abortions.[13]

Church teachings regarding lifestyle practices are followed only to a limited extent. As one official of the Catholic Intelligentsia Club explained: 'Many Poles are deeply religious, but this doesn't mean they follow church policies. The influence of the Church against such things as divorce, abortion, birth control and sex outside of marriage is only partial and indirect.'

The tension between the Church's teachings and religious practices on the one hand and the lifestyles necessitated by the conditions of People's Poland on the other induces much stress and guilt in many people. A 'cultured' person by Polish standards would never ask about the sincerity of a person's religious beliefs or details of his lifestyle. Devout Catholic women, married and unmarried, fervently waved at the Pope during his visits to Poland, steadfastly attend Mass, and yet have abortions, often doing so against their own beliefs. As one woman put in, 'Out of necessity, many people do what the Church teaches against, but no one is proud of it.' All this only further increases the tension between official ideologies and individual realities.

A rekindled Catholicism is one response to the national uncertainty of the 1980s. So is an understandable upsurge in fortune-telling and astrology and an emphasis on 'living for the moment'. Some people hold frequent parties, consuming rationed meat and spending scarce money on expensive liquor, saying, 'I earn so little money that there is no point in saving it,' or, 'Tomorrow there will be a war, and I will lose everything anyway.' Many of those I came to know seemed to think about the future rarely, if at all.

A renewed emphasis on 'life of the spirit' (*duchowe życie*) is another response to precarious national conditions. Employed as an adjective, *duchowe* means at once spiritual, intellectual, moral, mental, emotional, religious and 'of the soul', an embracing term absent in English. In Poland, emotional, spiritual or intellectual life is less compartmentalized. Life of the spirit is carried on within one's *środowiska* and provides the emotional and spiritual fiber of the private world. At small gatherings, people share their predicaments, telling stories about their own and others' experiences. It is life of the spirit, not the latest VCR or investment opportunity, that can make life in Poland worthwhile and allow one to escape from the psychological weariness of 'social schizophrenia'.

A crucial component of life of the spirit, regardless of one's social status, is intellectual pursuit. Slavic countries have strong literary traditions. People read not merely as a pastime, but also to compare their life experiences with those of the characters and to establish a basis for intellectual discussion. What one studies, reads, and writes matters: people value intellectual inquiry.

A heightened trust in 'fate' and 'destiny' are yet other responses to uncertainty and turmoil. People often explain events in their lives in such terms. The sense of a lack of control over their lives is related to romantic notions about destiny, fortune, happiness and love, with which Polish culture – both 'high' and popular – abounds. People say of themselves and others that they were 'destined to misfortune', 'destined not to find love', or 'destined to leave Poland'. One young engineer concluded: 'It doesn't depend on the individual how his life will be, only on a greater power.'

People are perpetually alert for overnight reversals of lifelong fortune. An 11-year-old boy whose sister had just been arrested by martial-law authorities exclaimed, 'This is just like the time of the Partitions [when Poland was broken up by three great empires], when people had no rights.' After reporting the event to the church network that was concerned with political detainees, he said, 'Oh, it's not so bad. Maybe she'll be gone for only a few months.'

This boy well knew that his great-grandfather had been deported to Siberia and that his grandfather had perished in Auschwitz. The partitioning powers of the eighteenth and nineteenth centuries, wretched exile in Siberia, murder in concentration camps and abrupt internment were not remote horrors from history books or movies but part of this youth's reality. Knowing there could be no appeal, he concluded simply: 'My sister has bad luck.'

Through generations

For Poles, two centuries of life-jolting, sometimes life-menacing turns of events have honed adjustment into an art. Poland has a long history of informal, extra-legal networking. From 1792 to 1918, when the country was partitioned among Russia, Prussia and Austria (the Prussian territories became part of Germany in 1871), the laws of these powers were regarded as instruments of alien sovereignty, defiance of which was a patriotic act. From 1918 to 1939 attempts were made to develop an effective state bureaucracy and a viable industrial base. The efforts to establish an independent, legitimate state were relatively successful, but not enough so as to preserve Poland against its two powerful neighbors.

Under German occupation from 1939 to 1945, Poles again were faced with a foreign government and had to rely on their native survival skills. Underground networks resisted both the occupying Germans and the advancing Russians. The extensiveness of the informal economy is well-documented in the diaries and memoirs of survivors where there appear many present-day terms for getting by – załatwić, for instance. Many of those who survived the concentration camps, slave labor and scarcities of World War II did so through bribery and the black market. In an article published at the moment of peace in the August 1945 issue of the literary journal Twórczość, the prominent critic Kazimierz Wyka characterized the many laws and policies implemented by the Nazis, including rationing and the prohibition of buying and selling agricultural products, as 'social fiction'. Wyka wrote:

> The population had to choose between eating what they were allowed to and starving to death (ration allocations were too small for actual needs), or managing somehow. Nobody considered the first alternative seriously – the only important question was *how* to manage in spite of the regulations.

As Wyka described it, the occupation years had actually developed an elaborate 'excluded economy'. Even in the most totalitarian of systems, 'the occupying force could not control everything'. Wyka observed that the 'excluded economy' persisted long after the extreme conditions (under which one-sixth of the population perished) that engendered it disappeared. The imposition of Soviet-style politicized economic institutions – state planning, centralization, and the one-party system – on a country of vastly different cultural institutions stimulated the continued development of informal networking and indirect clandestine outmanoeuvering of the state system.

More recently, Wojciech Pawlik's sociological research in one small Polish town shows that its people so intensified their use of informal channels during the economic slump of 1981–3 that they continued to reply on such channels even after the market possibilities recovered and goods could be obtained directly from stores through formal channels.[14]

Past experience has afforded Poles the ability to make the down-to-earth adjustments necessary for survival and for a certain moderate prosperity. They have become accustomed to dramatic and tragic situations. Despite military discipline at work and the threat of losing jobs, the internment of thousands and the dampening of expectations, Poles celebrated Christmas a week after the declaration of martial law in approximately normal fashion. This was not out of acceptance of martial law, but rather out of a seasoned ability to adapt. 'When you are among crows, you have to crow as they do,' says a Polish proverb.

Poems of contemporary writers such as Czesław Miłosz and those of the greatest Polish poet, Adam Mickiewicz (1798–1855), tell how Poles cope with hardship and contradiction. Poles appreciate the art of adjustment, but are forever critical of it as detrimental to the spirit

Consummate survivors, Poles have learned how to say one thing, do another, and entertain a consciousness between. 'It is necessary to survive the crisis,' shrugged a middle-aged woman who had survived a death camp, laughing as she swallowed her straight-up vodka. 'A person can adjust to anything.'

Poland's ongoing problems – the catch-all 'crisis' which so many voices assert is both cause and the manifold symptom of practically any trouble – will by no means disappear. And Poles of every age, occupation and class will go on working to expand their networks and to elaborate their exhausting mechanisms of private arrangements. The informal economy and its instruments will survive, responding and adjusting to the vagaries of the official economy and bureaucracy. 'Reforms' might make a few more refrigerators available, but queue committees will remain, adapting to each new demand. The efforts of independent associations, underground factions and the Church to compensate for fragmentation also might meet with limited success.

Ultimately discussions of reform must not address themselves simply to transforming the largely discredited visible mechanisms of the economy. Poland is not a nation of two societies, or economies, but of acknowledged and unacknowledged aspects of one society, which are much more complex than official and formalist doctrines concede. Thus any reform attempts also must anticipate and incorporate changes stemming from the curious hybrid that is the offspring of European history, Polish tradition, and Communist doctrine.

Notes

1 These numbers pertain to 1987. *Rocznik Statystyczny* (1987) was the source of the salary figure and Dr Joanna Sikorska, sociologist at the Polish Academy of Sciences, provided the price estimates.

2 See, for example, *Sisyphus* (vol. 2), 1982, Edmund Wnuk-Lipiński (ed.) on 'dimorphism' of values.

3 Nowak, Stefan (1979) 'System Wartości Spoleczeństwa Polskiego' (The value system of Polish society), *Studia Socjologiczne* 4: 75.

4 Beskid, Lidia (1987) *Warunki i Sposòb Życia Spoleczeństwa Polskiego w Sytuacji Regresu*, Warsaw: Instytut Filozofii i Socjologii Polskiej Akademii Nauk, 104, 109. The following study also confirms the fact that the level of consumption is higher than personal income: Goralska, Helena (1984) *Dochody i Konsumpcja Ludności Żyjacej w Niedostatku*, Warsaw: IPiSS, Studia i Materialy (zeszyt 3/209), 42, 49.

5 Economists Marek Bednarski and Marian Wisniewski came up with these figures independently, cited in the following sources: Bednarski, Marek (1984) 'Drugi Obieg' (Second Circulation), *Życie Gospodarcze*, 26 August, 35; Bednarski, Marek (1985) 'Podstawowe Problemy Funkcjonowania Gospodarki "Drugiego Obiegu" w Polsce', in P. Wòjciką, (ed.), *Problemy Patologii i Przestępczości, Położenie Klasy Robotniczej w Polsce*, vol. 4, Warsaw; Wisniewski, Marion (1985) 'Ekonomiczne Uwarunkowania "Drugiego Obiegu" Gospodarczego w Polsce', In P. Wojcika, (ed.), *Problemy Patologii i Przestepczosci, Polozenie Klasy Robotnicze w Polsce*, vol. 4, Warsaw, 524–68.

6 Moneys generated by black-market trade in hard currency, through hard-currency bank accounts (which Polish citizens have been allowed since the early 1970s), or by private legal enterprises (the operation of which usually

entails some illegal activities) are crucial to a state economy with perpetual foreign debt.

7 Poland has a substantial legal private sector, among the largest in eastern Europe. Nearly one-third of the population is employed in it, although predominantly in agriculture. The sector is dominated by agriculture, housing, small-scale enterprises and handicrafts such as restaurants and boutiques.

8 Barely two-thirds of Polish households occupy an entire apartment; almost one-third share an apartment with at least one other household, according to studies conducted by the Central Statistical Office and sociologists Lidia Beskid and Joanna Sikorska of the Polish Academy of Sciences. Not only is living space limited but many Polish homes also lack modern facilities. According to the Central Statistical Office, in 1984 approximately 89 per cent of the living quarters in urban Poland had a water supply; 77 per cent had a private toilet; 74 per cent had a shower or bathtub; 63 per cent had a gas supply and 63 per cent had central heating. In rural Poland, conditions were more primitive: 40 per cent of living quarters had a water supply; 25 per cent had an indoor toilet; 30 per cent had a bathtub or shower; 2 per cent had a gas supply and 21 per cent had central heating.

9 Nearly two-thirds of working-age women are employed.

10 In the 1980s women have carried the burden of significant increases in living costs, not fully compensated by wage increases. The threefold to tenfold increase in the cost of food, clothes, and other necessities over the late 1970s has driven women to make many goods at home – they can buy fruit and make their own jam preserves instead of buying poorer-quality products at higher prices. According to the Central Statistical Office, the general index of the cost of living in 1986 was almost five times higher than in 1980; pay adjusted for cost of living declined from 100 in 1980 to 83.2 in 1986. (Source: *Warunki Życia Ludności w 1986 Roku*, Głowny Urząd Statystyczny.)

11 Few people are actually prosecuted for 'economic crimes' – those who are, are prosecuted for small-scale illegal activities. Rarely are big operators – usually Polish millionaires or the so-called 'fat fish' (VIPs) – indicted. However, during the Solidarity and martial law periods, political elites (mostly former officials) were not exempt from scrutiny and prosecution. In 1981, representatives of the Prosecutor-General's Office and of the Ministry of Justice reported that in 1980 over 1,000 serious economic indictments were directed to the courts. In 1981 investigations were in progress against a number of former high-ranking officials, including four former ministers, seven former deputy ministers, five former first secretaries and two former secretaries of *voivodship* (district) committees. In 1982, General Jaruzelski granted amnesty to all former high-ranking officials accused of economic crimes, along with some imprisoned Solidarity activists and criminals.

12 Coffee, chocolate and cigarettes were frequently among relief items sent to Poland and particularly to political prisoners during martial law. Many of these items were distributed by the Church.

13 According to official statistics, over 300,000 abortions are performed in Poland each year. But official statistics include only those abortions carried out in state hospitals. Many more are performed privately and go unreported, and some knowledgeable Poles guess that only one-third are included in the official

count. The estimated actual abortion total is larger than Poland's annual birth rate – which in the 1980s has been one of the highest in Europe.

14 Pawlik, Wojciech (1985) 'The economy of everyday life in a local community', in *Umowa o Kartki* and Jacek Kurczewski (eds), Warsaw: Warsaw University.

Afterword

The chapters of this book were written in the years 1987–8. Although they stand remarkably well the test of events of the year 1989, a brief comment on these events is in order.

The January 1989 decision of the Polish Communist leadership to negotiate a power-sharing arrangement with Solidarity opened a new chapter in the unfolding Polish drama. Two reasons seem to lie behind this startling and tantalizing initiative. One was Gorbachev's policy which, while not lifting entirely the threat entailed in the Brezhnev Doctrine, removed an easy excuse for keeping the *status quo*. The other reason was the failure of reforms so far to bring Poland out of the economic crisis. Demoralized and disillusioned, the authorities, fearful of a new wave of social conflicts, offered Polish society what they still possessed and could give immediately: political concessions. These concessions led to the Round Table Agreements of April 1989 and to Solidarity's stunning victory in the June 1989 Parliamentary elections. These events in Poland (and the recent social upheavals in China, the USSR, and Hungary) seem to indicate that once the fear of state repression is removed, the Communist countries develop an inner dynamic which takes them relatively fast towards a fully-fledged parliamentary democracy and market economy. In effect, any intermediate institutional arrangement seems both unworkable and unstable. The key destabilizing force continues to be the poor economic performance. It would appear that the Communist leaders failed to realize that, in the economy, the only effective substitute for the controls of the central plan, however crude they may be, is the strict discipline imposed by competitive markets. Their reluctance to create such markets (and free prices) and to impose tight monetary controls (and eliminate deficits of all kinds), even if the result is closures and unemployment, has positively contributed to large consumer shortages and rapidly accelerating inflation: the origin of fires which now threaten to engulf the entire social fabric of Poland and the Soviet Union.

The political reforms have given the government of Poland a new opportunity. But there still remains the question of whether the present mood of national reconciliation is sufficiently well-established to impose reforms which will inevitably imply large social costs. The Paris economic summit of July 1989 decided to offer help to Poland and Hungary to meet some of these costs. However, the main part of these costs will have to be borne by the two countries themselves. Are they ready for this effort? It may well be that the present economic crisis will have to progress further still before they and the USSR find enough wisdom and political will to abandon decisively a system which has proved to be for them such a costly experiment. Major reversals, even a partial return to the old ways, cannot be excluded.

S. Gomułka and A. Polonsky
July 1989

Notes on Contributors

Stanisław Gomułka is Reader in Economics at the London School of Economics and Political Science, where he has been since 1970. Educated at the University of Warsaw, he has also taught at the University of Pennsylvania (1984–5), and held fellowship appointments at: the Netherlands Institute for Advanced Study (1980–1); the University of Stanford (1985); the University of Columbia (1986); and the University of Harvard (1989). His most recent books are: *Growth, Innovation and Reform in Eastern Europe* (1986–7) and, as editor and contributor, *Economic Reforms in the Socialist World* (1989).

Wiktor Herer is Professor of Economics at the Institute of National Economy at the Central Bureau of Planning, Warsaw. His books include: *Agriculture and the Development of National Economy*, (1962), *Development Tendencies in Agriculture*, (1970), and (with W. Sadowski) *Migration from Agriculture: Consequences and Costs*, (1978), and *Hitting the Growth Barriers*, (1989).

Maria Hirszowicz has spent the greater part of her life in Poland, where she held several posts at the Universities of Warsaw and Lodz. She left Poland in 1969, and is Reader in Sociology at the University of Reading. Dr Hirszowicz is the author of many books in Polish, and of the following in English: *The Bureaucratic Leviathan: A Study in the Sociology of Communism*, (1980), *Industrial Sociology*, (1981), and *Coercion and Control in Communist Society*, (1986). She is also co-author of *Class and Inequality in Pre-Industrial, Capitalist, and Communist Societies*, (1987).

Jerzy Holzer is Professor at the Institute of History at the University of Warsaw. He has written many books on Polish and German history, among them: *Parteien und Massen, die Politische Krise in Deutschland 1928–1930*, (Wiesbaden, 1975), *Mozaika Polityczna Drugiej Rzeczypospolitej*, (Warsaw, 1974), and *Solidarność, Geneza i Historia*, (Warsaw, 1983, Paris, 1984, Munich, 1985).

Jerzy Jedlicki is Professor at the Institute of History at the Polish Academy of Sciences in Warsaw. He has written on both social and economic history, as well as on the history of ideas in eighteenth- and nineteenth-century Poland. His books include: *Klejnot i Bariery Spoleczne (The Crest and Social Barriers)* (Warsaw, 1968), and *Jakiej Cywilizacji Polacy Potrzebuja (What Sort of Civilisation the Poles Need)* (Warsaw, 1988). He has been awarded a fellowship of the Woodrow Wilson International Center for Scholars in Washington DC for the year 1989–90.

Jan Jerschina is Associate Professor (docent) in the Sociology Department of the Jagiellonian University in Kraków. He has published widely on the role of the Catholic Church in Poland.

Lena Kolarska-Bobińska is Associate Professor (docent) at the Institute of Philosophy and Sociology, Polish Academy of Sciences. In the years 1971–6, she held visiting appointments at the Universities of Carnegie-Mellon and Stanford. Her books include: *Centralization and Decentralization: Decisions, Power, and Myths*, and as a co-author, *The Poles '80, The Poles '81, The Poles '84*, and *The Poles '88*, a series of empirical studies of Polish society during the years 1980–8.

Marcin Król is both a historian and a journalist. His books include: *Stańczycy; Antologia Myśli Spolecznej i Politycznej Konserwatystow Krakowskich. (The Stanczycy; An Anthology of the Social and Political Thought of the Kraków Conservatives)*, (Warsaw, 1985), and *Konserwatysci a Niepodlegość, (The Conservatives and Independence)*, (Warsaw, 1985). He is editor of the independent monthly review, *Republica*.

Mira Marody is Associate Professor (docent) in the Institute of Sociology at the University of Warsaw, specializing in social psychology. Among her publications are: 'Sens empiryczny a sens teoretyczny pojecia postawy' ('Theoretical and empirical senses of the concept of "attitude"'), (Warsaw 1976), 'Polacy '80', ('The Poles '80), (Warsaw, 1981), and 'Technologie intelektu', ('Technologies of intellect'), (Warsaw, 1987). She is co-editor of 'Rzeczywistość polska i sposoby radzenia sobie z nia' ('Polish reality and ways of coping with it') (Warsaw, 1987).

Antony Polonsky is Reader in International History at the London School of Economics and Political Science. His books include: *Politics in Independent Poland* (Oxford, 1972), *The Little Dictators* (London, 1975), and with Boleslaw Drukier, *The Beginnings of Communist Rule in Poland* (London, 1981). He is President of the Institute for Polish-Jewish studies, and editor of *Polin: A Journal of Polish-Jewish Studies*.

Jacek Rostowski is Lecturer in Soviet and East European Economics at the School of Slavonic and East European Studies, University of London. He has written articles on economic reform in Poland, and also on other aspects of the economies of Eastern Europe, such as material intensity and inflation, paying particular attention to East-West comparative analyses. He is co-editor of the journal *Communist Economics*, and Deputy Director of the Centre for Research into Communist Economies.

Władysław Sadowski is Professor of Economics in the Institute of National Economy at the Central Bureau of Planning, Warsaw. His publications mainly concern the theory of growth in socialist economy. He has also published works on the practical aspects of economic development, such as: *Migration from Agriculture: Consequences and Costs*, (1975), and *Hitting the Growth Barriers*, (1979). These books were written jointly with Wiktor Herer.

Jadwiga Staniszkis is an Associate Professor (docent) in the Sociology Department, at the University of Warsaw. Her books include: *Poland's Self-Limiting Revolution*, (Princeton, 1986), and *Ontology of Socialism*, (Oxford University Press, forthcoming).

Andrzej Walicki was Professor at the Institute of Philosophy at the Polish Academy of Sciences until 1981, and Senior Research Fellow at the Australian National University (1981–6). He is now O'Neill Professor of History at the University of Notre Dame, Indiana. He is a historian of ideas, specializing in Russian and Polish intellectual history, as well as being the author of seven books in English including the *History of Russian Thought From the Enlightenment to Marxism*, (Stanford, 1979, and Oxford, 1980). His other works include: *Philosophy and Romantic Nationalism: The Case of Poland*, (Clarendon Press, Oxford, 1982), and *The Enlightenment and the Birth of Modern Nationhood, Polish Political Thought from the Noble Republicanism to Tadesz Kosciuszko*, (Notre Dame University Press, Notre Dame, 1989).

Janine Wedel holds a Ph.D. in Anthropology from the University of California, Berkeley. She was affiliated with the Institute of Sociology at the University of Warsaw, as a Fulbright scholar. From 1985–6, Dr. Wedel carried out post-doctoral research under the auspices of the International Research and Exchanges Board, again in affiliation with the University of Warsaw. Her doctoral dissertation (U.C. Berkeley, 1985) and book, *The Private Poland: An Anthropologist's Look at Everyday Life*, (1986), resulted from this research.

Index

In the following index, 'Poland' is abbreviated to 'Pd' and 'Polish' to 'P'.

between 162–3
production apparatus, P. 124
productivity 98
professional standards 144–5
propaganda campaigns 99–100, 129
property reforms 183, 184–6
prosperity, inter-war islands of 130–1
Prus, Bolesław 8
Prussia 2, 29, 42
Prussian v. Byzantine cultures 125–7, 128, 132–3
'psychological well–being' 228–9
public opinion 155, 170; see also opinion polls
public service, ethos of 28, 32
publications, independent 101, 150, 153, 154–5
Pułaski, Kazimierz 60
Pyjas, Stanisław 101

quality of life 93
'queue committees' 247, 258

Racławice, battle of 44
Rakowski, Mieczysław 86, 172, 187
rationing 238, 256–7
raw materials 123, 181
realism, political 8–10, 34–8, 53–4
reconstruction programme, post–war 120–1, 128
Recovered Territories 81, 86
referendum of 1987   172
reform, economic 15–16, 104, 112, 156–8, 161–2, 163, 168–9, 171–2, 174–6, 182, 183, 209–210
refrigerators 244, 247, 248
registration court hearing of 24 October 1980   106
religion, teaching of 91–2
religious renewal 13, 91–3, 94, 101
Renaissance, Polish 26
repression 84–5, 110–11, 122, 133, 134
reprisals, Tsarist 58
research in Pd 91, 151
resistance movement, anti-Nazi 10
resourcefulness, importance of 232
revolutionary ideology, in nineteenth century 63–4
riots, spontaneous 103
risk–taking, importance of 232
romantic nationalism 5–7, 8–9, 10,

21–2, 23, 29–33, 34–5, 37, 43–8, 55–6, 58, 59–61, 73–4; rejection of 59–61
Rostowski, Jacek 16
Rousseau, J.-J. 27
Różewicz, Tadeusz 60
Rulewski, Jan 106
Rumania 136, 138
'runaround', ubiquity in P. life 249
Russia 2, 29, 32, 44, 64; see also USSR
Ryzhkov, Nikolai I. 187
Rzewuski, Henryk 65

Sadowski, Władysław 14–15, 194–5
'sanctuary', P. 55–6
savings 222–3
scepticism 59–61, 63, 67
schizophrenia, national 6–7, 234, 240
scientists, P. 91
Second Vatican Council 76–7, 91
Second World War 80, 87, 120, 256–7
secularization 84, 92
security, sense of 230
segmentation of economy 188
Sejm 2, 3, 23–4, 28, 29, 188
self-esteem 60, 232–3, 235–6; see also dignity, need for self fulfilment, need for 233
'self-limitation' of power 185–6, 191
'self-limiting revolution', concept of 105, 107
services sector 203, 204, 211
shortages 201
Sikorska, Joanna 259
Silesia 88
sixteenth-century Pd 23–5
Słowacki, Juliusz 5, 41, 45, 46–7, 50
Sobieski, King Jan 24, 232
'social circles' (srodowiska) 241–3, 248–9, 250
social Darwinism 8–9, 34, 35
'social insurance' 230, 232
'social vacuum' 240–1
socialism, decay of 198–223 and breakdown of Aasland's Law 201–3, 209–13; and ideological bankruptcy 210–11; and importance of private enterprise 199–201, see also Solidarity; democratic opposition; market economy
socialism, in nineteenth-century Pd 64–5